# Hacking the Electora

## *How Campaigns Perceive Voters*

*Hacking the Electorate* is the most comprehensive study to date about the consequences of campaigns using microtargeting databases to mobilize voters in elections. Eitan D. Hersh traces the path from data to strategy to outcomes. Hersh argues that most of what campaigns know about voters comes from a core set of public records. States vary in the kinds of records they collect from voters – and these variations in data across the country mean that campaigns perceive voters differently in different areas. Consequently, the strategies of campaigns and the coalitions of voters who are mobilized fluctuate across the country because of the different ways campaigns perceive the electorate. Data policies influence campaigns, voters, and, increasingly, public officials.

Eitan D. Hersh is an assistant professor of political science at Yale University. His research has been published in journals such as the *American Political Science Review* and the *Proceedings of the National Academy of Sciences*, as well as featured in news outlets such as PBS *NewsHour* and the *New York Times*. Hersh has served as an expert consultant in several election-related court cases.

*In honor of my parents*
*Kenneth M. Hersh and Leah Ehrenhaus-Hersh*

# Hacking the Electorate

## *How Campaigns Perceive Voters*

**EITAN D. HERSH**

*Yale University*

CAMBRIDGE
UNIVERSITY PRESS

# CAMBRIDGE
## UNIVERSITY PRESS

University Printing House, Cambridge CB2 8BS, United Kingdom

One Liberty Plaza, 20th Floor, New York, NY 10006, USA

477 Williamstown Road, Port Melbourne, VIC 3207, Australia

4843/24, 2nd Floor, Ansari Road, Daryaganj, Delhi - 110002, India

79 Anson Road, #06-04/06, Singapore 079906

Cambridge University Press is part of the University of Cambridge.

It furthers the University's mission by disseminating knowledge in the pursuit of
education, learning and research at the highest international levels of excellence.

www.cambridge.org
Information on this title: www.cambridge.org/9781107501164

First published 2015

*A catalogue record for this publication is available from the British Library*

*Library of Congress Cataloging in Publication data*
Hersh, Eitan D.
Hacking the electorate : how campaigns perceive voters / Eitan D. Hersh.
pages   cm
Includes bibliographical references and index.
ISBN 978-1-107-10289-7 (hardback) – ISBN 978-1-107-50116-4 (paperback)
1. Campaign management – United States.   2. Political campaigns – United States.
3. Voting – United States.   I. Title.
JK2281.H46   2015
324.70973–dc23        2014046688

ISBN 978-1-107-10289-7 Hardback
ISBN 978-1-107-50116-4 Paperback

# Contents

# Acknowledgments

The research contained in this volume began in 2009. In the six years since, I have benefited from a community of scholars without which I could not have completed this book. At its best, scholarly research is conducted not in solitary confinement but in a vibrant ecosystem in which students inspire, colleagues encourage, mentors nudge, and reviewers critique. I have been blessed with a community that has helped me in inspiration, encouragement, nudges, and critiques. I hope to primarily convey my gratitude through actions – by helping students and colleagues as they have helped me. But I also wish to acknowledge some of the individuals who were particularly important in making this book possible.

I first thank my teachers. Stephen Ansolabehere served as my graduate adviser. For his creativity, knowledge, friendship, and generosity I am overwhelmingly grateful. Claudine Gay and Gary King, who served along with Steve on my dissertation committee, offered terrific advice and encouragement in the early stages of this project. Ken Shepsle's engagement with my studies was also critical to this project's early development.

In addition to my teachers at Harvard, I have acquired teachers across the discipline who helped make this project a success. Barry Burden, Robert Erikson, Rick Hasen, Sunshine Hillygus, Brian Schaffner, John Sides, and Lynn Vavreck participated in a book conference in 2013. The book changed substantially in light of their comments and suggestions. I especially thank Sunshine, Brian, John, and Lynn for reading multiple versions of the manuscript. David Mayhew and Chris Mann also read full drafts of the manuscript and offered very insightful feedback.

I thank my graduate school colleagues, especially Katie Levine Einstein, Anthony Fowler, Bernard Fraga, Justin Grimmer, Elena Llaudet, Clayton Nall, and Joe Williams. I thank my colleagues on the Yale faculty, especially Peter Aronow, Deborah Beim, John Bullock, Dan Butler, Sam DeCanio, Alan Gerber, Jacob Hacker, John Henderson, Greg Huber, David Mayhew, Ellie Powell, Kelly Rader, Stephen Skowronek, Steven Smith, Susan Stokes, and Vesla Weaver. And I thank colleagues around the country who have been generous with their time and ideas, especially David Broockman, Ryan Enos, Peter Ganong, Seth Hill, Matthew Hindman, Daniel Hopkins, Gabrial Lenz, Chris Mann, Marc Meredith, Markus Prior, Todd Rogers, Jim Snyder, and Charles Stewart. My conversations with all of these individuals throughout the last six years have not only made my research better but they have also made this job fun.

For research support, I thank the Center for the Study of American Politics and the Institution for Social and Policy Studies (ISPS) at Yale. I thank directors Alan Gerber and Jacob Hacker for their generous support. For funding for the early stage of this project, I thank the Center for American Political Studies at Harvard as well as Stephen Ansolabehere. For hosting me during a year of research leave, I thank the departments of political science at Boston College and Boston University. For research assistance, I thank Nate Blevins, Ivan Fan, and especially Michael Young, all terrific graduates of Yale College. I also thank Pam Lamonaca and Pam Greene at ISPS for all their help.

Many campaign practitioners helped make this research possible. I especially thank Laura Quinn and Bob Blaemire at Catalist, Jim St.George at NGP VAN, and Ethan Roeder on the Obama campaign for their help. I also thank the Analyst Institute for its role in fostering dialogue between political scientists and political practitioners. And I thank the two dozen Republican and Democratic campaign operatives I interviewed whose anonymity requires my gratitude to be transmitted privately.

I owe special thanks to Robert Dreesen at Cambridge University Press for his enthusiasm and commitment to this project. Throughout the stages of review and revision, Robert has been a remarkably supportive, helpful, and calming force. I could not have asked for a better editor to guide me through it. I also thank Jenny Lederer for help with editing and for designing the cover.

I wish to acknowledge and thank the teachers who led me to a career in the study of politics, especially Mr. Edward Dirissio at Classical High School in Providence, and Nancy Bauer, James Glaser, Gary McKissick, Molly Mead, and Vickie Sullivan at Tufts University.

Many friends have graciously listened to my attempts at explaining this research in plain English. Through their patient questions, the research improved. I especially thank Joshua Cohen, Joshua Foer, Daniel Stuckey, Jeremy Sueker, Jessica Fechtor, and Eli Schliefer. Eli also deserves credit for coming up with the book's title. In acknowledging the help of my friends, I also want to honor the memory of my friend Daniel Abrams (Z"L), classmate from pre-school through high school, and a 2006 Yale graduate, whose creative spirit rubbed off on everyone who knew him, and so who shares in our accomplishments because they are his too.

I am blessed with a wonderful family. For their love and support, I thank Abraham and Marilyn Ehrenhaus; David (Z"L) and Claire Hersh; Kenneth and Leah Hersh; Ami, Loni, Micah, Zev, Noa, and Yael Hersh; Michael, Shayna, and Nadav Fel; Mel and Eva Hoffman, Claire Hoffman, and Alexander Hoffman.

For being my partner every step of the way since we were in college taking political science classes together, for her wisdom and her kindness, for her balance and her focus, for building with me a household that I cherish above all else, I thank a woman of great valor, Julia Elizabeth Hoffman. And for his wide-eyed enthusiasm for playing, learning, and growing, I thank my son, Levi Jacob Hersh, who entered the world halfway into this project and has made life more exhilarating and hopeful ever since.

And finally, I thank the two people to whom this book is dedicated, whose sacrifices for my education provided me with the tools to succeed, and who value professional achievements like this book but not nearly as much as they value integrity, generosity, family, and community. For their sacrifices, values, and love, I dedicate this book to my mother and father.

# I

# Introduction

What does an elected representative see when he or she sees a constituency? And, as a natural follow-up, what consequences do these perceptions have for his or her behavior?

– Richard Fenno, *Home Style*

Officials of the modern state ... assess the life of their society by a series of typifications that are always some distance from the full reality these abstractions are meant to capture ... These typifications are indispensable to statecraft. State simplifications such as maps, censuses, cadastral lists, and standard units of measurement represent techniques for grasping a large and complex reality.

– James Scott, *Seeing Like a State*

In the 1970s, political scientist Richard Fenno followed members of Congress on tours around their districts. Fenno observed how they interacted with voters so that he could study how politicians perceive their constituents and how these perceptions guide their behavior. As Fenno noticed, politicians have intuitions about which voters are supporters and which are opponents, what issues voters care about, and how the politicians ought to present themselves to the diverse audiences they encounter across their districts. But perceptions like these can be vague and distorted. Distorted as they may be, these perceptions guide politicians in their efforts to represent the public.

In contemporary politics, perceptions of voters are not merely vague ideas carried around in the heads of politicians; perceptions are also recorded in detailed electronic profiles that describe each constituent within a jurisdiction. As is now well known, political parties in recent years have built databases to facilitate targeting strategies. These databases list the names and contact information for all voters in a district, along with information about their personal traits, their neighborhoods, and their history of political participation. Politicians and their campaigns use these lists to perceive the electorate. The lists help them understand who their supporters are, what issues different voters care about, and how they should present themselves to voters in their campaign appeals. This large-scale collection of data influences how politicians perceive voters, and in turn, it affects how they interact with voters.

In this book, I examine how politicians, in the context of their campaigns, perceive voters and how those perceptions translate into the relationship politicians build with their electorates. During recent election cycles, I have looked under the hood of campaign databases and I have surveyed thousands of campaign workers who use these databases. I have done so in order to gauge the perceptions of the electorate that come from campaigns creating a digital profile of each voter, and to study how these perceptions affect the choices campaigns make.

The aspect of politics that is currently most influenced by these new databases is direct voter contact, which incorporates campaign strategies such as door-to-door canvassing, telephone appeals, and direct mail. These strategies of the "ground campaign" have become increasingly prominent in campaign politics, and the effectiveness of these strategies has been a topic of much scholarly research in the last fifteen years. Direct contacting efforts can accommodate fine-grained strategies in which one household receives a communication while the household next door does not. These strategies are informed by campaign databases that are used to estimate the political dispositions of voters. I focus on how the perceptions of politicians as captured in individual-level campaign databases affect which voters receive direct appeals and why they receive them.

However, the elite perceptions I study in this book have consequences for politics that extend far beyond strategies of voter contact. As I show, the way campaigns perceive voters in their databases holds important lessons for our understanding of public policy and the future of political representation. For example, I will describe how the data that are collected in political campaign databases are being used in governmental functions as well. The same individual-level databases used in campaign targeting have been widely adopted by congressional offices to field constituent service requests.[1] When constituents seek information or assistance from a Congress member's office, their personal information is often linked to the same targeting records that appear in campaign databases.

As another example, the federal government has recently used political targeting databases to estimate the racial composition of voters who lack photo IDs in order to evaluate the legality of voter identification laws.[2] In the coming years, one can expect that the databases studied here, which are designed primarily to facilitate campaign targeting, will be used increasingly in official government functions like these. Consequently, this book's attention to politicians' perceptions of voters as they appear in targeting databases is but a first step in studying the consequences of new, individual-level voter profiles. The same perceptions that affect the targeting decisions studied here are likely to influence decisions in official government business into the future.

Furthermore, though microtargeting databases are currently used primarily for strategies like door-to-door canvassing and phone banks, perceptions formed through these databases are already beginning to influence television advertisements and other avenues of mass appeals. Campaigns are just now beginning to aggregate individual-level databases to geographic levels that can be targeted with cable TV ads.[3] In the future, it is quite likely that ads will be targeted to individual cable boxes. As media appeals become increasingly amenable to fine-grained targeting, the perceptions of voters that are garnered from microtargeting databases will inform media appeals just as they inform direct contacting appeals. Accordingly, this study of elite perceptions applies not only to individual-level campaign contact but also to frontiers in congressional representation and mass media advertising.

A campaign's chief goal in perceiving the public is to form predictions about which members of the public are supporters, which are likely to show up to vote, and which are persuadable. What kinds of information do campaigns rely on to form predictions like these? As I assess how voters appear to campaigns in targeting databases, it immediately becomes clear that *public* records – primarily individual-level records from the voter registration system, but also data from the Census Bureau and state licensing agencies – play a key role in shaping their perceptions. Public records and the laws that generate them turn out to be *the* essential ingredient for understanding elite perceptions as well the consequences of those perceptions for political outcomes. Thus, the story told in this book is not just a story about campaign strategy; it is a story about how policy decisions affect politics.

The reasons why even sophisticated campaigns perceive voters through the lens of public records may be surprising. For one, alternative sources of data, like commercial records, have comparatively limited predictive

power in helping campaigns gauge voters' politically relevant characteristics. For another, public records can be *designed* to be helpful to campaigns. Administrative records are designed by election-seeking politicians who are cognizant of the data's political value. I uncover evidence
that politicians pass laws calling for the collection of personal data explicitly so that the data can be used by political campaigns.

Critically, public records used by campaigns to perceive voters vary
substantially across the U.S. states, because each state has primary control over the election system within its jurisdiction. This means that the
perceptions formed by elites about voters also vary by state. I exploit this
variation to investigate how different kinds of perceptions lead to different strategic decisions. I form predictions about how campaigns interact
with voters based on the laws that govern the flow of public records in
a given jurisdiction. These laws serve as *levers* that influence how campaigns interact with the electorate. When a particular data law is in effect,
campaigns perceive voters one way and engage with them one way; when
the law is not in effect, they behave differently. As with other aspects of
the law, seemingly small policy differences can have consequential effects
on the conduct of campaigns and the outcomes of elections.

For example, in some states, campaigns can obtain public records of
individual voters' race or party affiliation; in other states, they cannot.
When public records are available that provide a clear signal of partisanship, I hypothesize that campaigns focus more on mobilizing partisans
and less on targeting geographies or persuading undecided voters. I also
suggest that they have less unintended contact with partisans of the other
party. Similarly, when public records provide a clear signal of racial identity, I will show that campaigns focus more on mobilizing voters because
of the voters' race, and less on targeting geographic areas with homogenous racial groups. These decisions by campaigns are predicted to have
a number of downstream consequences for voter behavior as well. For
example, in places where campaigns do not have accurate, individual-
level signals of partisanship or race available from public records, the
population of mobilized voters tends to be concentrated in geographic
areas where voters are homogenous. In places where public records allow
campaigns to identify individual voters who are likely supporters, turnout
is less geographically contingent.

In short, the public information environment, which varies within
the United States, affects campaigns' perceptions of voters and in turn
affects with which voters campaigns interact. The goal of this book is to
reveal new explanations for how campaigns engage with the electorate by

developing an understanding of how they form perceptions of voters and how those perceptions guide their strategic choices.

By observing how elite strategies and mass behaviors vary based on the ways elites perceive the public, this book not only offers a new framework for understanding campaign strategy and not only draws a connection between the public policy of data collection and elite perceptions, but also explores a new way in which geography and federalism shape our politics. Voters experience elections differently across the country for a number of reasons. Voters who live in red states or blue states, battleground states or safe states, can have very different political relationships because of where they live. Here, I show that subtle, seemingly mundane data policies, which vary by state, have a clear set of ramifications for how voters experience elections. Campaigns perceive voters differently depending on the policies of the jurisdictions in which voters live, which helps us understand a new way in which geography shapes politics.

## An Example

To build some intuition of the case I will make in this book, consider as an example the attempt by the 2008 and 2012 Obama campaigns to mobilize young voters. Because young people so strongly supported Barack Obama in 2008 and 2012, his campaign attempted to mobilize voters under the age of twenty-five. In swing states, the campaign's volunteers and staff engaged millions of young voters and personally encouraged them to participate in the political process. The campaign *wanted* to mobilize youth because it knew young people were supporting its candidate. It *could* do this effectively because the public record identified the age of every registered voter. In nearly every state, the age of a registered voter is a matter of public record. This means that when campaigns perceive voters, they perceive an accurate estimate of each voter's age. They can use this perception to inform their strategy for door-to-door canvassing, phone banks, and mail and e-mail messages.

In the absence of individual-identifying age data, consider what the campaign might have done instead. It might have pursued a coarser strategy, like mobilizing residents of college towns. If it had done so, a different subset of the electorate would have been engaged. According to confidential strategy memos from the 2008 Obama campaign, the campaign actually focused specifically on mobilizing young voters who did not reside in college towns, including women in their twenties living in rural areas and African-American youth living in urban areas. Without individual-identifying age data, the campaign would have perceived its target audience differently, leading to a different set of strategies and a different set of voters who would be mobilized.

Thus, a twenty-year-old woman in rural Ohio may have received attention from the Obama campaign not just because she was likely to be a supporter but because a particular dataset enabled the campaign to find her. The existence of a public record about her birthdate affected the campaign's decision to contact her in the first place, and also affected how the campaign engaged her (through direct contact, such as door-to-door canvassing or phone calls) and the type of message she received (a get-out-the-vote message geared toward her identity as a young person). In contrast to perceptions of age, campaign perceptions of attributes like voters' party, race, and degree of persuadability are less precise and vary considerably across jurisdictions, which means there will be substantial variation in the strategies campaigns pursue based on the data available to them.

Relevant to this example are two important questions. First, why can campaigns perceive voters' ages in the first place? The main administrative rationale for the public collection of age data is that knowing a person's age is necessary to determine whether that person is eligible to participate in elections. But for this purpose, administrators actually need a binary measure: whether or not a prospective registrant is over the age of eighteen. There are auxiliary reasons administrators want to know birthdates (e.g., they may also use this information to validate the person's identity at the polls), but these reasons are separable from the need to make the information a matter of public record that can be used by politicians for electioneering. As I argue, a key part of this story is that through carefully crafted laws pertaining to election data, politicians have repurposed administrative personal information to serve their electioneering needs. Indeed, sometimes they seem to collect personal information for no other reason than to provide data to their campaigns.

A second question raised by the example is this: Why should age and not some other voter characteristic be used as the basis of campaign engagement? Age was correlated with Democratic support in Obama's elections, but so were educational attainment and ideology and attitudes about gay rights and positions on military intervention. However, none of these characteristics were utilized by the Obama campaign the way age was. The Obama campaign did not place phone calls and pay home visits because a voter was known to have an advanced degree, identify as a liberal, support gay marriage, or oppose foreign wars. Beyond small-scale surveys, no records existed that would identify individuals as having these traits. And no information that the Obama campaign did possess was particularly good at proxying for traits like these. The point is that the basis for voter engagement depends not on what campaigns would like to do in theory, but on the data they can access that allows them to form impressions about the electorate. Because the data that campaigns access often come from public records, the laws within a jurisdiction that govern how personal information is collected and disseminated serve as levers that affect how and why political campaigns engage with some voters but not others.

## The Perceived Voter

The theory of campaign contact that I present is labeled the Perceived Voter Model. The hypotheses I test about campaign strategy stem from understanding the perceptual biases inherent in strategic decisions that are informed by a limited set of information. I trace the path from the data campaigns gather, to the perceptions they form with those data, to the strategies they pursue based on those perceptions. When one starts from the perspective of elite perceptions, an entirely different set of hypotheses emerge about how elites make strategic decisions than if one ignores the informational roots of decisions. Campaigns are predicted to interact with voters not because the voters are, for example, strong Republicans, African American, or persuadable in their attitudes, but because a campaign uses a specific set of data to perceive which voters may have these traits. Their perceptions of these traits may be quite distorted and lead to a different set of voters being engaged by campaigns than one might otherwise expect.

To understand how campaigns think about voters, my focus is not on real *voters* per se, but rather on *perceived voters*. These are the people politicians think about when seeking office. *Perceived voters* compose the electorate from the *campaign's-eye-view*. They are not people; they are avatars generated from whatever data a political campaign, candidate, or party can surmise. By developing a model of campaign strategy based on *perceived voters*, I generate a set of predictions about strategic behavior different from prior research in this field, which has largely ignored the informational hurdle that campaigns face in perceiving the political dispositions of voters.

By distinguishing voters from *perceived voters*, I draw attention to the barrier that exists between a politician who seeks to represent voters and the voters he or she represents. Campaigns do not perceive voters as voters perceive themselves. This means that to understand the decisions campaigns make, one cannot study campaigns from the voter's-eye-view, such as through public opinion surveys. *Perceived voters* cannot be surveyed. They are rows in spreadsheets in computers in campaign offices. They are also stereotypes and generalizations that politicians carry in their heads, as Fenno (1978) noted. But increasingly, as the population grows and data become more available and usable, *perceived voters* are zeros and ones in computers.

To characterize the strategy of voter engagement, I study these zeroes and ones. The data I analyze in this book comes not from surveying voters but by studying *perceived voters*: I look at the actual data that campaigns are looking at when deciding which voters to contact and deciding how to communicate with them, and I survey the actual people who are using data to target voters. Through these resources, I am able to approach questions about the roots and consequences of elite perceptions. Elites no longer perceive the electorate simply by following gut instincts and taking occasional polls, but also by assembling large amounts of data to profile individual voters. I partner with the companies and organizations that build these profiles so that I may study how perceptions garnered from voter databases affect strategic behavior.

## 1.1 THEORETICAL ANCHORS AND EXTENSIONS

At the most basic level, this book will help readers understand why voters are targeted by campaigns in the way that they are. When a voter receives a phone call from a campaign with a certain message, why did that particular voter receive that particular message? Over the last fifteen years, experiments in political science have helped explain that individual-level targeted appeals such as door-to-door canvassing, telephone calls, and mailers do indeed have measurable effects on the behavior of voters (Green and Gerber, 2008). Collectively, we know much less about *why* some voters are targeted by real-world campaigns while others are not, and *how* targeted appeals to specific audiences might affect the composition of the electorate. In this book, I help shed light on why particular types of voters, bearing particular characteristics, are subjected to appeals while others are not. I focus on the strategy of voter contact, not the effectiveness of voter contact, and I demonstrate that strategic choices are constrained by the policy lever of public records laws.

In exploring this phenomenon, I contribute to a broader literature about campaign strategy and voter engagement. One major question in the study of campaign strategy is how strategic choices are constrained by institutional rules. For example, scholars have formed predictions about how campaigns pursue voters, given the constraints imposed by the Electoral College (Shaw, 2006), the party nomination process (Cohen et al., 2008), campaign finance laws (Box-Steffensmeier, 1996), and single-member districts (Cox, 1990). I build on this literature by focusing attention on a set of institutional rules to which scholars have paid little attention but which have a predictable and clear set of consequences for how political campaigns interact with the mass public. Public laws about the collection and distribution of personal information affect how politicians perceive their constituents and consequently how they engage with voters during their campaigns. I thus reveal a new link between institutions of American politics: the institutions that are responsible for collecting and distributing public records (i.e., state legislatures, election administrations) affect the institutions responsible for winning elections (i.e., political parties).

As a study of campaign targeting, this book also shares a theme with Hillygus and Shields (2008). Hillygus and Shields mainly study the subset of voters who are responsive to persuasive campaign appeals, but they also theorize about the informational roots of campaign contact decisions. I build on their research in microtargeting insomuch as I study the perceptual biases that result from the constrained set of data that inform elite perceptions and the consequences of these perceptions when campaigns microtarget voters.

Separate from themes associated with research on electoral campaigns, there are two other broad themes in political science that are closely connected to the argument of this book. The first theme that I build on relates to the institutions of government that generate the public records that become so crucial to campaign perceptions. I argue that among the reasons that political campaigns rely on public records to perceive the electorate is that politicians have designed the system of public records to benefit their campaigns. In doing so, politicians have taken the voter registration system and open record laws – two policy areas that were established with the intention of *limiting* political influences in governance – and transformed them into publicly subsidized campaign resources.

In crafting this argument, I build on research about the political influences in bureaucratic organizations (Keyssar, 2009; Waarden, 1992;

Lowi, 1979; Hasen, 2005; Tokaji, 2008; Balkin, 2008) and research about how public policies, developed over a long period of time, affect the ways citizens and organizations mobilize for political ends (Hacker and Pierson, 2011; see also Campbell, 2003; Mettler, 2002; Patashnik, 2008; Hacker, 2002; Baumgartner, Leech, and Mahoney, 2003; Lessig, 2006; Winner, 1980). To understand why organizations, such as parties or interest groups, build certain kinds of coalitions and not others, one must investigate how the policy environment affects their choices. I show that policies about the collection and regulation of personal data affect the ways political parties build electoral coalitions.

The second theme I build on deals with heuristics, or information "shortcuts." I characterize public records as shortcuts that help campaigns form impressions about a voter's political dispositions. A theory of information shortcuts can help explain why decision makers need to resort to certain informational inputs in the first place, why they end up using one set of inputs over others, and the consequences for their use of information shortcuts on decisions they make. Prior research engaging this line of inquiry begins with Downs (1957), but includes a diverse body of research on mass behavior (Popkin, 1993; Lupia, 1994; Bartels, 1996; Althaus, 1998; Alvarez, 1999; Lau and Redlawsk, 2006) and elite behavior (Krehbiel, 1991; Geer, 1996; Miler, 2009).

I argue that the way political campaigns use public records to evaluate voters is parallel to other types of decisions made using information shortcuts. For example, before they go into the voting booth and cast a ballot, ordinary voters use shortcuts like party affiliations, endorsements, and demographics to make quick judgments of politicians; they do not make voting decisions based on an encyclopedic knowledge of politicians' roll-call votes or policy platforms. The particular shortcuts that voters use can lead them to different voting decisions than if voters used alternative shortcuts or if they had encyclopedic-like knowledge of candidates' positions. Similarly, I argue that political campaigns operating in large populations rarely have encyclopedic knowledge of the dispositions of voters in their electorates. Instead, they cling to a particular set of shortcuts, which affect the way they perceive voters' dispositions and the way they act upon those perceptions. The consequences of their perceptions can be predicted once one has knowledge of the data that inform their perceptions.

It is not self-evident that public records, such as information found in voter registration files, should serve as a critical shortcut for campaigns' perceptions of voters. On the contrary, many historical and contemporary depictions of campaigns assume that campaigns have intimate knowledge of the political dispositions of voters such that they would not be reliant on crude shortcuts from public records. One might assume that through years of interacting with voters, the established political parties in the United States have acquired detailed records of voters based on secretive party lists or on extensive social networks of local party workers. Or perhaps campaigns can rely on new commercial databases to accurately predict voters' political dispositions. Although campaigns do use many alternative mechanisms to make sense of their electorates, I show that campaigns nevertheless rely primarily on public records as shortcuts to perceive voter attributes. A range of strategic choices can therefore be predicted simply with an awareness of campaigns' access to various shortcuts from public data resources.

## 1.2 THE INFORMATION FALLACY

In analyzing how data affect perceptions and how perceptions affect strategies, this study will serve as a corrective to an information fallacy that pervades conventional accounts of political campaigns. The fallacy is that modern campaigns are assumed to have accurate, detailed information about the preferences and behaviors of voters. When I dig into advanced campaign databases and show that much of what campaigns perceive about voters is a result of a limited set of public records, and even the most sophisticated campaigns often misperceive voter preferences, I hope to push back against the hype of the information fallacy.

The information fallacy manifests itself in both popular accounts of political campaigns and in academic accounts. In popular writing, there is a stream of stories trumpeting the genius of microtargeters: They "can figure out what John Smith at 286 Main Street is thinking" (Washington Post); "could divine my likely views on taxes, law enforcement, abortion, and global warming" (New York Times); "know you don't like anchovies" (Los Angeles Times); "know you better than you know yourself" (CNN); "talk directly to the exact voters they need to win" (ABC); and so on.[4] Even the more careful popular accounts of campaign technology, such as recent books by Jonathan Alter (2013) and Sasha Issenberg (2012), which indeed mention in passing the limitations of microtargeting, are nevertheless enamored by the hundreds of variables describing millions of voters that are used in top-secret statistical models that are all very complicated and advanced.

As a general matter, popular writing about new technologies tends both to oversell the promise of technology and to depict technologies in glowingly enthusiastic terms (Winner, 1986). Popular writing about campaign data and microtargeting is no exception. In describing the nuts and bolts of actual campaign databases, I demonstrate that beneath the surface, the inputs campaigns use to perceive voters are typically straightforward and are publicly available. This perspective has been voiced by others. Ethan Roeder, data director for the 2012 Obama campaign, for example, has articulated this view. Roeder was instrumental in granting me access to some of the data examined in this book. In a 2012 *New York Times* op-ed, he wrote:

> Virtually all of the offline data that people like me traffic in is boring, basic and publicly available. Want to know the year of birth for everyone who is registered to vote in Ohio? Just Google 'Ohio voter file download'....
>
> How do we predict whether people are going to vote or not? We look at the voter file. It tells us how often a person votes, although not for whom. Not all strategists agree about how to interpret this information, but the source of the data is no secret.

The 2012 Obama reelection campaign is widely considered to be the most sophisticated, data-driven campaign in the history of U.S. politics. And yet here in his own op-ed, as well as in the course of interviews described herein, the campaign's data director articulates both that the knowledge campaigns have is limited in general, and that it is limited specifically to information contained in public records. If this is true for Obama's presidential campaign, it is all the more relevant to less sophisticated races in American politics. Uniquely, one need not rely on just elite interviews to get this point. I have the campaigns' own data to prove it.

Importantly, the information fallacy lurks in academic research on campaign strategy as well. But it is more subtle. Consider a standard technique in which a researcher asks a sample of voters in a public opinion survey whether campaigns contacted them, and then studies the attributes of voters who answered yes and no. If the researcher infers from the characteristics of voters who reported being contacted that these were the characteristics that campaigns used as the basis for strategic electioneering, as classic works like Rosenstone and Hansen (1993) do, then one is setting aside the difficulty campaigns may have in estimating voters' attributes. When campaigns perceive voters, they do not see the opinions, traits, and behaviors that voters see in themselves. They see *perceived voters*, a simplified and distorted version of the electorate that is based on the data available to them.

## 1.3 CAMPAIGN TARGETING AS A NORMATIVE PROBLEM

Much of the public discourse about campaign targeting and the advent of large voter databases can be seen as a normative dialogue between two opposing sides.[5] One side holds that it is good for democracy when campaigns use these tools because the data help campaigns connect with voters in more meaningful ways than through bland television advertisements. Just as an Amazon.com shopper might appreciate Amazon's ability to show him books that, based on his data profile, he is predicted to enjoy, a voter might appreciate a campaign that targets her with an appeal suited to her tastes. On the other side of the debate are concerns that campaigns' collection of personal data is an invasion of privacy and that pinpointing different messages to different voters violates an egalitarian norm of democracy.

I aim to inform the debate about the virtues and vices of voter targeting. I distinguish between two normative problems. The first problem relates to conflicts of interest inherent when politicians either use campaign data for governmental purposes or use governmental power to provide data to their campaigns. I argue that because politicians typically have both administrative and political incentives in their oversight of public records, there is reason to be concerned about conflicts of interest and abuses of power in this domain. At the end of the book, I offer several policy prescriptions to help mitigate these conflicts of interest.

The second normative question is whether microtargeting strategies promote or undermine democratic values. This book offers no clear answer to this question; indeed, I do not believe there is yet a clear answer. On the one hand, collecting personal data can help politicians better understand their constituents. Instead of politicians carrying around in their heads vague perceptions of their constituents, they can use verifiable empirical data to guide their perceptions. Furthermore, when one digs into these databases and realizes that they are mostly compilations of public records, this may mitigate concerns about the invasion of privacy. On the other hand, when political campaigns obtain data about the electorate, they mostly use the data to characterize voters as either with them or against them. Voters are complex, and campaigns use data to perceive a simplified version of that complex reality. Their simplified version is a polarized version in which voters are divided into those who are valuable to the campaign and those who are not. While the tension between these two perspectives remains a tension throughout the analysis, the book leaves this debate on a more informed footing and focuses the

debate on how campaigns' use of *public* records in particular may further
or hinder democratic values. I show how understanding the policy roots
of targeting can help resolve the tension between the two sides in this
debate.

## 1.4 OPPORTUNITIES AND CHALLENGES IN THE STUDY OF ELITES

The argument that the data environment affects strategic behavior is
an elite-level argument. My focus is how elite organizations – political
campaigns – perceive voters in their databases and how these perceptions
affect strategic choices, such as the choice to engage with partisans or with
nonpartisans, to focus on geographies or on individuals, to try to mobilize
or to persuade. I explore some downstream consequences of these effects,
examining how these strategic choices might in turn affect voter behavior.
However, the main focus is on the perceptions and behaviors of political
campaigns.

Studying elite organizations presents a different set of methodological
challenges than studying the mass public. In studies of the mass public, one
might use a random-sample survey to gauge the opinion of voters or use
an experiment to simulate how individuals react to certain stimuli. One
cannot as easily sample from a representative population of campaign
organizations to gauge their opinions or, even less plausibly, conduct
experiments on complex campaign organizations.

How, then, does one study the perceptions and behaviors of elite
organizations? Past research has largely taken two approaches. The first
approach is to do what Fenno did back in the 1970s: follow politicians
and political strategists around, interview them, and observe how their
apparent perceptions affect their behavior. The chief drawback to this
case study approach is that it is difficult to know whether findings are
generalizable. Over the course of eight years, Fenno spent time with only
eighteen congressmen, and he went to lengths to explain that his cases
may not be representative of other members of Congress.

A second approach in the literature is to reformulate research questions
about elite decision making so that they can be studied by assessing
downstream, observable outcomes of the decisions. For example, one can
assess the television advertisements broadcast by campaigns and then try
to reverse-engineer the strategic choices that led to those advertisements.
Similarly, one can ask voters in mass opinion surveys about whether
campaigns reached out to them and then study the relationship between
the personal attributes of voters and the variance in reported campaign

contact. The drawback with these approaches is that it is difficult to understand how elites perceive the electorate and how they make strategic choices only by observing the outputs of their choices, especially when those outputs are filtered through mass surveys that are plagued with response biases and misreporting biases.

In this book, I chart a new methodological course. The data I have collected come from the perspective of elites, not the perspective of the mass public. This represents a return to the study of elite perceptions that has been somewhat lost with the sweeping influence of mass opinion research in the last fifty years. But instead of using case studies, I capitalize on a recent centralization of data resources in campaign politics that allows me to study hundreds of campaigns simultaneously. In recent years, politicians typically are not using their own data and technological resources to perceive voters and pursue their strategies; rather they are relying on private firms and national parties to supply the data and technology for them. By partnering with the data suppliers, I examine how hundreds of campaigns perceive voters and how those perceptions affect their strategic behavior.

The bulk of the empirical evidence comes from research partnerships with two of the most important companies on the Democratic side of politics. The first partnership allowed me to see voters as they appear to campaigns. The second partnership allowed me to understand how the provision of public records influences the decisions of political campaign workers who are involved in direct forms of voter contact.

In the first partnership, I contracted with a company called Catalist. Catalist maintains a continually updated national database of voters, wherein each voter is listed with more than 700 predicted characteristics. More than sixty-five members of Congress use Catalist's data, as do the major party organizations, such as the Democratic Congressional Campaign Committee and the Democratic Senatorial Campaign Committee; national unions, including AFL-CIO and the Teamsters; major issue organizations, such as the ACLU, Planned Parenthood, and the Sierra Club; and dozens of other organizations and campaigns, both local and national use Catalist as well. The 2008 Obama campaign also used Catalist data. By studying the content of records in Catalist's database, I am studying the voters as they appear to all of these campaigns. These are the voters as campaigns perceive them when they are deciding how to engage with the mass public. By studying how campaigns use Catalist's data in targeting voters, one can learn how perceptions affect strategies across a wide range of campaigns.

In the second partnership, I worked in conjunction with a company called NGP VAN. NGP VAN maintains a secure website through which nearly all Democratic campaigns access voter records. NGP VAN is not a database; it is a Web-based resource that enables campaigns to interact with data coming from Catalist, from the Democratic National Committee, or from other sources. In 2012, approximately 100,000 individuals associated with the Obama reelection campaign had log-ins to NGP VAN's secure portal, as did thousands of workers and candidates involved in races for down-ballot offices. My colleague Ryan Enos and I, in partnership with the 2012 Obama campaign and 25 state Democratic parties, embedded a survey into NGP VAN's secure website and interviewed more than 3,500 campaign workers from nearly 200 different campaigns, asking them about how they were engaging with voters in real time, as they were logged into the NGP VAN system. This survey allowed me to measure the effects of the public data environment on strategic choices of campaigns.

Once I explain these data sources in greater detail, I proceed to discuss the extent to which they are representative, what they can tell us, as Democratic data resources, about perceptions and strategies on the Republican side, and their various limitations as research tools. However, these sources enable me to study elite perceptions in a new way. The survey of campaign workers enables me to measure the behavior and opinions of a small number of individuals who, in the moment they are being surveyed, are actively engaged in direct voter-contacting strategies. The data from Catalist enable me to witness voters as they appear to political campaigns in the political campaigns' own data. Moreover, while campaigns vary substantially in their resources and strategies, my Catalist and NGP VAN partnerships leverage the fact that many campaigns are actually working with a common set of data and tools. By studying those data and tools, I am able to characterize the perceptions and strategic choices of hundreds of campaigns all at once. To buttress these data sources, I also collected data and interviews piecemeal from a number of individual campaigns. I did so to supplement my study of the Catalist and NGP VAN records with data and strategies from races either less sophisticated or more sophisticated than the typical campaign utilizing Catalist or NGP VAN.

## Which Campaigns? Which Years? A First-Order Analysis

As I describe in greater detail in Chapter 3, individual-level voter lists have been used by campaigns at least as early as the turn of the twentieth century, when local election offices began printing voter registration lists. The kinds of lists used by political campaigns have gone through several stages of development, the most recent of which can be pegged at the 2008 election, when campaigns operating in every state could easily and cheaply use data from the national parties or from private companies to target voters. While I discuss historic uses of voter data, my main focus is on the use of data in targeting strategies in the 2008, 2010, and 2012 election cycles.

In partnering with data and technology suppliers to campaigns, Catalist and NGP VAN, I aim to depict strategic behavior in as broad a range of campaigns as possible in the years since 2008. My focus is on the common perceptions of voters as they appear in microtargeting databases in these years. Which campaigns use targeting databases most actively? Campaigns that can cultivate staff and volunteers to make phone calls and knock on doors. Not every campaign has such manpower; typically it is competitive House, Senate, gubernatorial, and presidential races that cultivate the support necessary for large-scale canvassing operations. However, many campaigns without significant manpower can utilize direct mail and send messages to households based on targeting strategies that are also defined by voter databases. The financial barrier to campaigns using targeting databases in direct mail and in canvassing is far lower than the barrier to broadcasting television advertisements. As such, compared to TV ads, direct contact is a strategy applicable to a much more diverse set of campaigns.

Quite obviously, direct voter targeting is a more sophisticated enterprise in campaigns for the presidency than in races for Congress or for state legislative seats. And surely, campaigns have innovated in certain ways since 2008 such that their strategies have changed over the period I am studying. Given this variation over time and across races, how is it possible to generate hypotheses that will be applicable to all these kinds of races, as I hope to do here? Furthermore, to what extent will my analysis of 2008–2012 campaigns remain relevant as campaigns continue to innovate?

To answer these questions, it is worth distinguishing between first-order effects on elite perceptions and second-order effects on elite perceptions. Public records, I demonstrate, have a first-order effect on elite perceptions: across races and years, the provision of voter registration data affects how campaigns strategize in the context of direct voter contact. One might least expect public records to constrain the perceptions formed by sophisticated presidential campaigns, whose ample resources easily overcome the limits of public data in perceiving voter attitudes. But

I show that public record laws have dramatic effects on strategy even at the presidential level. I show that the presidential campaign that is widely considered to be the most sophisticated user of direct contacting strategies did indeed perceive the electorate quite differently across jurisdictions on account of the public data environment. The effects are even stronger in the down-ballot races, which do not supplement their data resources with as much information beyond public records.

Popular retrospectives written about presidential campaigns tend to focus on the tricks and novel methods that accompany each new election season. The Obama campaigns targeted voters on Facebook; they had analytics teams measuring how to phrase e-mail messages to solicit donations; they acquired data from more sources than any down-ballot campaign; and so on. Focusing on new tricks, one may miss that the 2012 Obama campaign had 100,000 staff and volunteers logging in to the NGP VAN website and engaging voters in ways very similar to campaigns for lower offices. In this book, I aim to focus on the campaign contacting strategies that are common across races, not the bells and whistles employed only by the campaigns at the cutting edge.

At the same time, I demonstrate that the bells and whistles of the cutting-edge campaigns have only second-order effects on elite perceptions. I show that while the 2012 Obama campaign perceived voter attitudes more accurately than did the 2008 Obama campaign, and while sophisticated campaigns that use microtargeting models perceive voters more accurately than do campaigns that only use public records, these differences are small when compared to the ways the availability of public records in any campaign and in any year affects perceptions. The cutting-edge strategies that presidential campaigns might use to help them perceive voters cannot substitute for the clear perceptions that campaigns have when certain public records are available to them.

In short, public records have a first-order effect on elite perceptions; innovations by technologically advanced campaigns have second-order effects. I emphasize this point, and show empirical evidence to support it, because this enables me to characterize a wide range of campaigns across multiple election cycles. I aim to develop predictions about elite behavior that are not applicable only to campaigns at this particular juncture in time, but rather to explain an element of campaign strategy applicable to election years in the past and in the future.

As a final matter of clarification, I emphasize that the perceptions and resultant strategies I study here are specific to individual-level contact. At a theoretical level, a model that takes seriously the perceptual biases of strategists is appropriate for understanding other forms of voter engagement, such as TV, radio, and Web-based ads. In the future, as these forms of advertisement become even more amenable to individualized appeals, the theory considered here will become more applicable to these alternative methods of campaign engagement. However, my empirical analysis is focused on strategies of the "ground campaign."

There are three reasons why I am particularly focused on individual-level strategies. First, these strategies can incorporate the most fine-grained decisions. In mass-media appeals, campaigns can decide between using one type of message or another or targeting one geographic area or another, but with direct targeting, campaigns decide which individual voters to target. Second, the same individual-level databases used in direct contacting strategies are also now being used in official government business, specifically in congressional offices to facilitate constituent services. Thus, the perceptions that campaigns garner from the databases which I study are the same perceptions that congressional offices are garnering in their constituent service databases. This fact connects my study of campaign strategy to a larger story of political representation in the United States. Third, I show that public records laws are a lever that particularly affects perceptions and strategies of direct contact, connecting this study of campaigns to broader effects of public policy on political relationships.

## 1.5 PLAN OF THE BOOK

In the next chapter, I lay out the logic of the Perceived Voter Model and generate testable hypotheses. I theorize about how campaigns perceive voters. For example, how do campaigns perceive which voters are likely supporters or which voters are persuadable? Many previous analyses of campaigns imagine campaigns as having encyclopedic-like knowledge of voters, from party machines presumed to have networks of precinct captains who know intimately the dispositions of voters in their neighborhoods to tech-savvy microtargeting campaigns, presumed, as CNN put it, to "know you better than you know yourself." I examine the circumstances under which campaigns could reasonably have detailed knowledge of voter dispositions, and I explain why campaigns operating in large-scale electorates do not have such detailed knowledge of voters.

Rather than possessing detailed knowledge of voters, campaigns use a set of heuristics to form rough predictions about voters' political dispositions. I consider the various heuristics, or shortcuts, that campaigns can use to perceive voters' dispositions, and I offer reasons why public records, such as records in the voter registration system, bear certain qualities that make them particularly useful as information shortcuts. Given the importance I ascribe to public records in helping campaigns perceive voter attributes, it follows that the provision of public records in a given jurisdiction will result in predictable strategic behavior on the part of campaigns. I offer hypotheses predicting a number of ways that the provision of key public records affects how campaigns target voters and how voters behave as a result. For example, campaigns want to perceive voters' likely partisanship. In some places, these perceptions are informed by voter registration records of party affiliation; in other places, they must be informed by alternative sources of data. Depending on the source of data, campaigns will perceive different voters as partisans and engage them accordingly.

The most controversial argument I make for why campaigns perceive voters through the lens of public records is that election-motivated politicians design public records to be useful to their campaigns. Before turning to the empirical tests of the key hypotheses, in Chapter 3, I take a historical view of public records in order to flesh out this argument. I show that, since the turn of the twentieth century, political campaigns have capitalized on public records in the voter registration system. I show evidence that laws governing the collection and distribution of voter registration data are sometimes made with political considerations in mind. The very existence of microtargeting databases can be explained in part by policymakers, over a long period of time, crafting data laws in ways that serve the needs of their political campaigns. Detailing the history of these data laws helps set the stage for investigating strategic choices in recent elections.

Following this theoretical and historical exploration for why public record laws bear on elite perceptions, I begin an empirical investigation of contemporary campaign strategy. In Chapter 4, I introduce the data sources that enable me to test how perceptions affect campaign strategy and voter outcomes. I discuss how data obtained from Catalist, NGP-VAN, and other sources enable me to describe the voters perceived through a campaign's-eye-view. The Catalist data offers a window into how voters are perceived in the hundreds of real-world political campaigns that use Catalist as a vendor. One of the key features of Catalist data I introduce in Chapter 4 and that I study throughout the empirical investigation is Catalist's targeting models. Catalist generates predictive models that estimate, for every voter in the country, attributes such as the likelihood they are a Democratic supporter or the likelihood they will vote in an upcoming election. The outputs of these models are quantitative representations of elite perceptions of voters. Campaigns turn to models like Catalist's to gauge whether a voter is a likely supporter, likely opponent, or likely swing voter. I study Catalist's targeting models as representations of sophisticated elite perceptions.

A second novel source of quantitative data stems from a survey of campaign workers that I conducted with my colleague Ryan Enos during the 2012 election season. Partnering with President Obama's reelection campaign, we programmed a survey into the computer system used by more than 100,000 campaign staffers and volunteers who worked on election campaigns from president on down to county commissioner. From June 2012 through the November Election Day, we surveyed these workers daily as they engaged with voters in the field. By studying how campaign workers interacted with the electorate, I examine the extent to which campaign efforts are predicted by features of the public data environment.

The key tests of the Perceived Voter Model are conducted in Chapters 5, 6, and 7. In Chapter 5, I focus on perceptions of partisanship. Campaigns have a clear interest in estimating which voters are likely supporters and which are not. However, their ability to perceive their core supporters varies by jurisdiction, since some U.S. states collect information about voters' party affiliation and history of voting in past primaries while others states do not. I first show how campaigns perceive partisanship differently in states that collect different types of public records that are indicative of partisanship. I then test how these perceptions lead to different strategic choices. Finally, I examine several implications for voting behavior consistent with the cross-state differences in campaign strategy.

In Chapter 6, I focus on perceptions of race. Because racial identity is highly correlated with party support, campaigns have a clear interest in estimating which voters are members of different racial groups. However, their ability to perceive voters by racial group varies by state, because some states require citizens to list their race on voter registration applications whereas other states do not. I first show how campaigns perceive voters' races in states that collect different types of records indicative of racial identity. I then test how these perceptions lead to different strategic choices. Finally, I examine implications for voting behavior consistent with cross-state differences in strategy.

In Chapter 7, I focus on perceptions of persuadable voters. Campaigns have a clear interest in identifying which voters are likely to vote but who are persuadable or undecided about their vote choice. However, unlike public records of partisanship and race, which, when they are available, are highly predictive of political support, there are essentially no records available to campaigns that are consistently predictive of persuadability. Persuadability is a psychological disposition that campaigns have no good way to estimate. In this chapter, I replicate the kinds of strategies that campaigns use to determine which voters should receive persuasion appeals. I then connect the voters who typically receive these appeals with survey data in order to demonstrate that typical voters targeted for persuasion do not resemble the kinds of voters that survey researchers would classify as persuadable. I argue that because no available record is consistently predictive of persuadability, campaigns cannot effectively target persuadable voters. As a result, persuasion efforts in direct contacting strategies are less efficient than mobilization efforts. The voters who are most ripe for persuasion cannot be pinpointed for individual-level contact.

Chapters 5–7 show that many voters perceived as partisan supporters, as African-Americans, or as persuadable do not actually bear these traits. And many voters who do bear these attributes are never contacted by campaigns. The *perceived voters* to whom campaigns make appeals are a rough and distorted approximation of the people to whom campaigns would like to address their appeals. Prior models of campaign strategy have predicted that in direct mobilization efforts, campaigns target individuals like partisan core supporters, persuadable voters, and racial groups that lean in their party's direction. But by focusing on the perceptions that campaigns have of groups like these – perceptions that lead to their actual contacting strategies – Chapters 5–7 provide an explanation for campaign contact that takes seriously the uncertainty that pervades strategic decision making even in highly sophisticated campaigns.

In Chapter 8, I return to a question that lingers from the analysis in the previous chapters. Why do the strategies of sophisticated campaigns vary so significantly across jurisdictions based on the availability of public records when these campaigns can supplement public records with access to hundreds of consumer microtargeting variables, proprietary party records, and rich social networks of supporters and activists? In Chapter 8, I offer evidence to support the claims that commercial records and proprietary records typically offer campaigns inaccurate perceptions of voter traits and that these records are typically not highly correlated with the political dispositions that campaigns care about. I also explain why campaigns have trouble reaching out to their supporters and to persuadable voters by leveraging social networks. Evidence for these claims helps explain why even in the most sophisticated campaign organizations, one can expect a campaign's strategic choices, now and in the future, to be predictable based on the data laws of the states in which they are operating. In essence, alternative data sources are no substitute for the basic descriptors that are publicly available in some jurisdictions.

In addition to summarizing the argument and findings, the final chapter, Chapter 9, evaluates the analysis in normative terms. How should we make sense of the use of microtargeting databases in political campaigns? Are these databases good for democracy or bad for democracy? As mentioned earlier, I distinguish between two normative questions. The first bears on the political co-optation of administrative data by political campaigns as well as the increasing use of political data in official government business. The second bears on whether microtargeting is good or bad for democracy. I believe there is a clear answer to the first normative question, and I offer some recommendations for safeguards against inappropriate uses of government data in campaign politics and inappropriate uses of campaign data in governance. As to the second question, there is no clear answer. I do, however, suggest that viewing campaign targeting strategies as consequences of specific policy choices adds substance to the debate about the value of targeting in a democracy. I point to future research and future policy reforms that can help address the question about whether targeted campaigning leads to better or worse democratic outcomes.

# 2

# The Perceived Voter Model

This chapter develops a model of campaign decision making. In an effort to win an election, campaigns seek to mobilize supporters and persuade undecided voters. In order to contact these voters and transmit mobilizing or persuasive messages, campaigns must predict which voters will be responsive to their appeals, and they must decide which voters should get which kinds of appeals. To make these decisions, campaigns gather data and form impressions about the voters. The Perceived Voter Model draws attention to how and why the particular set of data available to campaigns affects their assessments of voters, which in turn guides strategic decisions.

To draw the connection between data inputs, perceptions, and the actions taken by campaigns, this chapter aims to accomplish four tasks. First, as a preliminary matter, I define the aspect of campaign politics that is the focus of this study. Political scientists study a wide variety of phenomena that fall under the heading of campaigns; my first goal is to situate direct voter engagement in the context of campaign politics. Second, I define the *perceived voter* as consisting of the attributes of voters that campaigns consider when making strategic decisions. I discuss this concept as it relates to prior research on campaigns. Third, I define information shortcuts, or heuristics, that campaigns use to perceive voters, and I discuss the features of public records that make them important shortcuts for campaigns. I compare the use of public records as a shortcut in perceiving voters with two alternatives. The first alternative is *not* using shortcuts; the second alternative is using plausible shortcuts other than public records. Fourth, I generate hypotheses about how the use of public records as shortcuts is likely to affect the strategic decisions of campaigns and the turnout behavior of voters.

## 2.1 THE STRATEGY OF DIRECT CONTACT

The term "campaign" takes on multiple meanings in the study of elections. A campaign can designate the formal organization of a political candidate seeking office (as in the Obama campaign); a campaign can also designate a period of time leading up to an election (as in the "campaign season"). Voters can be influenced by both the formal organization of a campaign and the informal absorption of information from the news media and from peer-to-peer discussions ahead of an election (Brady, Johnston, and Sides, 2006). Unlike the informal influences on voters, however, the formal campaign organizations select specific strategies to influence voters' judgments. These strategies are the focus of this book.

Campaign organizations have multiple avenues of strategic influence. A campaign may try to influence voters by paid media advertisements, by drawing news media to planned events, and by volunteer-based and staff-based canvassing. For political scientists studying campaign effectiveness, most research has investigated canvassing techniques (e.g., Green and Gerber, 2008). But in studies of strategy, the focus has largely been on mass appeals and candidate events (e.g., Shaw, 2006; Vavreck, 2009). Presidential campaigns spend most of their budgets on paid media, and since these are broadcast, advertisements generate a paper trail that can be archived and studied. On the other hand, door-to-door, telephone, and mail appeals are largely volunteer-based (and therefore do not generate a money trail), and they are not broadcast (and therefore are not generally documented and archived). While political scientists can replicate canvassing efforts to study their effects on voters, it is not easy for them to study real-world canvassing strategies. As John Sides has written, "[T]his is the toughest part of the campaign to watch, since much of it is invisible."[1]

In spite of the difficulty in studying direct contact, it is important to pay attention to these sorts of strategies. Campaigns, even presidential ones, are increasingly putting effort into direct contact, according to accounts by the campaigns themselves (e.g., *2012 Obama Campaign Legacy Report*, 2013), popular accounts (e.g., Issenberg, 2012), and scholarly accounts (e.g., Darr and Levendusky, 2009; Masket, 2009). The 2012 Obama campaign claimed they recruited 2.3 million volunteers to engage in direct voter contact: roughly one of every hundred adults in the United States. The 2012 Romney campaign reported having contacted voters more than 225 million times (*Voter Contact Summary*, 2012).

When campaigns use volunteers and staff to interact with individual voters, what does this strategy look like? In campaigns for offices as low as county commissioner to offices as high as the presidency, direct contact has some common features across races. Campaigns often start with a prediction of voter turnout in the upcoming election. From there, they subset the electorate into different categories of people that merit attention. Some subgroups need to be IDed – identified as a supporter or an opponent; some need to be mobilized on Election Day but do not need to be persuaded to vote for the candidate; others will surely vote but their vote is up for grabs and so they need to be persuaded; and still others may be solicited for volunteer opportunities or for donations (Malchow, 2008). With varying degrees of sophistication, campaigns decide how to classify and prioritize these voters. No matter the campaign, strategists will decide which voters to approach and which to ignore, and which messages to give to voters they do approach.

Once they have a "field plan" outlining these decisions, campaigns send staffers and volunteers to talk to voters. Figure 2.1 shows an example of an actual script used in a volunteer-based voter contact effort. The script is from a state senate campaign, but its format is quite similar to scripts used in campaigns for nearly every level of office. At the top, we learn that this script is being used on 663 voters who live in 465 homes. Volunteers are asked to record detailed information about the interaction with each contacted voter. Data from these scripts are collected and fed back to the campaign so that the campaign can estimate how well it is doing, and also so it knows which voters to contact to get out the vote on Election Day.

Compared to ads or campaign events, direct voter engagement elicits a very concrete form of feedback. Campaigns know how many voters have been reached and where those voters stand with respect to the candidates. Furthermore, this form of engagement can accommodate complex strategic decisions. Broadcast ads and even community events are blunt strategic tools compared to the process by which campaigns can direct contact to one household but not another. A campaign can easily design different scripts for different houses, or use different kinds of volunteers to engage with different kinds of targeted voters.

It is because campaigns can use detailed, individual-level profiles to guide their direct contacting strategies that I pay particular attention to

```
Script: General Election Call Script

People: 663

Doors: 465

Hi is _____ available?

My name is _____ and I am a volunteer with [redacted]'s campaign for State Senate. [Redacted] is the [redacted] candidate
running against [redacted] in the [redacted] Election on [redacted].

[Redacted] is a doctor and a health care policy expert who lives with his wife [redacted] in [redacted]. I'm supporting [redacted]
because we need truly new and independent leadership to make a real difference on [redacted]. [Redacted] is a doctor who works
every day with people who are struggling to find jobs, to gain access to affordable health care, and have good schools for their
children. And he is committed to standing up to special interests on [redacted] and I know he will always put the families in
the district first.

Action: Can we count on you to vote for [redacted] in the [redacted] Election, Tuesday [redacted]?

        1 = Yes voting for [redacted]
        2 = Leaning towards [redacted]
        3 = Undecided
        4 = Leaning against [redacted]
        5 = Not voting for [redacted]
        0 = Not Voting
        R = Refused

IF YES:
Great! We really appreciate your support. The Election is on [redacted].

Action: Can you volunteer to help [redacted] get elected?

        Y = Yes
        N = No
        M = Maybe

Action: Would you be interested in a lawn sign?

        Y = Yes
        N = No
        M = Maybe

IF Undecided:
Are there any questions or concerns that you have? (If you don't know the answer, take down their info and have the campaign
contact them later.)

IF NO:
Thank you very much for your time. Goodbye.
```

FIGURE 2.1 Example of a Real Targeting Script Used by Campaign Volunteers.

these strategies here. The content of personal information in campaign databases will affect their strategies in this domain. The informational inputs that campaigns use to target television ads will theoretically affect their behaviors in a similar way as I outline here, but my focus is on direct contact because it can accommodate the finest-grained strategic choices, it is particularly affected by variations in public data policy, and it relies on databases also used in constituent services and in other governmental functions.

## 2.2 THE PERCEIVED VOTER

Prior to having contact with voters through mail, phone, or in-person canvasses, campaigns must predict the personal attributes of voters. They need to know which voters they ought to prioritize and what messages different voters should receive. The main predictions campaigns try to make are the probability that a person will show up to vote and the probability they will support one candidate or party over the other. But campaigns can make more specific predictions as well, such as predictions about which voters support specific issues. Sophisticated campaigns have begun thinking not just in terms of likely support and likely voting but also in terms of "treatment responsiveness." In predicting responsiveness, the campaigns do not merely want to estimate which voters are undecided; rather they want to predict which voters will be moved in their attitudes by an appeal aimed at persuading them.[2]

When I refer to campaigns' perceiving voters, it is the campaigns' perceptions of a voter's likely partisan support, issue support, turnout likelihood, persuadability, treatment responsiveness, or other such attribute that I have in mind. The *perceived voter* refers to voters as they appear in these predictions made by campaigns. The *perceived voter* is contrasted with either objective indicators or with self-reported indicators of voters' attributes. For example, a campaign may perceive a particular group of voters to be persuadable, but this does not necessitate either that these voters think of themselves as persuadable or that these voters are actually persuadable.

The perceptions that campaigns have about voters can range from hunches carried around by strategists to predictions from statistical models. The perceptions offered by the Congressmen whom Richard Fenno studied were sometimes rooted in hard data, but were often based on gut feelings that politicians get as they interact with community members. In more recent years, campaign organizations develop statistical models that generate a score for each voter, which estimates the probability that they support a particular party or candidate or that they will be likely to vote. These scores are a contemporary version of a campaign's perception of voters that will affect the campaign's strategic decisions.

Whether a campaign's perceptions of voters' attributes come from gut feelings or statistical models, two obvious points about these perceptions deserve emphasis. First, a campaign's perception about a voter's attributes is likely to be different from a voter's own perception of his or her attributes. And second, all strategic decisions about voter engagement are based on campaigns' perceptions; they are based neither on voters' perceptions nor on some objective truth about voters' actual attributes.

These two claims are intuitive. But they point to hypotheses about campaign behavior that are quite different than one would consider if it is assumed that campaigns perceive voters as voters perceive themselves or if campaigns perceive some objective truth. Hypotheses that take seriously the perceptions of elites will focus on the data and tools that campaigns have at their disposal, and on the biases and limitations of those tools that affect campaign decisions. Hypotheses not rooted in perceptions are more likely to consider what campaigns would ideally like to do rather than what they actually can do given their informational limitations.

Consider alternative answers to the following question. Most strategic campaigns do not focus on transmitting appeals to young adults or to citizens not registered to vote. (Incidentally, the Obama campaign was an exception.) The question is: Why would the typical campaign choose to ignore these groups? From a perspective that is not focused on perceptions, one might simply reason that because young citizens and unregistered citizens tend not to vote regularly, campaigns would not want to waste resources on trying to engage them. From the perspective of the Perceived Voter Model, one might look to an entirely different set of explanations.

It turns out that young voters are just as responsive to appeals as older voters, but young people change residences so frequently that it is hard for campaigns to keep track of them (Nickerson, 2006). Nickerson found that younger voters were three times more likely to have an invalid phone number listed in campaign databases as older voters. Similarly, unregistered citizens may be responsive to campaign appeals; however, because campaign databases are frequently based on the registered population, it is difficult for campaigns to generate accurate contact lists of citizens who are not registered. In both cases, then, the reason why campaigns might not engage these voters is not necessarily because of the voters' true propensities, but because campaigns face challenges when trying to perceive the propensities of these voters.

In focusing attention on how available data affects a campaign's perceptions of the electorate and in turn affects its strategies for engaging with the electorate, the Perceived Voter Model emphasizes the role of uncertainty in elite decision making. A model of this kind has its roots in Anthony Downs's *Economic Theory of Democracy*. Downs writes:

> From the basic economic nature of becoming informed emerges the necessity of selection among data. Immediately there arises the crucial question

of how to decide which data to select and which to reject. The question is crucial because the answer chosen determines what type of information is used in making decisions and therefore shapes the decisions and their effectiveness. Furthermore... selection can be carried out by someone other than the decision-maker. Obviously, whoever carries it out has a potentially enormous influence upon decisions even if he does not make them himself. (p. 211)

Campaigns are actors that must select data in order to form impressions about the electorate. The data they select might be gathered from outside entities, like the government or commercial data aggregators. Whatever the data's source, the data that inform their perceptions will affect the decisions they make.

Many scholars have followed Downs in studying how information affects political decisions. They have studied how information and perceptions affect the ways that voters decide which candidates to support and which positions to take on issues (e.g., Key, 1966; Zaller, 1992; Lupia, 1994; Alvarez, 1999; Popkin, 1993; Lau and Redlawsk, 2006; Schaffner and Streb, 2007; Burden and Hillygus, 2009). They have also studied how polls and other sources of information affect how elites choose to represent voter interests (Geer and Goorha, 2003; Butler and Nickerson, 2011; Maestas, 2003) or how elites choose which issues to pay attention to (Jones and Baumgartner, 2005). In all cases, these studies have productively refocused attention away from what an actor would decide based on complete knowledge about a given situation, and toward how an actor actually decides based on the information that is available.[3]

The Perceived Voter Model adds a new wrinkle to the existing literature on information and political decision making. Previous studies of elite decision making, starting with Downs, have focused on the uncertainty that politicians have over questions of policy. For example, politicians are not sure which policies will attract a winning coalition of voters, and they may be uncertain about the position the median voter holds or the position their opponent holds. The form of elite uncertainty studied here is even more elementary than this. Even if politicians know what policy will attract a winning coalition, they still might not know how to mobilize that coalition. To do so, politicians need to know who their supporters are, and the task of determining which voters are supporters and which are not may be a difficult undertaking. To understand how campaigns endeavor to perceive their supporters, one must look at the data they use to inform their perceptions.

## The Voter and Perceived Voter in Past Research

In the study of American political campaigns, some scholars have been more attentive than others to the effect of elite perceptions on campaign strategies. In their landmark study, Huckfeldt and Sprague (1995) were particularly attuned to the difference between the campaign's view of a voter and the voter's view of a campaign. Their study of mobilization through social networks focuses on the latter. From that perspective, voters are not rows in campaign spreadsheets; they are people embedded in networks. But if one is to study voters from the campaign's perspective, as I do here, voters are perceived only by way of the data that campaigns are able to collect. Campaigns engage voters based on crude identifiers like those found in voter registration files. This type of data, Huckfeldt and Sprague (1992) note, "is the best the parties can do, because it is, in essence, all the information that is available (p. 74)." Hillygus and Shields (2008) and Shaw (2006) are similarly attentive to the idea that to understand how campaigns are interacting with voters, one must take the perspective of the campaign's-eye-view.[4]

However, a large class of research on campaign strategy conflates *perceived voters* with voters. Specifically, research that studies campaign strategy by surveying the mass public about their interactions with campaigns tends to conflate the attributes that voters report about themselves with attributes of voters that are perceived by campaigns. The most prominent work that uses this research method is Rosenstone and Hansen's (1993) book on mass mobilization. But other scholarship follows their lead, including, for example, Wielhouwer and Lockerbie (1994), Shaw, de la Garza, and Lee (2000), Goldstein and Ridout (2002), Gershtenson (2003), Wielhouwer (2003), McClurg (2004), Leighley (2005), Hillygus (2005), Parry et al. (2008), and Beck and Heidemann (2010), among others. Because Rosenstone and Hansen's research is the most prominent among these, I consider in more detail the kind of inference they make about campaign strategy related to direct voter engagement. I focus on their work to help clarify how the Perceived Voter Model leads to different predictions about campaign strategy than have been offered in previous scholarship.

Part of Rosenstone and Hansen's project is to develop a model of direct mobilization. By direct mobilization they have in mind the same kinds of strategies as I do here. They write:

> Leaders mobilize people *directly* when they contact citizens personally and encourage them to take action. Door-to-door canvasses by campaign

organizations, direct mail solicitations by political agitators, television appeals for aid by presidents, and grass-roots letter drives by interest groups are examples of direct mobilization. (p. 26)

Rosenstone and Hansen's theory of direct mobilization suggests that to maximize the impact of their efforts, campaigns will mobilize people who they already know, who are at the center of social networks, who are powerful, and who due to their "resources, interests, preferences, or beliefs" are likely to participate in politics. Rosenstone and Hansen offer this model not just as a theory of mobilization in small-scale elections but primarily as a model of large-scale electioneering. Indeed, they test their hypotheses in the context of large-scale elections like presidential and congressional campaigns.

Rosenstone and Hansen generate a set of specific hypotheses: employees of large companies, members of associations, organizational leaders, the wealthy, the well educated, and core partisans will all be mobilized because they are centered in social networks and are likely to take part in politics. However, without accounting for the idea that campaigns act upon their knowledge of *perceived voters* rather than knowledge of real voters, Rosenstone and Hansen's model of strategic mobilization is more aptly characterized as a model of what political campaigns may want to do rather than a model of what campaigns actually do. Their model sets aside that campaigns may not know which voters are employed or unemployed, well educated or poorly educated, members of organizations or not, likely to participate or not, and centered in social networks or not. Whether campaigns know these attributes of voters is a testable question. When I test it, it becomes clear that typical campaigns cannot mobilize voters on the basis of many of these characteristics.

Other prominent theories of campaigns also ignore perceptual biases. Kramer (1966), for instance, investigates the relative value to campaigns of geographic-level mobilization strategies and individual-level mobilization strategies, but he sets aside how perceptions of partisans might vary in their accuracy. As another example, Bartels (1998) devises a measure of a social group's "mobilization value" from the perspective of a campaign. But the model ignores the campaign's difficulty in connecting with groups it wishes to. Certain education cohorts, religious cohorts, and partisan cohorts are considered to have mobilization value in Bartels's model, regardless of whether a campaign can figure out how to reach them. Groups thought to be of mobilization value, like individuals who attended a couple of years of college but did not graduate, do not identify with a major religion, or are "pure" independents, may have hypothetical mobilization value, but they have no real value in direct engagement strategies if campaigns cannot actually find them.

Because of the frequent, implicit assumption that campaigns know about voters what voters know about themselves, scholars tend to utilize public opinion surveys and infer campaign strategy from the perceptions of voters. A common approach has been to use the National Election Study (NES) survey that asks respondents the following question:

> The political parties try to talk to as many people as they can to get them to vote for their candidates. Did anyone from one of the political parties call you up or come around and talk to you about the campaign? Which party was that?

This is the survey question that Rosenstone and Hansen use to test the hypotheses of their model. Since self-reported church attendees, high-income earners, homeowners, members of unions, Southern blacks, and voters possessing other traits report being contacted by political campaigns, Rosenstone and Hansen infer that campaigns strategically mobilize these groups. But again, campaigns may not be able to perceive these traits as voters perceive them.

To be clear, my critique of mass survey-based studies of campaign strategy is theoretical, not methodological. Previous critiques of survey-based approaches to the study of campaign strategy have focused on methodological problems, like misreporting bias: respondents answering questions about contact with campaigns misreport their contact at high rates (Bradburn, Rips, and Shevell, 1987; Ansolabehere, Iyengar, and Simon, 1999; Vavreck, 2007). My critique is that there is an informational gap between what campaigns know about voters and what voters know about themselves, such that one could not possibly reverse-engineer campaign strategy from the perceptions of voters as generated from mass surveys, even if there were no survey biases. Voters simply do not know what campaigns know about them.

## 2.3 PERCEIVED VOTERS IN SHORTCUTS AND ENCYCLOPEDIAS

If one way to anticipate strategic choices is to investigate the perceptions of strategists, the next question is: How do strategists form their perceptions? What are their data inputs? I posit that campaigns use a particular set of *shortcuts*. The choice of which shortcuts are used affects perceptions of voters, which affects the strategies employed. In the empirical analysis, I show how the use of particular shortcuts affects strategic behavior and

I show evidence for the reasons why certain shortcuts matter more than others do. But here, I explain why I refer to campaign data as shortcuts and how one might alternatively view the inputs to a campaign's perceptions.

The idea of information shortcuts, or heuristics, that are used in political decision making is rooted in research on voter behavior. Researchers of mass political behavior have asked how citizens can make decisions in the voting booth when most of them know very little about public policy or candidates' positions. Researchers' answers have focused on the strategies voters use to make decisions in the absence of encyclopedic knowledge of politicians. Scholars have studied how voters use the party affiliation and demographics of the candidates, and the endorsements made by influential elites, among other such shortcuts, to help them make their decisions (Lupia, 1994; Rahn, 1993; Bartels, 1996; Lau and Redlawsk, 2001). This scholarship has asked both about the kinds of shortcuts voters use and the effect of using these shortcuts on voting decisions.

In the study of voter decision making, it is straightforward to assume that voters do not have encyclopedic knowledge of issue positions and roll-call votes of politicians ahead of Election Day. Voters' political knowledge is easily verifiable in public opinion surveys. Because of this assumption, studies of voter decision making can proceed to questions about the plausible shortcuts voters may use and the consequences of their use.

With campaigns, one cannot assume that political organizations do not have encyclopedic knowledge of voters in their electorates. In fact, from popular and scholarly accounts of campaigns, the opposite is often assumed – that campaigns know everything about each voter that they would like to know. Old-fashioned party machines evoke the sense that party bosses, through their armies of precinct captains, kept detailed records on each voter (Gosnell, 1933). Contemporary party organizations, with their microtargeting databases, are described as having complete profiles of voters as well. As *Washington Post* columnist Dana Milbank claimed, politicians "know not just your name, address, and voting history but also your age and the age of your children, whether you smoke cigars, where you shop, where you attend church, what kind of car you drive, how old it is, whether you're on a diet, and what type of pet you have."[5] If campaigns know so much, then perhaps one could contemplate strategic decisions without worrying about how a limited set of data informs elite perceptions. On the other hand, if campaigns mostly rely on information shortcuts, then understanding how campaigns pursue voters necessitates an investigation into the shortcuts.

There are thus two ways to conceive of campaign perceptions of voters. In one view, campaigns perceive voters through crude shortcuts. In another view, campaigns and parties have encyclopedic knowledge of voter dispositions. Political scientist James Scott (1998) might call this encyclopedic knowledge *metis*, defined as an intimate knowledge that comes from direct experience interacting with a local population.

To make this distinction concrete, imagine John Doe, who is registered as a Democrat and lives in a highly Democratic area. Suppose that John Doe nevertheless personally identifies as a Republican and that he even tells all of his friends and neighbors that he is truly a Republican in his heart. Under the encyclopedic framework, a presidential campaign or national political party might be able to ascertain John Doe's true Republican leanings; under a framework that suggests campaigns are reliant on shortcuts like public registration records, the campaign organization would perceive him as a Democrat no matter how he perceives himself and no matter that all of his friends know he is a Republican.

There are three conditions under which a campaign could reasonably approach this kind of encyclopedic knowledge and not be reliant on shortcuts. One condition is that if the campaign is operating on a small scale, it might indeed have something akin to encyclopedic knowledge. In a small electorate, like a school board district, a candidate may easily ascertain the landscape of voters and nonvoters, base supporters, opponents, and swing voters. In such an electorate, shortcuts that could help predict who is a likely supporter or a likely voter are of little use because with so few voters, these attributes do not have to be modeled – they are simply known (Oliver, Ha, and Callen, 2012). Similarly, if the objective of a campaign is to recruit not large numbers of voters but rather small numbers of volunteers, political caucus participants, protesters, or donors, then it is possible to use private knowledge rather than statistical data mining to find prospective participants (see Verba, Schlozman, and Brady, 1995; Brady, Lehman, Schlozman, and Verba, 1999; Hersh, 2012). Along these lines, Geer (1996) argues that in small electorates, it is reasonable for politicians to perceive citizens' policy preferences, and thus no informational barrier exists that could lead the politician to use polling to understand voters better. In small-scale environments, personal relationships and social networks can be the basis for campaign strategy. However, when an electorate contains 400,000 registered voters, as in a congressional district, or 185 million registered voters as in a presidential election, the sheer scale makes it difficult to perceive voters based on intimate local knowledge.

A second condition that might allow campaigns to perceive voters without relying on shortcuts, even in large-scale electorates, is if the campaigns can learn over time. If a campaign or party can interact with voters over an extended period of time, and if they can retain information about each voter, they might be able to build profiles of voters that are based not on crude shortcuts but on more intimate knowledge. However, in the context of large-scale electorates, there are a number of reasons why it is difficult for an organization, even a long-standing political party, to retain information about individual voters.

First, the electorate is in flux: new voters come into the electorate, old voters die, and many voters move across jurisdictional lines, thus limiting a candidate's ability to track people over time. Second, arguably the most valuable information campaigns could know about the electorate is the outcome of each citizen's vote choice in past elections, which is private. Third, owing to the size of large electorates, few personal connections are possible between a party organization and a voter, and even when personal connections are made, it is difficult for campaigns to ascertain a reliable estimate of the voters' dispositions. In part, this is because campaign workers who are interacting with voters are biased in their perceptions of voters and often overoptimistic about where voters stand (as I show). In part, it is also because when voters talk to a campaign worker who has approached them, they might misreport their opinions so as to avoid an uncomfortable conversation. Fourth, voters' opinions are in flux; their level of support may be candidate-specific. Fifth, owing to the candidate-centered nature of American politics, information that a party's candidate gathered in one year may not be shared with the party's candidate in the next year (Shaw, 2006). Because of limitations like these, it may be quite difficult for campaigns or parties to build up detailed profiles about individual voters.

A third condition under which a campaign could engage with voters based on practical knowledge rather than shortcuts is if the campaign could leverage social networks to transmit messages. Even in a large population, and even in the absence of learning, a campaign might still pursue a strategy of direct contact with voters based on networks rather than relying on lists of voters and informational shortcuts. Campaigns do indeed use network-based strategies, but any observer of a congressional or presidential campaign's direct contacting operations will surely notice that most of the contact that occurs in in-person canvasses, phone banks, and mailers is not network based. Rather, it involves volunteers contacting voters who they do not know, but who are perceived by strategists as being a likely supporter or an undecided voter. I offer some empirical evidence that explains why social network–based strategies are not the main pursuit of direct-contacting efforts. But the logic of why network strategies are limited can be summarized as follows.

First, social network–based campaigns rely on their activist supporters to transmit messages. Given the size of networks of influence and the number of people willing to engage other citizens on behalf of a campaign, the networks to which activists are tied contain too small of a population to be the main focus of a large-scale campaign.[6] Later, I report on a case study of a campaign that put substantial resources into recruiting voters through networks, and it found that it could engage less than 1 percent of the electorate in this way. Second, given the political homogeneity of the social networks in which activists are often embedded, activists are not connected to many of the sporadic and undecided voters to whom campaigns most want to appeal. And finally, recent campaigns that have attempted to leverage social networks of activists have found that campaign volunteers prefer to interact with strangers rather than to try to engage their personal acquaintances in conversations about politics.

Because campaigns for offices such as congress member, senator, governor, or president want to engage many thousands or millions of voters, and because they face challenges in learning about the preferences and dispositions of individual voters either by building up proprietary records of voters over time or by leveraging social networks, they tend to rely on shortcuts found in databases. They collect personal data from available sources and use these data to inform their strategic choices. This is not to argue that campaigns never have encyclopedic knowledge about voter preferences. Rather I posit, contrary to the image of the all-knowing campaign with its vast databases, the conditions under which campaigns can obtain intimate knowledge of voters are rarely met in large-scale elections. Just as most voters do not have the kind of encyclopedic knowledge about candidates that enables them to clearly perceive candidates' positions, candidates rarely have this kind of knowledge about voter preferences either. Thus, if one seeks to understand strategic choices of campaigns, the shortcuts campaigns use to make predictions about voters are a useful place to look.[7]

## Choice Among Shortcuts

Given that large-scale campaigns rely on shortcuts to form perceptions of voters, why would they rely on one type of shortcut over another? Useful shortcuts will bear some obvious characteristics. First, campaigns will foremost seek out shortcuts that are predictive of the attributes they care most about, such as how supportive or persuadable a voter is likely to be. Second, since campaigns are interested in predicting the attributes of many people – in the case of the national campaigns and parties, they are potentially interested in perceiving the entire U.S. electorate – they might prioritize data that are available for a large segment of the public. Third, as articulated by Downs in his theory of information acquisition, decision makers will prioritize information that is low in cost.

In considering plausible shortcuts that campaigns might use, then, it is useful to think about how predictive those shortcuts are of traits campaigns care about, how much of the population they cover, and how expensive they are for campaigns to acquire. Consider a piece of data that campaigns may be able to obtain from commercial aggregators, such as a consumer's preference for anchovies, which the *Los Angeles Times* highlighted all the way back in 2006 as being in the Republican Party's secret database. Is this consumer preference a useful shortcut that will help campaigns perceive the political dispositions of voters? Upon reflection, it is clear that this kind of information is unlikely to be relevant to campaigns' perceptions. Why? For one, there is no evidence that preferences for anchovies are highly correlated with the political preferences that campaigns care about. Even consumer attributes that appear more politically relevant than anchovy enthusiasm often tend not to be predictive of political attributes, once demographic variables are taken into account. For example, owning a boat may be correlated with being a Republican. But once one accounts for the basic correlates of partisanship (like neighborhood wealth, age, race, and region), commercial predictions of boat ownership do not explain additional variance in a model of partisanship or turnout, as I will confirm.

Even supposing that a consumer habit like anchovy consumption was predictive of some political attribute, there is yet another problem a campaign faces: a campaign's perception of which voters like anchovies might be very inaccurate. Just as campaigns do not know, ahead of their first contact, which voters are supportive of their candidate, they similarly do not know which voters are actually anchovy enthusiasts. Commercial aggregators that supply information to campaigns about consumer preferences do not actually tell them which specific individuals buy anchovies or own boats. Aggregators supply campaigns with predictions from statistical models. An aggregator might form this prediction by administering a consumer survey to a small sample of the population, predicting a self-reported preference for anchovies with demographic and geographic characteristics from the sample and then applying the predictions to the rest of the population whose preferences for anchovies are unknown. Predictions that come from models like these tend to not be very accurate, a claim that I also confirm empirically.

On top of these limitations, there are the limitations of coverage and cost. Because anchovies are a niche product, even if this preference was correlated with political preferences, it would only be predictive for a small number of people. This does not mean that this preference could not be used by campaigns, but it means that this sort of correlate, even if predictive of political attitudes, might be of secondary value to a campaign. Finally, perceiving the electorate through consumer preferences may be costly. A campaign or a political data vendor not only must pay a commercial aggregator for the data, but it must then pay to link the data to the personal identifiers in campaign databases that continually change as voters move around and as they enter and exit the election system.

To generalize beyond this silly example of anchovy consumers, then, a data input might not help campaigns perceive voter attributes for a number of different reasons. The data might be costly and it might provide information limited to a small segment of the electorate. The attribute captured by the data might not be predictive of a politically relevant trait. And the data available about the attribute might be a poor predictor of the attribute itself.

In comparison to predictions of consumer preferences that stem from commercial databases, it is easy to understand why public records from the election administration would be more useful shortcuts for campaigns when they form perceptions of voters. Consider that in many states, when citizens register to vote, they are asked to indicate their political party affiliation, which becomes a public record. In a prediction of likely partisan support, a voter's party registration status is quite informative; not every registered Democrat or Republican votes for their parties' candidates, but registration and partisan support are highly correlated. Moreover, this piece of data is wide in coverage and low in cost: local governments assemble registration lists with contact information for every voter along with a party affiliation, and they often supply this information about all the voters in the jurisdiction to campaigns for free.

Importantly, personal information about voters that is collected in public records is useful to campaigns not only because these records are accurate, predictive of politically relevant attributes, and low in cost, and not only because the alternatives, such as consumer records, tend not to bear these characteristics. In the next chapter, I also make the case that public records are often *designed* to be useful to campaigns. Unlike commercial records that are generated by private companies and used mostly in consumer marketing, public records are generated by politicians who can collect data for the benefit of their campaigns. At the very least, politicians can ensure that policies regulating the dissemination of administrative data permit political organizations to acquire the data that will be useful in their campaigns. It is not by accident that a system of personal data regulated by politicians serves the informational needs of these same politicians.

However, in some jurisdictions, campaigns lack key public records such as party registration. In these cases they can attempt to perceive voters' attributes by turning to alternative information shortcuts. As I show, they can perceive voters by focusing on voters' geographic location, consumer habits, or by using other data. But when estimated through these alternative mechanisms and even when estimated through high-tech statistical models, the perceptions that come from data will not be perfect substitutes for the perceptions that come from government data. The *perceived voters* are estimated from one kind of data will be different from the *perceived voters* estimated from another kind. Because perceptions vary, strategies vary. And because strategies vary, the class of voters who are mobilized to participate varies. Thus, to predict how campaigns engage with voters, one can trace the causal chain from available data to perceptions to strategies. This is the purpose of the Perceived Voter Model.

## 2.4 HYPOTHESES

I have so far explained why campaigns need to rely on shortcuts (i.e., they do not have encyclopedic knowledge of the electorate) and why public records containing personal information about voters may serve as particularly useful shortcuts. If a campaign wants to perceive how persuadable or supportive a voter is so that the campaign can decide how to, and whether to, interact with the voter, personal data collected by the election administration will contribute to that perception. Consequently, public data laws that regulate the kinds of information collected and distributed by governments are a lever that will likely affect strategic choices. Governments decide the kinds of data to collect about voters in public records. These decisions affect how campaigns can perceive voters and how these perceptions translate into strategies.

In formulating specific hypotheses, I focus on strategies of mobilizing supporters and strategies of persuading undecided voters. I posit that strategic decisions for mobilization and persuasion can be explained by variations in public data laws. Broadly, I hypothesize that the availability of public records that are predictive of partisan support or persuadability will affect whether a campaign utilizes a geographic-level contacting strategy or an individual-level contacting strategy; which voters receive attention, such as partisans or independents; and the basis for campaign contact. By the basis of contact I mean, for example, that given the availability of a public record, a campaign might appeal to a voter because she is a Democrat; given the unavailability of that record, a campaign might appeal to the same voter because she is female or because she is white.

There are two kinds of public records that are highly predictive of partisan support and vary in their availability across states. These are records of party affiliation and racial identity. When campaigns can utilize public records that indicate a voter's party registration, I hypothesize that campaigns will focus more on mobilizing individual voters because of their partisan identity, and they will focus less on the geographic areas that are highly concentrated with partisans. (In Appendix A, I consider in more detail this hypothesis about how a campaign's use of geographic or individual-level strategies depends on the data environment that informs its perceptions of voters. I do so by taking Kramer's [1966] classic theoretical model of canvassing and extending it to accommodate perceptions that vary in their accuracy across jurisdictions.) When party data are available in public records, I further hypothesize that campaigns will focus more on mobilizing supporters and less on trying to persuade undecided voters. Furthermore, because party registration data signals which voters are likely supporters or opponents, when these data are available, I hypothesize that campaigns will have less accidental contact with voters of the opposite party. As a downstream effect of the data, I expect that turnout will be higher among partisans in environments in which public records of partisanship are available, but lower in geographic areas concentrated with partisans.

When voter registration records contain information on individual voters' races, I hypothesize that campaigns will focus more on mobilizing voters because of their racial identity, and they will focus less on mobilizing voters because of the racial composition of their neighborhoods. Because blacks are a racial group that supports one party at a very high rate and because, as I show, it is difficult for campaigns to predict which voters are black absent individually identifying public records, I hypothesize that blacks in particular will be mobilized to vote more in states with public race data. In states without public race data, I expect turnout to be lower among blacks but higher in areas in which blacks are concentrated, since campaigns must use a geographic strategy rather than an individual strategy for mobilizing blacks in these states.

In predicting the effects of public data availability on strategies of persuasion, the expectations are of a different sort. Unlike public records of race and party affiliation, which are highly predictive of partisan support, it turns out that no data available in public records, and indeed no data available in any campaign records, are highly predictive of persuadability. Persuadability is a psychological disposition that is very difficult to predict with demographic, geographic, or even consumer identifiers available to campaigns. Therefore, with respect to persuasion strategies, my hypothesis is simply that because available data do not permit campaigns to perceive accurately the disposition of persuadability (which I will confirm empirically), campaigns are not able to direct their contacting efforts to persuadable voters. In other words, persuadable *perceived voters* are such a poor approximation of voters who are actually persuadable that campaigns essentially cannot target persuasion messages to individual persuadable voters. (In Chapter 7, I discuss this hypothesis as it relates to some of the innovations in persuasion targeting that were pioneered by the 2012 Obama campaign.)

After testing these claims, I return to some of the reasons that I offered for why public records play an outsized role in campaign perceptions. In particular, I made three claims in this chapter that I attempt to confirm with either quantitative or qualitative evidence from campaigns. First, I suggested that, compared to public records, alternative data that campaigns use as shortcuts, such as commercial records, are typically less accurate and less predictive of the political traits that campaigns care about. Second, I claimed that campaigns tend to be reliant on shortcuts because in large-scale electorates, it is difficult for campaigns to keep proprietary lists in which they track, encyclopedically, the preferences of voters. Third, I claimed that in large electorates, it is also difficult for campaigns to leverage the social networks of their supporters as a means to contacting voters. After showing how public data laws serve as a lever on campaign strategy, I then show evidence for these claims in order to advance the case for why public records play the role that they play. In other words, because of the limits of consumer data, proprietary data, and social network data, these informational resources are imperfect substitutes for public records when public records are unavailable. This is why campaign strategy varies by jurisdiction depending on the public data context, and why it will likely continue to do so in the future.

## 2.5 SUMMARY

In this chapter, I developed the Perceived Voter Model of strategic voter contact. To characterize the strategic choices campaigns make, it is necessary to understand the perceptions that campaigns form about the characteristics of voters. In some circumstances, such as in small electorates, it is possible for campaigns to build up a detailed knowledge of the political dispositions of voters. However, in larger-scale electorates, campaigns rely on information shortcuts to gauge the dispositions of voters. Campaigns ought to rely most heavily on shortcuts that accurately describe characteristics of voters, that describe characteristics that are predictive of voters' political dispositions, that characterize a large percentage of the electorate, and that are inexpensively obtained. I argued that public records, such as individually identifying data stemming from voter registration records, often meet these criteria. Other types of campaign records offer less clear perceptions and therefore do not substitute for the perceptions formed by public records when public records are absent. This implies that variations in the kinds of personal records gathered by the government and distributed to campaigns should result in variations in campaign strategy. I articulated a series of hypotheses that predict how campaigns engage with voters as a consequence of the public data environment in which they are operating.

Briefly, I also posited that politicians over time have crafted data policies to suit their campaigns' informational needs. Of the reasons I offered for why public records play an important role in strategic campaigns,

# 3

# The Policy Roots of Elite Perceptions

Voter registration records, as well as other public records containing personal information, do not merely happen to be useful for campaigning. The data are useful by design. This chapter demonstrates how public policies about data are purposefully shaped in ways that affect campaigns' strategic communications with voters. Political campaigns are waged in a particular policy context. To understand how political campaigns interact with voters, it is necessary to examine that context.

When investigating campaign perceptions and strategies in contemporary politics, it is striking how reliant campaigns are on public institutions for their data. Parties and vendors receive real-time updates from election authorities about which voters have newly registered, which voters have cast early ballots, and which voters bear key demographic characteristics. They receive a steady stream of data from state and federal authorities that manage lists of licensees and subsidy beneficiaries. They also obtain detailed neighborhood characteristics from the Census Bureau. The thesis of this chapter is that campaigns are able to perceive voters through these resources in part because politicians have designed data laws for this very purpose. Laws about the collection and dissemination of public data are often tailored so that politicians can repurpose the data in service of their campaigns. This repurposing often happens with little public awareness.[1]

From nearly the moment voter registration laws were enacted, the records that compose the voter registration system were co-opted by political parties to help them mobilize their supporters. Other sources of public data have been similarly co-opted by campaigns for electioneering. The decennial Census, meant to count the population for the purpose of allocating congressional seats, now caters not only to private industry by providing detailed information about every neighborhood in the United States but also to campaigns that use these same data to target political messages to segments of voters. Similarly, open-record laws, which allow citizens to request government documents, are co-opted by political campaigns that petition agencies for administrative data in order to facilitate political targeting.

In reviewing the political nature of public data, two points of clarification are in order. First, I do not mean to implicate the practice of using public records for electioneering as corrupt. At the same time, I do mean to point out a tension between the incentives of political campaigns and the incentives of public officials in this domain. There is a conflict of interest inherent when governments collect administrative data and repurpose those data for political ends. I return to this conflict of interest in Chapter 9. Second, in arguing that politicians generate data laws to serve their campaigns, I am not arguing that most politicians are actively trying to manipulate public records laws to suit their political needs. If they were, campaigns would likely have much more data about voters than they already have. Most political actors operate passively in the policy environment they are given. The few actors who actively attempt to alter the policy environment do not always succeed. They may also have interests other than their electoral campaigns, such as an interest in good governance, that contribute to their policy agenda. Public policies change slowly, and even though they have an electoral incentive to have the government collect data useful for their campaigns, political actors typically have other priorities as well. Nevertheless, the evidence I uncover does suggest that electoral incentives can drive policy change with respect to laws about the collection of personal data.

### 3.1 EARLY POLITICAL USE OF REGISTRATION DATA

The following transcript appeared on page 2 of the *New York Times* on Monday, October 26, 1891:

> A large, clerical-looking man entered 51 West Thirty-fourth Street and wished to register [to vote]. He gave his residence as 24 West Thirty-Third Street, was immediately asked "which floor?" and when he said the entire house, had a Bible thrust into his hand and was compelled to swear to this astounding fact. The rest of the conversation was as follows:
>
> "Your name?"
>
> "Henry A. Stimson."

"Henry, Henry," said his inquisitor, "a good old-fashioned name. A family name I suppose, most families have old names. My name is Henry," and after entering the number of years that Mr Stimson had lived in the state, &c he said:

"Now I am going to ask you some serious questions, Your color? White, I suppose, shall I put down white?"

"Well, that is a matter of taste," said Mr Stimson, and he was entered in the book as a white man.

"Age?"

"Fifty-three years," replied Mr. Stimson, and the register commented upon that. "Height?"

"Six feet two."

"Huge! Pretty big man, ain't you? How much do you weigh?"

"Two hundred pounds"

"Sure of that? Don't weigh any more? You look as though you weighed more, well, you ought to know. Two hundred pounds; well all right. Color of your hair? Gray, light gray – we'll put it down for gray." And Mr. Stimson, without another word, reached the street as quickly as possible.

This article, written in the early days of the voter registration system, sought to explain why few citizens were registering to vote ahead of a particular election. The author suggests, "it may well be that many hesitate to register because they do not want to be interrogated about their age, color, height, weight, and distinguishing marks." Reflecting on the data collection practices of early registration systems, political scientist Joseph Harris, writing in the 1920s, says that the first principle of improving registration is "to avoid cluttering up the record with useless information, which is at present a common practice (Harris 1929, pp. 39–41)."

Throughout the history of the voter registration system, administrators have collected information that goes far beyond the administrative need. Of course, contemporary registrars no longer ask voters for their weight and height, but they do often ask for other information not obviously pertinent to one's right to vote. In certain eras of American history, registration forms have been far more invasive. For example, in an Alabama registration application from 1964, which is reproduced in Appendix B, voters are required to list, in addition to their name and address, their length of residence in the state, county, and precinct; whether they are or were in the armed forces, in what branch, and what their serial number was; whether they are a college student and if so, where; whether they have ever voted in any other state or county; how many years of schooling they completed and where they attended high school and college; where they were born; whether they have been married and divorced; the names, addresses, and birthdates of spouses; all places of residence in the last five years; the names and addresses of all employers of the last five years; history of past registrations; references of two people who can vouch for their identity; and records of legal infractions.

Why does the election administration keep records of personal information that seem unnecessary for authenticating eligible voters? Some extraneous information appears on voter registration forms, I argue, because the information has political value to parties and campaigns in facilitating direct contact with voters. To perceive voters, campaigns seek information. And for as long as voter registration has been a part of the U.S. election system, much of that information has come from government-generated voter lists that were designed in part to help campaigns.

Between 1860 and 1900, and especially between 1880 and 1900, at a time of rapid population growth that spurred many other Progressive Era reforms, cities and states began implementing versions of voter registration (Keyssar, 2009). As Keyssar notes, reformers hoped that voter registration would clamp down on fraud that was being perpetrated by urban party machines and would make precinct voting more streamlined. In some polling places, fights were breaking out on Election Day because parties disputed the eligibility of voters who came to cast their ballots. Reformers advocated registration as a means of maintaining order.

The hopes of reformers can be found in news reports of the day. As an example, the *Alton Telegraph* (Illinois) reported ahead of the 1868 general election:

> The fact is that the Democrats have always succeeded in Pennsylvania and other . . . states by fraudulent voting, and have always opposed a Registry Law. Enforce a Registry Law and they would loose New York city the next election. They carried this county last fall by illegal voting, and the *Advocate* knows they will loose it as sure as fate if the Union men see that the Registry Law is enforced.[2]

According to Keyssar (2009), political parties initially opposed voter registration. But once the registry laws were passed, party machines realized the enormous value of a publicly subsidized system that allows politicians to keep track of voters. Part of the value of the registration system to the parties was that it offered a new way to perpetrate fraud. To the dismay of reformers, the voter registration system simply changed the locus of election fraud rather than curbing it. Instead of stuffing the ballot box, the parties padded the registration rolls. In 1892, *The World* reported about the Democratic Party in New York that "Tammany Hall captured the organization of every board of registration, and there are 1,137 of them."[3]

While parties and reform groups battled over alleged fraud in the registration system, the parties also began using registration within the law as a tool of electioneering. The registration rules that went into effect at the end of the nineteenth century provided politicians with a precious new resource: data.[4] There are two clear ways that the parties made legal use of registration data. First, parties started incorporating registration statistics into their understanding of electoral competition. As Tammany leader Richard Croker told *The World* in 1892,

> All I care to say is that I am more than ever convinced that Cleveland and Stevenson will have 75,000 majority in this county . . . We have gained nearly 50,000 registered voters in New York and Kings Counties over the registration of 1888, and there is every reason for our claiming 32,000 votes out of this increase . . . [W]ith our normal majorities in New York and Kings, and the thousands of new converts and recruits, should send Cleveland and Stevenson to the Westchester line with nearly 100,000 majority.[5]

The registration tallies gave the parties something concrete to count during the campaign. The parties did not have to wait for Election Day to get an official indication of their strength relative to their opponents; they could see the record of how many of their supporters were registered versus how many non-supporters were registered. The data helped parties *perceive* the electorate in the aggregate.

More importantly, the second way that parties used registration data was as a tool for direct voter contact. The registration system changed the nature of mass mobilization by restricting the universe of people that campaigns had to convince to vote. Anyone not listed in the registration record was not eligible and therefore did not merit further attention during a given election campaign. Furthermore, a campaign could sort voters according to their probable support; if the records contained information about the voters' party affiliations and demographic traits, parties could use these data to narrow the scope of their voter engagement efforts. The data, therefore, also helped parties and campaigns *perceive* the electorate, voter by voter.

In his study of the voter registration system, Joseph Harris noted that even early registration lists were used by parties for canvassing, mailings

to supporters, and checking voters at the polls.[6] Long before the digiti-
zation of registration records and inexpensive data storage made use of
registration data easy, the parties nevertheless used these data for direct
contact. As Harris writes about the parties' use of registration data,

> Election offices are generally agreed that the printed lists are of little use to
> the public and are provided in the interest of the political parties. The cost
> of printing the lists of registered electors is substantial. (p. 180).

Harris found that most cities were providing lists of registered voters
to party workers so they could use them to facilitate their canvassing.
As he indicates, sharing these lists with the parties did not make the
election system more orderly, prevent fraud, or help administrators. But
the parties latched on to the lists, which soon became a fixture of their
campaign efforts.[7]

## 3.2  DATA FOR THE SAKE OF THE PARTIES

Evidence from the early part of the twentieth century suggests that administrative data in the form of voter registration were used by parties for
the benefit of their campaigns. But it is difficult to demonstrate that the
registration data was collected, in those early years, precisely for the sake
of the parties. However, one need not go far back in history to find examples of politicians crafting registration laws to benefit their campaigns.
It is a common practice that can be uncovered with a little digging into
contemporary, state-level lawmaking.

The contemporary voter registration system is written by politicians
who consider the interests of their campaigns when writing the laws.
Electioneering is not their only consideration, but laws about voter registration are clearly made with political considerations in mind. Legislators
pass laws that require administrators to collect personal data from the
mass public. The laws are written in ways that give administrators discretion in how the data can be used. Because the administrators are overseen
by election-seeking politicians, they tend to consent when a campaign
asks them to use the data for political purposes. Attempts to rein in the
political uses of administrative data are prevented by the politicians who
oversee the system.

Consider some examples. In December 2009, the Ohio State Senate
passed Senate Bill 8, a lengthy bill addressing a number of election
reforms. The bill made it through the Senate but was never reconciled
with a House version and thus did not become law. This bill is of interest

because buried in it is a provision that would allow Ohio voters to register with a political party when they submit an application to become a registered voter. Like many states, Ohio currently does not ask its registrants to declare a party publicly at the time of registration. There is no administrative need to do so, because Ohio's party primaries are open to anyone who wishes to participate. But this bill would have begun the mass collection of party affiliation for a non-administrative purpose. On the floor of the Senate, but with little other public mention, Republican Senator Bill Seitz, the bill's lead sponsor, indicated a singular rationale for the data collection:

> [W]e will give voters that opportunity that frankly works for both this side of the aisle and this side of the aisle [pointing] as we will now be able to target our new voters that are more likely to lean your way or my way.

The bill sponsors wished to change the law in Ohio and ask voters to report their party affiliation because the voters' declaration would be a public record and it would make it easier for campaigns to target their voters. No other rationale was provided.[8] The provision was inserted into the bill not because there was an administrative need, but because parties benefit from knowing which voters are with them and against them.

For another case, consider a 2003 bill in the California state legislature that would require voter registration applications to give citizens the option of indicating their race when registering to vote. Representative Mark Ridley-Thomas, a Democrat from Los Angeles, sponsored the bill with the support of the California chapters of the NAACP and Urban League.[9] In introducing the bill, Rep. Ridley-Thomas stated the following:

> The increasing racial and ethnic diversity of California's population has made attracting voters from all demographic groups a top priority for most political parties and recent campaigns. To achieve electoral success, broad-based multi-racial and multi-cultural coalition building is now essential. Therefore, it is anticipated that this information would actually be used to increase voter outreach efforts to these historically underrepresented populations.[10]

Again, the use of voter file information for campaign purposes here is not merely a secondary benefit to public data collection; it is the explicit purpose for the data collection.

The desire for election-seeking politicians to repurpose administrative data is nowhere more apparent than when proposals are offered to restrict political use of public data. Consider two recent instances, one in Utah and one in New Hampshire, in which bills seeking to provide voters with more control of their personal information have been rejected in order to protect political use of administrative data.

In 2012, Representative Becky Edwards, a Republican state legislator in Utah, offered a bill that would permit voters to limit public access to their date-of-birth information. Birthdates are collected as part of the registration application, but Edwards's bill would have allowed voters to opt out of having their data shared with political parties and others seeking the data. Edwards spearheaded this effort out of concern about fraud and violations of privacy and also to provide voters with more control of their own personal information.

As Edwards stated on the floor of the state house,

> This bill attempts to balance the importance of protecting sensitive personal information as well as the public's right to have access to that important information... There are some reasons why this information is being used appropriately: governmental reasons, election of potential jurors, public safety, redistricting. All of those governmental uses would still be available... There are political uses for this information: phone banking, political campaigns, data vendors, and voter profiling. Many of those can still be utilized using either the information from those who will maintain their information as public or... if there were entities who wanted to verify a petition or something like that they would be able to[11]

Edwards lays out the administrative uses of personal data and distinguishes uses that are governmental in nature from uses that are political in nature. Edwards's bill aims to give voters control of whether their birthdate information can be used for the latter set of purposes.

The bill was passed by the House but was eventually rejected by the state Senate. Edwards identified the bill's opponents as "the political parties and others with an interest in commercial uses for this private information."[12] Interviewing the state Democratic Party chairman who opposed the law, Utah's *The Daily Herald* wrote that the chairman "conceded that [the bill] would hurt databases put together by political parties that contain large amounts of voter information, which they use to market to specific voters."[13] Thus, the voter data that came into existence to serve an administrative need was not permitted to be more narrowly tailored to meet that need because campaigns wanted the data for electioneering.

The New Hampshire case is similar. In 2008, a proposal came before the New Hampshire House that would allow voters to opt out from having their personal information transmitted to political parties when the parties seek lists of registered voters from the election administration. Many jurisdictions allow certain classes of voters, such as victims of domestic violence, to be registered without having their information made public. But the proposal in New Hampshire, similar to the Utah case, called for a more general opt-out from having one's personal information distributed to political parties. The proposal never made it out of committee. As the official minutes of the committee hearing read,

> The committee believes that there is a strong public interest in having candidates being able to directly contact potential voters. Voters are free to throw away unwanted mailings, but candidates should have the opportunity to make themselves known to potential voters.[14]

The sense of the committee is that voters should not be allowed to register to vote and at the same time restrict their personal information from being used by political parties. The committee believes that campaign applications of registration data are in the public interest. From a particular viewpoint in which higher turnout is, in and of itself, a public interest and political parties are entities that can increase turnout, registration data ought to be used in this way.

From a different viewpoint, however, the New Hampshire legislative committee makes a subtle leap in logic. Few would argue with the committee that it is important for political candidates to be able to "directly contact potential voters." But the question is not whether campaigns should be permitted to contact voters; it is whether the public records should be made available to candidates for this purpose. Why, one might ask, can the parties not collect their own data? Why do they appear to cling to public sources of data, making laws that enable them to piggyback off of administrative records? Recall that the answer to this line of questions was given in Chapter 2: the parties need shortcuts in order to perceive the characteristics of voters. The electorate is too populous, voters move too often, candidates of the same party do not share enough information with one another, and so on. Repurposing publicly subsidized registration data is a clever way for campaigns to access informational shortcuts that enable to them to perceive the dispositions of voters.

## 3.3 CAPTURING NON-REGISTRATION-BASED PUBLIC DATA

Politicians have taken advantage of many forms of public data, not just registration records. While the hypotheses I test in this book are focused on the perceptions that stem from voter registration data, it is worthwhile to show how other types of public records have been transformed by politicians to aid campaigns' perceptions of voters. One could formulate additional testable hypotheses about how perceptions stemming from these data affect strategic decisions, a point I return to in Chapter 9. Like election data, these other data are ostensibly collected for some administrative purpose, but they are regulated by policies that make it easy for campaigns to use the data for electioneering. In some cases, politicians have explicitly carved out legal permissions for campaign uses of public data, such as in exempting political solicitations from "Do Not Call" restrictions. In most cases, however, the laws are implicit about permitting political uses for public data.

A chief mechanism by which campaigns access public data is through state and federal open-record laws. Like the federal government's Freedom of Information Act, or FOIA, each state has regulations that govern public access to administrative data. In general, there are limitations imposed on petitioners seeking government data. States often forbid commercial uses of data acquired through their open-records laws, and they forbid the sharing of data that is considered sensitive, personal, or privileged.

Many open-records laws were passed by states following the Watergate scandal, and they are meant to provide the public with enhanced oversight of their political leaders. Just as registration laws were passed in the wake of party corruption in order to limit the strength of parties, open-records laws were passed in the wake of partisan overreach in order to curb secretive, abusive government action. But a careful look at contemporary political databases reveals that political parties are active petitioners of public records through state and federal freedom of information laws. Acting as private entities, parties request from states every list of voters that they might find useful to their contacting strategies. In most states, administrators consider this political use of public records to be appropriate within the parameters of open-records laws.

Consider examples from the database generated by Catalist, the data vendor to left-of-center campaigns that I study in subsequent chapters. Catalist maintains a record of each registered voter in the country. It appends to this record all relevant information it can find about the voter. Much of the information Catalist appends comes directly from public records, including records obtained by state and federal FOIA requests.

From the Federal Aviation Administration, Catalist obtains records to identify which voters are pilots, control tower operators, mechanics, and other aviation workers. From the U.S. Department of Agriculture's records of farm subsidies, Catalist identifies 1.5 million registered voters who are likely to be farmers. From licensing board data from twenty-six states, Catalist knows hundreds of thousands of voters who are registered teachers, school support staff, and school administrators. Catalist's database also includes records for 27,000 voters who are licensed child care workers. Catalist individually identifies voters who are doctors, nurses, and other health care workers, because like school workers, medical professionals require state licenses to perform their work. Similarly, Catalist acquires data from wildlife administrations to figure out which voters have fishing and hunting licenses. More than 2 million individuals in the database are listed as hunters and more than 3.5 million are listed as fishers.

Long before companies such as Catalist had the technology and resources to make large-scale requests of licensing data and append these data to their lists of registered voters, political campaigns have been using public licensing data compiled at the local level. This is an important point because it reinforces that the technological progress of the last few decades is not the only enabler of list-based targeting strategies. Loose regulations about the reuses of public records are a more important enabler.

In a *New Yorker* article written in the 1960s, Calvin Trillin reports, "Almost anything that requires a license or a permit – dogs, marriages, barbers, swimming pools – is a matter of public record and is probably being noted down by a list compiler or an energetic part-timer."[15] Public records in this era were public in principle but were hardly accessible. Trillin explains that local administrators who happened to have access to these public records regularly engaged in a side business of selling their lists to marketers and political parties. The local bureaucrat responsible for dog permits, for example, would copy the list of dog owners and sell it, for personal gain, to marketing firms. With Catalist and other modern list providers, this process is simply scaled up and routinized.

Ironically, laws ostensibly passed to help private citizens track the government's action turn out to be laws that help political campaigns track private citizens. Government administrators need to keep records about individual citizens. To protect the public safety, licensing boards maintain lists of which individuals are permitted to teach children, provide medical care, and fly airplanes. To provide subsidies to farmers, administrators need to know where the farms are. To maintain sustainable gaming populations, administrators record which individuals can hunt and fish. The open-record laws allow campaigns to use these data in their electioneering efforts. Once a voter is known to be a teacher, a nurse, a farmer, or a hunter, a political party can perceive what that voter cares about.

Campaigns latch onto these data because they are legally permitted to use them for this purpose and because the data help them sort and segment the electorate in ways they find useful.

While election administration data and licensing data have been repurposed by political campaigns, no source of data has been more fundamentally repurposed than information produced by the U.S. Census Bureau. The U.S. Census serves a particular purpose, as laid out in Article I of the Constitution: to count the population for congressional apportionment. Just as registration data was immediately put to uses other than helping regulate elections, within a couple of decades of America's founding, the Census data, too, were widely repurposed.

The Census was first repurposed for governmental reasons that were unrelated to apportionment. In 1810, for example, Congress required the Census enumerators to collect data on manufacturers in addition to the population of residents. Today, Census population data is frequently used to allocate federal dollars to local regions (Prewitt, 2000). But data produced by the Census Bureau also has unrivaled commercial value (see Reed, 1937; Cohen, 1965; Eckler, 1970; Ellis, 1979; Mancini, 2010). Writing in 1914 in *Political Science Quarterly*, Walter Willcox explains that the Census Bureau was made a permanent entity in the early 1900s in part because of lobbying efforts by the National Board of Trade, which promoted the "need of a permanent census office as an aid to business men" (Wilcox, 1914). The business applications of the Census have only grown in the last hundred years.

In promoting participation in the 2010 Census, the Nielsen Company writes that "the U.S. Census drives business intelligence in America – even though many, if not most, of its users are not fully aware of this fact."[16] Nielsen's detailed report about the use of Census data in modern businesses makes clear that the business community knows much of what it does about U.S. consumers on account of data collected by the Census Bureau. Along the lines of Nielsen's promotional report about the Census, the business community contributes funds to advertising the importance of Census participation so that they can benefit from data that is collected from as many people and neighborhoods as possible (Hillygus et al., 2006).

The political uses of Census data are a direct extension of the business applications. Marketing campaigns and political campaigns seek detailed information about segments of the population that might be responsive to specific appeals. Since 1990, both businesses and political campaigns have been able to study characteristics about very localized areas (Issenberg, 2012). In 1990, the Census Bureau began publishing data on socioeconomics and other personal characteristics aggregated to the block group. With the country divided into more than 200,000 block groups, the Census Bureau gave businesses and campaigns tools for detailed segmentation strategies.

The federal government produces Census data that have uses far beyond what is necessary to apportion districts to states. Some of those uses are governmental, but many are private. The private uses are regulated by laws that grant wide latitude to private citizens, companies, and organizations to make use of neighborhood data produced by the Census. Like businesses, political campaigns are prominent beneficiaries of these data. By collecting and publishing statistics that are reliable, universal, and correlated with political outcomes, the Census Bureau, like the election administration, provides campaigns with key data that enable them to perceive the public and consequently affects their strategic choices.

### 3.4 POLICY CHANGE AND THE SUPPLY AND DEMAND OF PUBLIC DATA

Political parties as far back as the turn of the twentieth century were using registration records in canvassing efforts, but these records were difficult to use, poor in quality, and quite different across local and state jurisdictional boundaries. For citizens who happened to be registered to vote, who happened to live in jurisdictions that collected politically relevant demographic information about registrants, and who happened to live in jurisdictions that shared this information with the political parties in usable ways, campaigns could engage with these voters based on traits listed in voter files. But these conditions did not apply to all voters until fairly recently. Furthermore, until voter files were used in telephone and mail campaigns, and not just in door-to-door canvassing, utilization of individual-level data required massive coordinated efforts of volunteers or precinct-level workers – resources that were available to some urban party machines, but were not necessarily available to run-of-the-mill candidates scattered across the country. Thus, although voter registration records were available to the parties and candidates for political use and certainly were used in some places for the last 120 years, throughout this lengthy period of American history, politicians sought other sources of election-specific information that were either higher in quality or easier to use than voter registration records.

A chief alternative to individual-level targeting based on registration records was, and still is, geographic-level targeting based on past election returns. Soon after elections are held, administrators have long published records of votes aggregated to key levels of geography, such as the number of votes cast for each party's presidential candidate in every county, ward, or precinct. Johnson (1980) compiled public precinct returns in Missouri dating back to the 1850s. By obtaining maps of precinct boundaries as well as precinct-level returns, campaigns can decide which precincts to target in the subsequent election. To mobilize the base, campaigns might send canvassers to precincts that had previously voted overwhelmingly for their party; to persuade the undecideds, campaigns might send canvassers to precincts that had split their vote in the previous election or to precincts that swung back and forth over the last several elections.

As with registration-based targeting, precinct targeting in the pre-digital era was not without its challenges. Some of the challenges are the same as with early registration-based targeting: lack of consistency in data quality across election offices and the need for significant manpower to execute precinct-to-precinct canvassing strategies. Precinct-based targeting also presented, and continues to present, some unique challenges that limits its usefulness to politicians. These challenges are informational in nature. For one, the implementation of a precinct-level strategy entails indiscriminately canvassing all households in a precinct. Many of the households will actually contain non-registrants, nonvoters, and non-supporters. This coarse geographic strategy can thus be inefficient and possibly counterproductive from the perspective of a partisan campaign if it mobilizes some of the wrong voters.

A second informational shortcoming of precinct-level targeting is that strategists succumb to the ecological fallacy, meaning that they draw conclusions about individuals from the analysis of aggregations of those individuals. For example, campaigns often want to gear messages to persuadable, or swing, voters. Campaigns that have relied on precinct-level data, such as Democratic campaigns since the 1970s that have utilized data from the National Committee for an Effective Congress (NCEC), look to precincts that have swung back and forth over previous election periods or to precincts that are split evenly between Democratic voters and Republican voters. The campaigns transmit persuasion messages to these volatile precincts. However, the volatility of a geographic area is a poor measure of the volatility of individual voters. Precincts may be volatile without voters in them being volatile.

A third informational shortcoming of precinct-level targeting is that U.S. voters are not well sorted geographically into Republican neighborhoods and Democratic neighborhoods. Most voters live in areas that are quite mixed in their partisan composition. For this reason, a voter's precinct is a very noisy predictor of a voter's partisanship. Consider some examples from recent elections. Republican strategist Michael Turk, who held a senior position in George W. Bush's 2004 reelection campaign, reports that an internal analysis of the Bush campaign revealed that "only 15 percent of its voters lived in solidly Republican districts" (Turk, 2012). Similarly, a veteran Democratic congressional campaign manager told me that precinct information is rarely useful to him because so few precincts are solidly Democratic or Republican in the districts he competes in. In Chapter 5, I review my own analysis of this issue: by looking at vote returns in more than 120,000 precincts, I show that voters overwhelmingly live in districts that are split between Democrats and Republicans. As a result, knowledge of where a voter lives is by no means a sufficient signal of partisanship or persuadability to allow political campaigns to perceive voters' preferences accurately.

Prior to the broadcast era, then, campaigns seeking to engage in direct contact had suboptimal alternatives. Registration was individually identifying and in many jurisdictions provided campaigns with information about each voter's age, gender, race, partisan affiliation, vote history, occupation, and more. But the data were difficult to use and only available in some jurisdictions. Precinct data were also available to campaigns, but provided, and continue to provide, a very noisy signal of politically relevant, individual-level attributes. Other forms of public data, like data from the Census Bureau and licensing agencies, were even more difficult to use in the pre-digital era because their value rests in linking these records with either eligible voters or politically relevant jurisdictions. Given the difficulty in using any form of public data on a large scale, it is no surprise that party contact was often characterized in terms of networks and informal mobilization rather than in terms of data and strategic targeting (Huckfeldt and Sprague, 1992).

It is also no surprise that when broadcast advertising became widely available as a campaign tool, television ads were an attractive alternative to canvassing for the campaigns that could afford them. These ads did not require large numbers of volunteers or local campaign workers, and they allowed campaigns to connect with many voters all at once, though not in a targeted fashion. When television advertising became an option for candidates, candidate campaigns began to rely less on individual-level forms of targeting, and therefore less on state and local party operations, and more on broadcast media. To an extent, direct strategic mobilization went into hibernation and with it the volunteer base of campaign targeting (see Rosenstone and Hansen, 1993; Aldrich, 1995; Bimber, 2003).

In an interview, Massachusetts Democratic Party Chairman John Walsh explained to me: "Because for a long time the macro campaign worked well, there was atrophy in organizing campaigns."[17] The shift to television had obvious consequences for the kinds of strategies employed by campaigns. A campaign that relied on canvassing and then shifted to broadcast advertisement would need to move away from targeting specific demographics, such as ethnic groups, sporadic voters, age cohorts, and partisan identifiers, and instead generate messages that would resonate with the typical, television-viewing voter.

## The Reemergence of Direct Targeting

After a period of time in which mass-media appeals dominated campaigns, changes in supply and demand reversed the strategic course back to individual-level engagement. The seeds for this change were planted as early as the 1960s, concurrent with the growth of TV. On the supply side, direct mail firms emerged in the consumer marketing sphere that targeted products directly to individuals throughout the United States. Marketing firms blossomed in the 1960s with the aid of primitive computer technologies that enabled them to link databases of phone numbers and addresses, such as those produced in phonebooks, with public and private commercial lists and demographic contextual data. As Trillin wrote, "A list of eighty per cent of the families in the United States is of practically no value unless it can be refined into categories of people who have more in common than ownership of a telephone or an automobile. The greatest single aid the compilers have for making this refinement is the Census Bureau." Census data merged with geo-coded households provided direct-mail firms with the resources they needed to divide the country into distinctive market segments (see Weiss, 1988). To communications firms already engaged in direct marketing, applying their techniques for politics was a logical extension of the business model. Direct-mail firms thus represent the supply-side shift that led to more individual-level targeting.[18]

The demand side came from campaigns that were shut out of broadcast advertising because they lacked sufficient financial resources. Even in today's money-infused political campaigns, most federal campaigns broadcast zero television ads, to say nothing of the thousands of state and local races. The same was true in the middle of the twentieth century. The costs were prohibitive for most candidates competing for office. When television ads became a dominant form of campaign engagement at the highest tiers of political campaigns, the typical campaign needed an alternative. Direct mail presented a form of individual-level engagement that was less expensive than television and did not require an army of volunteers.

Bob Blaemire was a pioneering direct-mail vendor in the 1980s and 1990s. According to Blaemire, a certain segment of candidates were desperate for direct-mail technology and for consultants who could cater specifically to their political needs. Congressional candidates in Los Angeles who were priced out of broadcast options were the prime movers. These candidates, who could not afford broadcasting, not only fueled the direct-mail business applications to campaign contact but, according to Blaemire, were the loudest voices advocating for improvements in voter registration data. Unlike commercial marketers who used telephone lists as their primary data file for direct mail, political campaigns wanted to use registration lists as their data file. Voter registration records may have been unruly, but registration data often informed campaigns of whether a registrant was a regular voter or not, voted in primaries or not, and was a Democrat or Republican. For commercial marketing, these fields were generally inaccessible for commercial uses and irrelevant to most marketing interests. In a similar vein, consumer information was not particularly relevant to the political outcomes that candidates cared about.

For political campaigns to really benefit from direct mail lists and to use such lists as a method of voter engagement, they needed direct mail vendors to use voter registration data, not telephone books or company mailing lists. However, even into the 1980s and 1990s, registration files were still difficult to use. In some states, particularly in New England where election authority was situated in hundreds of town governments rather than in counties, mail vendors needed to acquire voter files on a town-by-town basis in order to send mail to all the voters in a congressional or statewide electorate. In some jurisdictions, records were stored in paper files that needed to be entered into computers by mail vendors at great expense. The data were also still highly variable in quality. Election authorities did not have a standard set of protocol for removing obsolete records from the voter files. Files were filled with "deadwood" – records of people who have moved away, lost interest in voting, or died.

And different states had their quirks. Take Alabama, where probate judges were responsible for maintaining voter registration lists. The judges were compensated for their work based on the size of the list they managed, which incentivized them to inflate the number of registrants on the lists.[19] The result was lists that were not only difficult to assemble but also inefficient to use as the basis for voter contact. Nevertheless, in the 1980s, political mail vendors began assembling town and county voter files and creating complete statewide lists of registered voters. Blaemire created one of the early statewide lists on the Democratic side, in 1984, for Al Gore's Senate bid in Tennessee.

When mail vendors began asking election administrators for clean, computerized records of registered voters, town and county governments realized they had an asset they could sell. Rather than campaigns paying vendors to assemble clean records from the messy files held by local election offices, the election offices could invest in better data and generate revenue. Once the local governments realized they had a constituency ready to buy data, they had an incentive to computerize their files. In fact, in the 2000s, when states moved to centralize control of voter registration, they did so over complaints of county and town election officers who lamented the loss of a revenue stream they had secured over the previous two decades (e.g., see debate over New Hampshire HB 1230, 2006). The financial support to administrators in the form of fees for lists made local election offices "clientele agencies," as Lowi (1979) might have called them. Local election officers became vendors of political data to campaigns. As noted early on by Harris (1929), the provision of public data to political campaigns was outside the intended role of election administrators, but the administrators could sustain and expand their roles by catering to the needs of campaigns, who were in turn willing to support the agencies through fees for services rendered. That election administrators are often themselves partisan politicians no doubt contributed to their role as political data vendors (see Hasen, 2012).[20]

With the emerging clientelism involving election authorities and campaigns, which was made possible by laws that sanctioned the political applications for administrative data, and with technological progress in computer storage capacity, by the 1990s voter lists improved in accuracy and were used more frequently for direct mail and other forms of individual-level contact, like canvassing and phone-banking. Firms that started off in the mail business were compiling individual-level lists from election records that could be used for all these forms of targeting. Because counties and towns were still responsible for the data, however, there was variability in the quality of records. This cross-jurisdictional variability piqued the interest of Congress in the 1990s, which used its authority under Article I, Section 4 of the Constitution to impose national standards on voter registration for the first time.

In 1993, Congress passed the National Voter Registration Act (NVRA). The NVRA is best known for its requirements for government offices, like motor vehicle registries, to offer opportunities for citizens to register to vote (a.k.a. "motor voter"). But in Section 8 of the NVRA, Congress stipulated national requirements for registration list maintenance. States were required to "conduct a general program that makes a reasonable effort to remove the names of ineligible voters from the official lists of eligible voters," or in other words to keep the lists free of "deadwood." The states were also given instructions for how they could purge obsolete records so as to avoid removing eligible voters from the rolls without their consent. The purging regulations were meant to facilitate lists that were "accurate and current," according to the law.

Perhaps the most important aspect of the registration reforms in the NVRA was not in the requirements themselves but in putting the onus on state governments for implementing the changes in their jurisdictions. When the federal government stepped into the realm of voter registration, it stepped into an area of administration dominated by towns and counties rather than states. The passage of the NVRA resulted in within-state centralization of authority (see Keyssar, 2009). For political parties with an ambition to create a national list of voters, this was an important milestone. Centralization to the state level meant that list vendors and their campaign clients no longer were at the mercy of thousands of local election offices, but only of fifty states.

Even though voter registration records may have improved in the 1990s on account of technological changes, the NVRA did not result in vastly improved voter files. This was in part because the list maintenance requirements in the NVRA were modest and in part because some of the other stipulations in the NVRA, like a voter's new ability to register by mail, complicated the job of registration administrators (see Alvarez, 2005). Bigger improvements came only after the next landmark piece of national legislation bearing on voter registration: the Help America Vote Act of 2002. The Help America Vote Act, or HAVA, was passed in the wake of Florida's election mishaps in the 2000 presidential election. Among its key provisions, HAVA required every state (except North Dakota, which has no voter registration) to develop a "single, uniform, official, centralized, interactive computerized statewide voter registration list defined, maintained, and administered at the State level."[21] The deadline for state compliance with this requirement of a statewide digital file was January 1, 2006. Twelve states missed the deadline,[22] and so it was not until the 2008 election cycle that, for the first time, every voter in the country was listed in a statewide digital registration database.

The state-by-state implementation of statewide registration databases, digitally stored and constantly maintained, lays the groundwork for the individual-level targeting that dominates contemporary campaigns. The data, improved by federal regulations, and the technology, improved by computer innovations, caught up to the permissive regulations on political applications of election data that had been on the books for more than a century. Registration data, precinct data, Census data, and licensing data had long been available to politicians and had been put to use in certain jurisdictions by particularly enterprising and well-financed campaigns. In the 1990s, the national parties and presidential campaigns acquired data files that were maintained by state parties and state-level consultants, but these files varied in quality considerably across states. It was not until 2008 that virtually any candidate running for any office could easily and cheaply access a complete list of registered voters – a list that was also easy to merge with other sources of politically relevant personal information. And that is where my empirical investigation of data-driven campaign perceptions picks up.

### 3.5 SUMMARY

In this chapter, I have explained why public records, especially those collected in the voter registration system, serve as information shortcuts that assist campaigns in perceiving the dispositions of voters. Since the time when the voter registration system was implemented, these data became a fixture of campaign strategy. Over time, lawmakers have tweaked registration data to better serve their electoral interests. They have proposed laws to collect data that are useful not to election administrators but to election campaigns, and they reject laws that limit the political use of registration records. I have shown how other forms of public data, like state licensing records and Census neighborhood records, are made available to the public, and can be used as inputs to campaign targeting strategies as well.

This chapter has provided background so that I can evaluate modern election databases in a new light. I have explained how the combination of permissive data regulations, national policy demanding better-quality records, parties and campaigns petitioning government administrators for data, and technological improvements together enable politicians across the country to interact with voters on the basis of publicly recorded personal information. This confluence of factors does not mean politicians can accurately perceive the true dispositions of voters; it means that campaigns can easily perceive some estimate of voters' dispositions by using the shortcuts accessible in public records. If voters are characterized in public records by a particular set of traits, then a politician will be able to mobilize or persuade the voters on the basis of those traits. If the public records are silent on those traits, the politician will have to find alternative means to perceive voters and to engage with them. Because political campaigns rely on public records to perceive voters, variations in public records influences how campaigns strategically engage in voter contact.

# 4

# Campaign Perceptions Quantified

Since 2008, every major campaign in the country has had the ability to engage with voters based on an array of individual-level characteristics that are stored in national voter databases. These databases offer a glimpse at how campaigns perceive the dispositions of voters and act on those perceptions. My empirical investigation takes me behind the scenes to the data and perceptions of campaigns in order to examine how the policy environment affects campaign strategy.

This chapter introduces the primary sources of data that are the focus of the next four chapters. Among these sources are two of the most prominent and sophisticated data resources on the Democratic side of politics. The first is the national campaign database used by many Democratic and progressive campaigns that is put together by a company called Catalist. The second source is NGP VAN, a company that provides a user interface that allows campaign workers to interact with databases. With my colleague Ryan Enos, I fielded a survey of campaign workers who use NGP VAN, a project done in partnership with Obama for America and twenty-five state Democratic parties. This survey, as well as other data from NGP VAN and data from Catalist, will allow me to see voters in a new light: from the perspective of campaigns themselves.

## 4.1 VOTER DATA IN THE INFORMATION AGE

Because technology allowed for it, HAVA required it, and political campaigns demanded it, state election authorities made great strides between 2001 and 2008 in developing up-to-date, computerized, statewide voter registration files. Concurrently, private firms and political parties began building an infrastructure to connect this abundance of data to thousands of political campaigns across the country. Since election administrators were increasingly making available to political candidates a complete digital list of registered voters in their jurisdictions, one might wonder: Why did campaigns obtain data from intermediary vendors or political parties rather than retrieving a list directly from the election authority?

The reason campaigns use intermediary data suppliers is that registration lists can be augmented substantially to increase their usefulness. As I have written about elsewhere with Stephen Ansolabehere (2014), vendors engage in a variety of data-cleaning activities. They identify duplicative records, incorrect addresses, deceased voters, and voters who have changed residences. They also locate addresses in Census geographies and match voter records to commercial records as well as to other sources of data. These sorts of tasks can make a political campaign's use of registration data far more efficient, but they require special expertise and computer power beyond the reach of typical campaigns. Thus, even though registration records have become readily available to any campaign that seeks them, control over the cleaned and augmented voter registration lists is centralized to the firms and parties that invest in list maintenance.

Both national political committees, the Democratic National Committee (DNC) and Republican National Committee (RNC), maintain national voter databases, which they can make available to presidential candidates, state parties, and local candidates. The current iteration of the Democratic database is called VoteBuilder; the current iteration of the Republican database is called Voter Vault. The Republicans began developing Voter Vault in the 1990s and had a working version of it in the field in 2002.[1] Democrats had predecessors of VoteBuilder functioning in 2004.[2] However, until every U.S. state began generating statewide digital files, which happened between 2004 and 2008 as a result of HAVA deadlines, these national databases were incomplete.

In order for typical campaign workers to use augmented voter registration records for their direct contacting efforts, they need a user interface (UI) that will permit them to crunch massive amounts of data without knowledge of computer programming or advanced statistics, and without having to store large databases on local machines. As a result, both the Democratic and Republican parties needed to find a way to grant access to their new databases that could accommodate average campaign users, dispersed across hundreds of local offices. For their UI, the Democrats rely on an independent company called NGP VAN. Before a 2010 merger with NGP, a Democratic fundraising technology firm, VAN, which stands for Voter Activation Network, spent nearly a decade helping Democratic campaigns interact with voter data. VAN's work continues as NGP VAN. NGP VAN does not own voter files; rather, it processes its customers' data so that the customers can have a better experience interacting with the records. The DNC, NGP VAN's primary customer, transmits its data (called VoteBuilder) to NGP VAN, and campaign workers who have access can manipulate the data in a Web-based interface. The Republican system is more straightforward, since Voter Vault is both the name of the data and the user interface, and both pieces are operated by the Republican Party.

Because they are owned by political parties, VoterBuilder and Voter Vault can be accessed by affiliated candidates and local parties. For these affiliated campaigns, the parties' data are cleaned and made available inexpensively in order to further a common political agenda. Use of the parties' data by candidate campaigns is widespread. On the Democratic side, for example, thousands of campaigns in all but one state (California) access VoteBuilder. Because campaigns across the country are all using the same data resources in their direct contact strategies, by gaining special access to the national party data resources, I can learn about strategic behavior across a wide range of campaigns.

Because VoteBuilder is not accessible to nonpartisan campaigns, there emerged a demand on the liberal side of the political spectrum for data owned by an entity other than the Democratic Party. A company called Catalist began meeting this demand in 2006. Catalist is a for-profit company that vends political data to organizations on the political left. Like the DNC, Catalist builds a regularly updated national voter file that incorporates public records, commercial records, and any other records that Catalist or its clients can incorporate into the database. Catalist is used by labor unions such as AFL-CIO and the Teamsters, and a slew of interest groups such as Emily's List, the ACLU, the League of Conservation Voters, NAACP, Planned Parenthood, and the Sierra Club. Catalist data is also available for purchase for candidate campaigns. It is more expensive than the party-subsidized data contained in VoteBuilder, but still many Democratic campaigns and parties purchase Catalist data to be used in place of, or as a supplement to, party data. The Obama campaign used Catalist data in 2008, and so do many federal candidates as well as the Democratic Senatorial Campaign Committee (DSCC) and the Democratic Congressional Campaign Committee (DCCC). Catalist has build its own Web-based UI, called the Q Tool, that allows campaigns to interact with the data. Catalist data can also be used by campaigns through the NGP VAN interface. For example, a candidate campaign can contract with Catalist and ask it to feed its voter records to NGP VAN, so that the campaign can use Catalist data through the NGP VAN interface. A Republican company quite like Catalist had not emerged by 2012. However, Republicans and allied groups have been working to establish parallel data systems for future elections.[3] For a detailed history of firms like Catalist and NGP VAN, see Kreiss (2012).

## 4.2 RESEARCH PARTNERSHIPS

The research partnerships that represent the empirical evidence of this book come from Catalist and NGP VAN. Data from Catalist and NGP VAN enable me to examine how campaign perceptions follow from public records and correspond to strategic decisions. These are the data sources that a range of campaigns employ in order to perceive the electorate. The voters as they appear in Catalist and NGP VAN are *perceived voters*.

### Catalist

In 2009, Stephen Ansolabehere and I became interested in new campaign databases, such as Catalist, that were emerging in national politics. We had a joint interest in using these sources of campaign data to study the voter registration system (Ansolabehere and Hersh, 2014), political behavior (Ansolabehere, Hersh, and Shepsle, 2012), and political methodology (Ansolabehere and Hersh, 2012). We also had separate interests in studying redistricting on his part (Ansolabehere and Rodden, 2011) and campaign strategy (Hersh, 2011) and voting behavior (Hersh, 2013; Hersh and Nall, 2015) on my part. Catalist had never previously engaged in a major contract with an academic institution, and it took seven months of work to secure the data in such a way that it could be used in academic research. The following year, in 2010, Ansolabehere and I worked with Catalist to generate a standardized academic subscription for their data, which, in addition to Yale and Harvard, has now been purchased by a number of other academic institutions.

There are three types of Catalist data that will be analyzed here. The first is a sample of 1 percent of all individuals in Catalist's database. The sample includes approximately 1.9 million registered voters from a simple random sample of all voters listed in all fifty states. Catalist calls this its "analytics sample." The analytics sample is an individual-level dataset in which each person is characterized by slightly more than

700 data points. The variables come from a variety of sources, including voter registration records, Census neighborhood statistics, commercial records that are merged into the database, information about the partisanship and religion of voters' counties, information about other registered voters in each voter's household, public license data from state and federal sources, and Catalist's own predictive models, called scores, that evaluate each person in the dataset for their likelihood of bearing a particular political characteristic. In my analysis, I utilize three independently drawn 1 percent samples from Catalist records, two of which were drawn in the spring of 2010 and the third of which was drawn in the fall of 2012.

The second type of Catalist data analyzed here is a smaller set of variables that are available for Catalist's full database of all individuals. As of this writing, this set includes records of 189,109,168 registered voters and millions of other individuals, such as those who were once registered but have been dropped from the rolls and those who are found in consumer databases but not in registration records (and are presumed to be unregistered citizens). This full-population dataset is what standard campaign clients use for building lists of voters to engage in direct contact.

For Catalist's full-population records, Catalist does not provide all 700 variables in its database. Instead, it permits its clients to review a subset of those variables, which include: each person's district information (all the political and nonpolitical jurisdictions in which they live); their voter turnout histories in all past elections for which the data are available; public records obtained from FOIA requests (e.g., which voters are identified as farmers, hunters, and fishers); demographic information either stemming from voter registration applications or, in some cases, from predictions based on voters' names and geographies (e.g., religion is predicted by name and geography); a few basic predictions from commercial records, such as a prediction that a voter has children living in their home; Census block–group level neighborhood data; and Catalist's key predictive models, such as a prediction of how likely a voter is to be a Democrat or to participate in an upcoming election.

There is one class of data that is available to Catalist's standard campaign clients but not to researchers. Catalist partners with the National Committee for an Effective Congress (NCEC) to locate each registrant's address in his or her voting precinct. NCEC supplies election history information for that precinct, such as the percentage of the vote going to the Republican versus Democratic candidates in the prior presidential election. Campaigns can use the NCEC variables when deciding which voters to contact, but NCEC has not permitted researchers to see its data as part of the Catalist academic subscription. For my own analysis here, I merge Catalist's individual records with precinct returns to recreate a semblance of what NCEC offers to campaigns. But apart from the NCEC precinct-level variables, the data that researchers see in Catalist's records are the same as the data that Catalist's campaign clients see.

When typical campaigns engage voters, they query on variables that are available for the full population, and they make custom lists of voters who they want to call, e-mail, canvass, or otherwise contact. They will log into Catalist's user interface, the Q Tool, and select certain demographics of voters that are strategically valuable to them. For example, they might begin with all registered voters in the state of Connecticut (2,107,948 records), restrict their search to just those who are registered in New Haven (69,632 records), and just those who are political independents (17,711 records), and just those under forty years of age (10,898 records), and just those who are male (4,886 records), and just those who are predicted based on their name and Census block group to be white (2,302 records), and just those who showed up to vote in the 2008 Presidential election (844 records), and just those who live in Census block groups where more than half the population has earned college degrees (464 records). A campaign worker could then export the names, addresses, and telephone numbers for these 464 voters and attempt to engage them via direct contact.

The analytics sample, with its more comprehensive set of variables, is not used directly by campaigns in contacting efforts. Catalist's modelers and other organizations' modelers incorporate the detailed records in the analytics sample when they attempt to predict, for example, how likely a person is to vote Democratic. Suppose a voter is registered independent, but in the analytics sample this voter is listed as likely married to someone else who is a registered Democrat. Catalist might predict that this type of independent voter leans Democratic.

Catalist can improve its predictive models further with a special set of data that it gathers from its clients. Catalist stores proprietary data from its political clients. The proprietary data typically takes one of two forms; field IDs and membership lists. An example of field IDs: for voters who told an Obama campaign volunteer that they were supporting Obama for president, the campaign might store a field indicating this self-reported attribute. Catalist links the attribute to the voter's larger profile and thus knows which voters are marked with a variety of identities gathered from the field. One example of a membership list might be if a pro-choice group has a list of its organization's membership and uploads this list into Catalist's records, Catalist would have an indicator of this affiliation appended to each voter's record. An interest group uploads its data into Catalist's records so that it can query on Catalist's other variables, for example by contacting its members who are women over fifty years of age – demographic information that is obtained from Catalist.

Catalist aggregates proprietary data points like these from its clients and uses them to build superior predictive models. For example, if someone is registered independent but is a member of a pro-choice group and has told an Obama volunteer that he or she is supporting Obama, then Catalist might use these data points to predict that this person, despite being a registered independent, is likely to be a Democratic supporter. Each of Catalist's clients can see their own proprietary data linked to Catalist records, but only Catalist sees the full profile of every data point on every individual voter. As a researcher, I can see the output of Catalist's work, in the various predictive models about voters that have been shared as part of the academic subscription, but I see none of the input field IDs or membership lists.

Catalist's predictive models, especially its models of partisanship and vote choice, will play an important role in my empirical investigation. As such, it is important that the reader develops a clear understanding of these models, which, again, are also referred to as scores. Scores represent a fairly recent development in strategic campaign contact (Malchow, 2008; Strauss, 2009; Hillygus and Shields, 2008). Before scores were developed, individual-level targeting decisions were made based on discrete divisions of voters. Registered Democrats might be targeted for mobilization; registered independents might be targeted for persuasion; registrants who voted in the last election would get more attention than would voters who did not vote in the last election. These discrete methods are being replaced by continuous, nuanced measures, at least in the more sophisticated campaigns. Instead of knowing only that a voter is a Democrat or a Republican, a campaign will pay a firm like Catalist to make a continuous predictive score. A voter is not mobilized because she is a Democrat, but because on a score predicting Democratic support, she is at least an 80 out of 100.

Catalist makes targeting scores for a variety of politically relevant traits, such as marriage and education, but the flagship scores that Catalist makes for its clients are a prediction of partisanship and a prediction of turnout likelihood. Both of these models are built based on dozens of variables, including public records like party registration and vote history. The models also include as predictors commercial variables and proprietary client data.

Catalist makes its prediction about voter partisanship by using an algorithm that assesses both the correlates of party registration in states that register by party as well as self-reported party identification from a large telephone sample of voters in every state. Catalist's prediction of partisanship is modeled based on more than 150 variables. Once the model is complete, Catalist applies the model to all voters in its database, thus generating a predicted value for each voter based on the voter's listed personal traits.

In Catalist's turnout propensity scores, the dependent variable is an individual record of turnout in a previous, similar election. Suppose Catalist is predicting turnout in 2014. Its model might begin with voters who were eligible to vote in 2010, the last midterm election year. It will then predict turnout in 2010 based on demographics like age and gender, as well as geography, the types of races on the ballot, and commercial and proprietary data. Thus, both of these flagship models rely on public records augmented with commercial and proprietary party records.

To offer some intuition for what these targeting scores look like, Figure 4.1 represents the joint distribution of predicted turnout likelihood (for the 2010 general election) and predicted partisanship for 166.5 million citizens, nearly all active registrants in the United States.[4] The height of each point indicates the number of registered voters in that location. Each party's core supporters are reflected in the front corners of this distribution. But to achieve a plurality of voters, the campaigns must descend from these peaks to find the less avid partisans and less likely voters who may support them.[5] Remember: Figure 4.1 does not tell us the distribution of actual voters' partisanship and turnout likelihood, but only the campaigns' best guess. This is the distribution of perceived voters on two critical dimensions from the campaign's-eye-view.

To get a sense of how these scores are used, consider Figure 4.2. Similar to Figure 4.1, this figure lines voters up along the partisanship scale (x-axis) and the turnout likelihood scale (y-axis). The color shades indicate actual contacts in the state of Ohio from the 2008 Obama campaign and from left-of-center allied groups. If a voter was contacted by the campaign, this was recorded in Catalist's database, so the figure shows the relative degree of being contacted based on where a voter is located on these two dimensions. The heatmap shows areas with the most number of Democratic contacts per person and areas with the fewest number of Democratic contacts per person. The darkest regions of the heatmap indicate the campaign focused targeting on nonpartisans and Democratic partisans who were likely to vote as well as Democratic

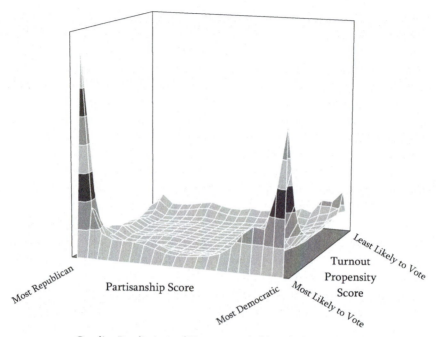

FIGURE 4.1 Catalist Prediction of Turnout Likelihood and Partisan Support for the 2010 General Election for Registered Voters in the United States.
*Note:* 166,492,316 observations. All active registered voters are included, except for those in the state of Virginia on account of legal restrictions on the use of vote history data in that state. Within each cell, every shaded tier represents between 0 and 1,000,000 registrants. Data based on 2010 version of Catalist models.
*Source:* Catalist, LLC.

partisans who were less likely to vote. The strong relationship between location in these distributions and attention from the campaigns is attributable to the campaigns using these scores as the basis for voter contact.[6]

Catalist's scores will be utilized in the empirical analysis of this book because they represent, in essence, the best a campaign can do in perceiving key voter attributes, such as partisanship. Not all campaigns use Catalist's data and modeled scores. But to approximate what perceptions look like in a sophisticated campaign – perceptions informed not just by public records but by commercial variables and proprietary organizational and party data – Catalist's models are a useful tool for study. These models are not merely an academic exercise. They are used as the basis of voter targeting by a variety of real-world campaigns, including the campaigns of federal candidates, unions, and nonprofits. The exact calculation of Catalist's models is proprietary. But that is not a concern

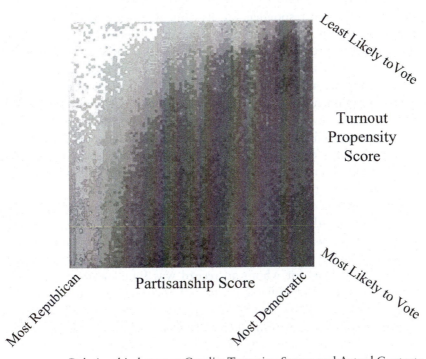

FIGURE 4.2 Relationship between Catalist Targeting Scores and Actual Contacts from the 2008 Obama Presidential Race in the State of Ohio.
*Note:* This heatmap, generated by Erik Brauner, former chief scientist at Catalist, is replicated with permission. This graphic is also reproduced in Nickerson and Rogers (2014). The relationship between propensity scores and actual contact from the Obama campaign as well as from allied groups working in the state of Ohio is shown. The color spectrum ranges from white (fewest contacts) to black (most contacts).

here. I treat the output of Catalist's behind-the-scenes work – the scores it assigns to each voter – as a strategic ranking, or sorting, of the electorate. The way that scores vary by person and jurisdiction will help explain how perceptions of voters vary as well. I also examine how Catalist's models changed from 2008 to 2010 to 2012, as the tweaks to these models shed light on the pace of change in this area of campaign technology.

A final data resource generated from my partnership with Catalist is a series of public opinion surveys that have been matched to Catalist's records. In 2010, Stephen Ansolabehere and I worked with Catalist and the survey firm Polimetrix, which conducts the Cooperative Congressional Election Study (CCES), to match CCES respondents to Catalist records. We asked Polimetrix to transmit to Catalist the identifying information it knew about respondents. Catalist then matched this identifying information about respondents to its campaign records. The output for researchers is an anonymous survey matched with public, commercial, and proprietary data. We matched 2008, 2009, and 2010 surveys to Catalist's records. We received the greatest number of Catalist fields appended to the 2008 survey. For example, I was able to connect 2008 survey respondents to Catalist's partisanship models and to precinct returns. As such, when it will be necessary to compare Catalist records with self-reported information, the 2008 CCES survey will be the main source of evidence. Consult Ansolabehere and Hersh (2012) for detailed information about the matching procedure between CCES respondents and Catalist records.

Of the 32,800 respondents to the 2008 CCES, Catalist identified about 75 percent as either registered or formerly registered.[7] The remainder of respondents were not matched to registration records and are thus thought to be unregistered respondents. Although it is possible that some of the respondents for whom no record was found were in fact registered but were not identifiable because of bookkeeping issues at election offices, it is more likely that these respondents are simply unregistered. Seventy-two percent of respondents are identified as actively registered; this closely resembles the rate of self-reported registration on the 2008 Current Population Survey, which estimated 71 percent of citizens were registered. However, even if some individual respondents who were not found by Catalist are actually registered voters, one might expect biases that could result from comparisons among those who *were* identified as registered to be minimal.

As with all research endeavors, it is important to be aware of possible sources of error. In this case, I am studying a probability-sampled, opt-in survey matched to public records, and there are opportunities in the sampling and matching procedures for biases to encroach. For information of the reliability of the CCES survey, consult Ansolabehere (2011) and Hill et al. (2007). Note that because of its sampling design and sample size, the CCES is generally well-suited for studying populations within states, as will be required for some of my analysis (Ansolabehere, 2011). On the quality of registration records, consult Ansolabehere and Hersh (2014) and Ansolabehere and Hersh (2012).

## The Ground Campaign Project

My second main data source allows me to examine how perceptions translate into strategies. This data source is a survey I ran with my colleague

Ryan Enos. We call this survey the Ground Campaign Project, or GCP. The GCP is a survey of campaign field workers that was conducted during the 2012 election cycle with the cooperation of Obama for America, NGP VAN, and twenty-five state Democratic parties. The impetus for this study is that it has been difficult for political scientists to understand the behaviors, attitudes, and motivations of political activists and campaign workers. These individuals represent a small fraction of the U.S. population, so a nationally representative public opinion survey will never contain enough of them to permit rigorous statistical analysis. Furthermore, campaign workers and volunteers are scattered in hundreds of communities across the country and, since they are highly mobile, are difficult to reach by phone or mail. It is because campaign staffers and volunteers are so difficult to interview on a large scale that past research on strategic campaign activities has attempted to reverse-engineer what campaigns do by asking average voters about the campaigns that contacted them (i.e., studying campaigns from the voter's-eye-view).

Campaign strategy recently changed in a way that enabled Enos and me to conduct a large-scale survey of campaign operatives. Namely, nearly every Democratic campaign in the country, from the presidency down to the county commissioner races, now uses NGP VAN as its user interface. When campaign workers want to generate lists of voters to target with a home visit, a phone call, a postcard, an e-mail, or any other form of direct contact, they log on to NGP VAN to generate their lists. The data they see in NGP VAN is typically the DNC's VoteBuilder database, but it could also be data from Catalist or from a state party or local vendor. By surveying campaign workers *through* NGP VAN, we could get unparalleled access to volunteers, staffers, and even candidates all across the country.

As with my initial contract with Catalist, the task of getting all of the key players to agree to do this survey took about a year. I first reached out to NGP VAN's managing partner, Jim St. George, on May 5, 2011. The proposal was simple: when campaign workers log in to NGP VAN, we would randomly select workers and ask them to participate in the survey. We would conduct the survey every day for the months leading up to the election, gathering data from a range of campaign workers (candidates and campaign managers down to interns and volunteers) and a range of races (presidency on down). St. George was excited about the project. All we needed, he said, was a sign-off from the Obama campaign. And, if we wanted to survey campaigns below the presidential level, we would need permission of the state parties in which those campaigns were operating,

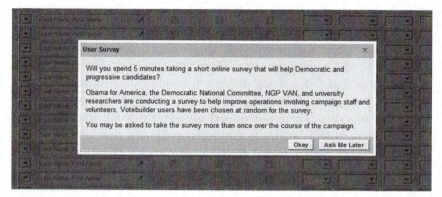

FIGURE 4.3 Screenshot of Initial Survey Prompt from the Ground Campaign Project.

since state parties manage access to NGP VAN and VoteBuilder for sub-presidential campaigns operating in their states.

Like St. George and his colleagues at NGP VAN, the Obama campaign's data team, led by Ethan Roeder, was enthusiastic. They helped craft questions and design the survey. We were also able to convince twenty-five state parties to let us engage with campaigns in their states. Thirteen months after our first contact with NGP VAN, we gained approval and started collecting data from the Obama campaign on June 11, 2012. We began surveying the down-ballot races on August 22, 2012. From each of those dates until the November 2, 2012 Election Day, we surveyed more than 3,500 campaign workers in 193 races.

The mechanics of the survey worked as follows. When campaign workers logged in to NGP VAN during the 2012 campaign season, they often worked in a "grid view" screen. In some Obama campaign field offices, designated staff and volunteers did much of the NGP VAN data entry and list management, but 80 percent of the campaign workers we surveyed said they spent at least five hours directly interacting with voters in the prior week. When Obama workers were in the "grid view" of NGP VAN, there was a 1-in-100 chance they would receive a prompt for our survey. For campaigners in all other races, there was a 1-in-33 chance to receive the prompt. Because the Obama campaign had so many active volunteers and staff relative to other campaigns, we used a higher sampling rate for down-ballot races.

The survey prompt, as it appeared in the "grid view," is displayed in Figure 4.3. If a campaign user clicked "Okay," a browser window popped up that included an informed consent page and then our survey.

Once a campaign worker had taken a survey, they were put in a separate pool and thereafter had a 1-in-1,000 chance of being asked to take a short follow-up survey. If a user clicked "ask me later," they retained the original 1-in-100 or 1-in-33 chance of being prompted again.

Together, Enos and I used the GCP survey to answer a number of research questions related to political campaigns and elite activists (Enos and Hersh, 2015a, 2015b). However, several questions were placed on the survey specifically for this book, as they offer insights into the Perceived Voter Model. The first of these questions asks campaign workers:

> Below are some characteristics that might be used as the basis for contacting voters. Rank the following voter characteristics in order of their importance to strategies in your state. Use "1" to indicate the most important characteristic, "2" to indicate the second most important characteristic, and so on. Use "0" to indicate characteristics that are not available about voters in your state.

- Party
- Race/Ethnicity
- Gender
- Previous precinct results
- Previous voter turnout
- Age
- Income
- Predictions from targeting models
- Other

This question will help me measure how campaign operatives in different policy environments react to varying availability of public records. The second question asks:

> How would you characterize the campaign's main strategy at the present time in your area? Select all that apply.

- Paid advertisement geared at persuading undecided voters
- Paid advertisement geared at mobilizing supporters
- Volunteer Field Contact geared at persuading undecided voters
- Volunteer Field Contact geared at mobilizing supporters
- Registering voters
- Recruiting voters through social networks (i.e. contacting friends and colleagues)
- Building party support
- Other

This second question will help me gauge the extent to which the information environment affects the kinds of strategies employed, at least according to the perspective of campaign workers. Note that to make sure that the survey took workers less than five minutes to complete (a requirement of our agreement with the parties involved), some questions on the GCP were only asked of half of the sample so that we could increase the number of questions we asked. The first question listed above was among these branched questions.

In the analysis of the GCP survey in this book, I primarily focus on campaign workers associated with the Obama campaign and working in swing states. This is by far the largest cohort of GCP respondents. Of the campaign workers who answered questions in the GCP, 85 percent logged in from accounts managed by the presidential campaign. Of Obama campaign respondents, 60 percent were working in one of nine swing states: Colorado, Florida, Iowa, Nevada, New Hampshire, Ohio, Virginia, and Wisconsin. In our joint work, Enos and I are studying workers in down-ballot campaigns, but here I use the GCP to study how a single campaign alters its strategy depending on its data environment.

By restricting the analysis to the presidential race, I can hold constant many confounding considerations, like financial resources, candidate traits, and opponent traits, and I can focus just on how the presidential campaign varied its approach by jurisdiction. This restriction also accommodates the limitations of the data. Because the down-ballot races were only surveyed in twenty-five states, and because respondents only compose 15 percent of the total interviewees, there are too few respondents on many of the questions I ask for a rigorous investigation. For example, only thirty-six down-ballot respondents in nonparty registration states answered the question about the characteristics used in direct contact. These workers are spread out across different campaigns in different states, and so controlling even for simple confounders like the office for which the campaign is working stretch the down-ballot data too thin. In contrast, the GCP interviewees include between 75 and 422 Obama-affiliated workers in each of the nine swing states.

Of course, using the GCP survey to focus on 2012 Obama workers raises a question of external validity: Do the results from the Obama campaign apply to other campaigns? My underlying assumption is that the effects of the public-records laws on the Obama campaign are at least as strong in down-ballot races. The basic argument I lay out is that when public records do not provide clear signals of traits such as a voter's partisanship, campaigns alter their strategy because their other data resources do not permit them to perceive voters in the same way. If any campaign was able to compensate for limitations in public records with other forms of data, it would be the 2012 Obama campaign, which was the wealthiest campaign in history and considered the most technologically sophisticated to date. Thus, if even the Obama campaign was affected by the public data environment, other campaigns surely would be affected as well. Additionally, down-ballot races use NGP VAN, the exact same interface as the Obama campaign used for direct voter contact, lending credibility to the assumptions of external validity. Finally, I use tools other than the Obama responses on the GCP to examine the effect of public data on campaign strategy in other kinds of races, thus further mitigating concerns of external validity.

The reason to restrict the GCP analysis to workers operating in swing states is because many of the campaign workers operating outside of swing states were actually working to facilitate efforts in swing states. For example, 40 percent of Obama workers who claimed to be working in "safe" states like California were actually working to recruit volunteers and to engage with voters in nearby states like Nevada and Colorado. It is not always possible to tell in which swing state an out-of-state respondent was actually working. As a result, I focus most of the analysis of GCP respondents on the 1,918 Obama workers located in the nine battleground states.

### GCP Sample Representativeness
Counting both Obama workers and down-ballot workers, the GCP solicited 15,953 individuals. Of these, 5,608 (35 percent) entered the survey. However, not all of these individuals clicked through an informed-consent page and answered every question. For most survey questions, the sample sizes are in the 3,000–3,500 range, resulting in an item-level response rate of approximately 20 percent.

The GCP respondents consist of 3,095 workers associated with Obama for America, and of these 1,918 were actively working in swing states. Of the Obama workers in swing states, 19 percent were paid staffers and the remainder were volunteers and interns. The average Obama worker in swing states (staffers and volunteers) spent twenty-five hours per week on the campaign, and spent twelve of those hours engaged in direct voter contact.

The GCP sample of Obama workers is dominated by low-level staffers and volunteers. The Obama workers in the sample are clearly not strategists; they are implementers of strategy. One question that may arise is whether these workers in the sample are aware enough of the campaign's strategy that one can infer that their responses are consistent with the overall strategies pursued by the campaign. After all, the purpose of studying the GCP respondents here is to measure how perceptions generated from public records translate into strategies pursued by the campaigns.

These workers are assumed to be sufficiently aware of the strategy to make their responses useful to study, for the following reason. Low-level Obama workers in the GCP sample are engaging with voters on a daily basis. I assume they are aware of whether they are interacting with Democrats or independents, with racial minorities or with whites. Indeed, the computerized and printed lists in front of them report these classifications explicitly. I assume the workers are aware whether the scripts they are using contain messages meant to drive up turnout among known supporters or to persuade undecided voters. Indeed, any cognizant person in this role would have a general sense of what types of voters they are engaging and what kinds of messages they are delivering, even if they are not the ones making high-level strategic decisions. The low-level staffers and volunteers should be thought of as agents of the campaign (Enos and Hersh, 2015b). They are carrying out the strategy chosen by the decision makers and should not be presumed to be completely blind to what they are doing. They need not be aware of the nuanced, high-level, strategic game plan to have a basic understanding of what they are actually doing when they are engaging with voters.

Another question that arises from the GCP is whether the workers in the sample who are logged into the NGP VAN website are representative of campaign workers in general. Unlike surveys of the American public that can be compared against, and benchmarked to, the observable demographic features of the U.S. population, there is no baseline akin to the U.S. Census to which the GCP survey can be compared. In its attempt to study campaign workers engaged in direct contact with voters, the GCP is the first survey of its kind. From speaking with high-level staffers associated with the Obama campaign, it is clear that essentially all workers who were seriously engaged in direct voter contact (the strategy studied in this analysis) had log-ins to the NGP VAN website. NGP VAN reported that the Obama campaign had approximately 100,000 unique user accounts by the end of the campaign. The GCP survey was sampled from the universe of all users. Thus, while there may be unknown selection biases resultant from certain workers being more willing than others to participate in the survey, it seems that the strategy of sampling from the pool of NGP VAN log-ins was the best method available for asking questions of the individuals who were engaged in direct voter contact.

See Enos and Hersh (2015b), appendix, for further information about selection bias in the GCP.

## Query Records from NGP VAN

A third source of data that, in a small way, will help evaluate campaign perceptions and strategies comes from a partnership with one state Democratic party in the 2010 general election season. This data collection effort was done in conjunction with my colleague Brian Schaffner. The name of the specific state party we worked with must remain confidential.

In my joint effort with Schaffner, we collected all query parameters of every voter list drawn during the 2010 election season by a statewide race, three congressional races, twelve state senate races, and seven state house races. The congressional and state house races were selected to include a range of contests based on the number of candidates registered and the demographics of the districts. The data needed to be obtained one query at a time, and so the data collection was quite time-intensive, which is why we did not collect data on all races in the state. Combined, the Democratic candidates in these races drew more than 6,400 voter contact lists over the course of the primary and general election campaigns.

Figure 4.4 shows one example of the 6,400 lists in the database that Schaffner and I captured and coded. This query represents one row in the spreadsheet. In this row, we learn that on October 26, 2010, a particular campaign went into the NGP VAN website and selected all voters in county X that were predicted to be African American, over the age of sixty, and who did not vote early. This list consisted of 1,931 voters. We recorded the parameters of lists like these that campaigns created without us seing the names of voters who were included on the lists. This data collection was small in scope, as it only pertains to a small set of races in a single state in a single election year. We cannot disclose the name of the state or many of the details. But I will refer to the "VAN query data" later, as it provides a window not into the data available to campaigns (which I learn from Catalist) or perceptions of campaign staffers who use that data (which I learn from the GCP), but into some concrete, conventional uses of the data.

## Interviews and Other Campaign Data

The final resource that will help me explain how campaign strategies vary predictably according to the availability of data is interviews with

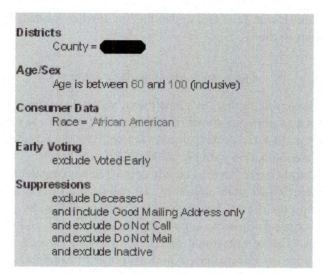

FIGURE 4.4 Screenshot of Query Parameters from NGP VAN.
*Note:* This screenshot shows parameters from one list queried by a state senate candidate. In addition to the information listed above, we were able to collect the date this query was generated (October 26, 2010), the number of people included in this list (1,931 voters), as well as the campaign worker who made this list and the exact time of day. Data generated from a joint project with Brian Schaffner.

campaign workers. I have sought out campaign workers who have worked on local, congressional, and presidential races. In particular, I have spoken with campaign workers who are familiar with the data at the root of strategic direct contact. In several cases, these campaign workers not only shared with me information about how they use data but also handed over computer files from old campaigns. For example, several campaign workers who had access to John Kerry presidential campaign data files and Barack Obama presidential campaign data files shared them with me. I reference these interviews with various campaign operatives, as these interviews can help further explain how data inform strategic choices.

Part of the value of these interviews and supplementary data is that they allow me to show additional uses of data that are not captured by Catalist or NGP VAN. In particular, presidential campaigns in the United States are unique in the amount of resources they are able to pour into voter contacting strategies. Whereas most of the campaigns in the country have no more tools than are provided by their parties in the VoteBuilder and Voter Vault databases, presidential campaigns do have additional resources. These additional resources might take the form of consumer data, but they are also often supplementary forms of public data. For example, I found a computer file from the Obama campaign that listed which voters lived in Section 8 housing, and an Obama field organizer from New Hampshire told me that the campaign figured out which voters received a state veterans tax benefit so they could compose a list of New Hampshire veterans. By shedding light on these nuances, the interviews help fill in some missing pieces about what voters look like from the campaign's-eye-view in sophisticated campaigns.

### 4.3 WHY FOCUS ON DEMOCRATS?

The research partnerships just described, one may have noticed, are all collaborations with Democrats and Democratic organizations. The exception to this is a small number of interviews I conducted with Republican data experts, none of whom agreed to be mentioned by name. When I investigate what voters look like from the campaign's-eye-view here, it will mostly be what they look like from the Democratic campaign's-eye-view. Why is this the case, and how does it affect my analysis?

When I went to Washington, DC back in 2009 to begin this research, I had every intention of gathering data from Republicans as well as from Democrats. I was a registered independent and, prior to graduate school, I had worked both for Democrats and Republicans in menial political jobs. However, when I began immersing myself in this project, I was received much more warmly on the Democratic side than the Republican side. Democratic operatives not only talked openly with me, but in some cases handed me sensitive data files from prior campaigns. I built relationships with staff at Catalist and NGP VAN, but I was not able to get phone calls returned by the Voter Vault team at the RNC. Why did this happen?

I can speculate three reasons for my lopsided access. The first reason was suggested to me by a political scientist who is involved in Republican campaign work. He figured that because most academicians are politically liberal, unless one is actively engaged in Republican politics or else works at a university that has strong conservative leanings, one will be met with suspicion when asking Republican operatives for information.

The second speculative reason why I had difficulty obtaining campaign data from Republicans was suggested to me by consultants for both Democratic and Republican campaigns. These consultants suggested that the Democratic side has more of an open-source culture than the Republican side does. The fact that the database business on the Democratic side involves third-party companies like NGP VAN and Catalist whereas data on the Republican side is more centralized at the RNC is telling. The Democratic side has more openings for collaboration because more individuals and organizations are involved in political data and can grant access. The Republican side is more closed and controlled by the national political party.

The third reason is that the Democratic Party in the Obama years was widely viewed as having the advantage in data and technology. Indeed, most of the popular press articles and books written in this period focused mainly on the Democratic side. One might speculate that the Democrats were more open to researchers because they liked the storyline that emphasized their advantage.

Whatever the reason for my one-sided access, I have tried to assess how it affects the empirical evidence here. I asked a leading Democratic targeting consultant, Hal Malchow, whether he thought the Democratic and Republican data resources looked similar. Malchow responded, "Yes – they get their data from the same sources." He then reviewed all the public sources, such as the voter registration system, that campaigns turn to. He said the parties turn to the same commercial data aggregation firms to match public records to consumer data. He said that databases may differ in how accurate they are and how up-to-date they are, but as a matter of the data fields, he expects that Democrats and Republicans are looking at a similar set of variables.

The similarity between the Democratic and Republican databases is easy to confirm. Just as one can search the Internet for "VoteBuilder training" and see, in detail, what campaigns see when they are logged into NGP VAN, it is easy to find out the basic structure of Voter Vault by using the same strategy. One can find screenshots from the Voter Vault Web interface that contain exactly the same basic options for generating voter contact lists as are contained in VoteBuilder. Users can select voters in particular geographies, like precincts, with particular demographic attributes, like gender, age, and political party affiliation. In short, both parties have built UIs that allow standard campaign workers to generate contact lists with the same set of querying options.

Thus, while the evidence presented here comes almost entirely from Democratic sources, I expect that the Republican data sources look similar and are equally dominated by public records. Nevertheless, it bears acknowledgment that I can be much more confident, given the data, about how Democratic campaigns see voters as compared with how Republicans see voters. That stated, since 2008, the Democrats have been widely acknowledged as having the edge in data and technology. My focus on the Democratic side arguably means that I am taking on a difficult case to test my hypotheses about how perceptions vary across jurisdictions. If there is one side of the political aisle that, since 2008, would be more likely to move beyond mere public records in forming their perceptions of voters, it is the Democratic side. And here I am showing that the strategies pursued on the Democratic side are well predicted by the public data environment.

## 4.4 SUMMARY

In this chapter, I have laid out several tools that can help me examine how information – particularly public information – affects the perceptions campaigns have of voters and the strategic decisions they make. With Catalist, I have a comprehensive database including hundreds of characteristics about every American voter; with the GCP, I have a survey of campaign workers engaged in direct contact; with the NGP VAN query project, I have thousands of list queries generated in one state; and I have interviews with campaign specialists that offer a window into conventional strategies for engaging voters. These data resources together provide new insights into the strategic capabilities and perceptions of political campaigns. Through these resources, I can measure how voters appear from the campaign's-eye-view. I can examine the American public, not as voters, but as *perceived voters* – the avatars that exist in campaign databases.

# 5

# The Perceived Partisan

The purpose of the Perceived Voter Model is to predict campaign strategies and their subsequent effects on voters by paying attention to the perceptions that political campaigns have of their electorates. In Chapters 2 and 3, I explained why public records of personal information, such as those that originate in the voter registration system, contribute to campaign perceptions. I offered specific hypotheses that explain how the provision of data about voters' racial identities or party affiliations, and the lack of data predictive of persuadability, will affect campaign strategies. In Chapter 4, I reviewed the data sources that will allow me to examine these hypotheses.

In this chapter, I begin to test hypotheses by focusing on the provision of public data about voters' partisanship. States differ in their public collection of personal data about partisanship. Some states collect data from voters that, when transmitted to campaigns, provide campaigns with effective tools for predicting which voters are going to support Democratic or Republican candidates in upcoming elections. Other states do not collect these data. In all states, voters cast secret ballots, but in some states, a campaign can use public records to predict a person's choices in the voting booth with a high level of accuracy. In this chapter, I examine how the availability of public records relevant to predictions of partisanship affect how campaigns perceive the electorate, how they strategize given those perceptions, and how their strategic choices affect voters.

## 5.1 PUBLIC RECORDS OF PARTISAN SUPPORT

There are two forms of party information that are available to campaigns on voter files in different states. The first form is party registration, whereby voters have the option of registering as a member of a political party and this designation becomes public information. The second form is party primary data. For each primary in which a voter chooses to participate, the party's ballot that the voter selected is noted on the public record. In 2010, in seventeen states, both forms of partisan information were available.[1] These states offer the greatest signal of party identification. In thirteen other states, party registration data were available but partisan primary data were not recorded on the voter file.[2] In eleven other states, the primary data were recorded, but no party registration data were made available.[3] Finally, in the ten remaining states, no partisan data were included in the public record.[4] As is evident from the map in Figure 5.1, which depicts these state categories, there is geographic variation, though data-rich states are found primarily in the northeast and west and data-limited states are found primarily in the midwest.

These designations of state law are somewhat fluid. In 2011, Idaho became a party registration state to accommodate a change to its primary system. As of 2012, following legal disputes, Michigan began publicly reporting primary data for presidential primary voting.[5] Because the evidence provided in this book comes from elections between 2008 and 2012, I count both of these states in the category of providing no party information in the public record. I do so not only because of when the bulk of my data were collected but also because there is a lag between when a jurisdiction like Idaho begins to collect data and when that data has wide enough coverage to be very useful as a tool for campaigns.

Why do some states collect party registration and party primary data while others do not? The most straightforward answer is that these laws stem from the structure of primaries within the states. If a state has a closed primary, meaning that only affiliated members can participate in the primary election, then the election administration must know which voters are affiliated with each party. Likewise, eleven states hold runoff primaries.[6] In a runoff primary, if no candidate receives more than 50 percent of the vote share, as is sometimes the case in multi-candidate races, then the two candidates with the highest vote shares face off in a second-round primary. If a jurisdiction requires second-round primaries, it may want to restrict voting in the second round to voters who participated in the first round. Under this kind of system, the election administration

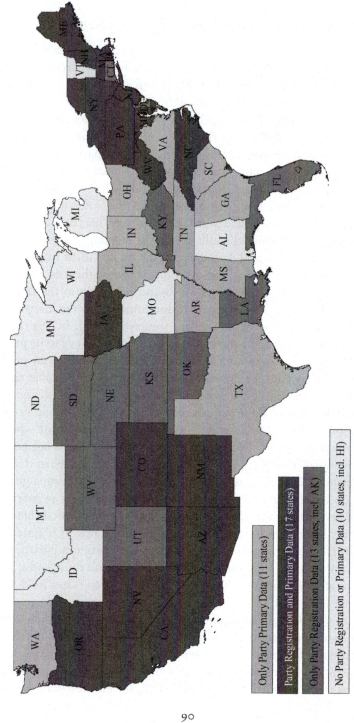

FIGURE 5.1 The Availability of Party Registration and Party Primary Data in the U.S. States in 2010.

Only Party Primary Data (11 states)

Party Registration and Primary Data (17 states)

Only Party Registration Data (13 states, incl. AK)

No Party Registration or Primary Data (10 states, incl. HI)

would need to track which voters participated in the Republican versus Democratic primaries, thus generating a public record.

The justification for collecting partisan information in the public record is not always so clear-cut. Whereas only eleven states hold runoff primaries, twenty-eight states list in the public record the party of the primary in which a voter participated. For example, Massachusetts permits independent voters to participate in either party's primary. If an independent voter chooses a Democratic ballot, she is listed in that election as having voted in the Democratic primary, and if she chooses a Republican ballot, she is listed as having voted in the Republican primary. Why is this a public record? There are some plausible administrative rationales. Primary vote history might be used as a metric for gauging the accurate counting of votes: the number of people listed as having voted in the Democratic and Republican primaries should equal the number of ballots counted in voting machines for each party. Along these lines, in a 2010 Michigan Appeals Court case involving disclosure requirements of primary party data, state judges were persuaded by FOIA petitioners that these data allow citizens to fulfill a watchdog role in holding election administrators accountable for running accurate and fair contests. At the same time, personal information about partisanship might find its way into the public record because of its use as a campaign tool, as I discussed in Chapter 3. It turns out that the FOIA petitioners who were plaintiffs in the Michigan case were not public interest watchdog groups but political data vendors who had an interest in using the data for the purpose of campaign voter contact.

Whatever the explicit state rationale for publicly recording party registration and partisan primary voting records, there are clear political benefits from having the data. The origins of the data, such as their relationship to primary election laws, is an interesting topic of study in its own right, but here, as I examine the perspective of a campaign strategist, the origin story is of secondary importance. Campaigns operate in a particular information context, and when that context permits them to see political identifiers for each voter, campaigns latch onto them. When they are available, these records provide campaigns with strong signals of the partisan preferences of voters.

Just how strong of a signal do public identifiers offer? In 2012, among validated voters who were registered Democratic, 88 percent voted for Barack Obama and 85 percent voted for the Democratic congressional candidate. Ninety percent of registered Republicans voted for Mitt Romney and 89 percent voted for the Republican congressional candidate.

This level of party voting was the same in 2008. In 2008, 90 percent of registered Democrats voted for Barack Obama and 91 percent of registered Republicans voted for John McCain. At the congressional level, 87 percent of registered Democrats and 89 percent of registered Republicans voted for their party's candidate. These statistics come from Catalist records matched to the 2008 and 2012 Cooperative Congressional Election Studies.

Records of primary participation are also highly predictive of outcomes. Among registered voters who are not listed with a political party but have been noted in the public record as voting in a Democratic primary anytime between 2000 and 2008, approximately 76 percent reported voting for Barack Obama and 78 percent reported voting for the Democratic congressional candidate. Voters who are listed in the public record as having voted in Republican primaries exhibit even higher rates of fidelity to their party's nominees across offices.

These two pieces of information that originate from public records thus provide campaigns with a strong signal of how a voter is leaning before the campaigns make any contact with the voter. But in many states, campaigns cannot access these signals. Here, I explore how the availability of these signals affects strategic decisions and, consequently, affects voters. The presence or absence of partisanship information about voters forces campaigns into differentiated strategies across states. In turn, those differentiated strategies affect how voters are incorporated into the political process.

## 5.2 PERCEIVING PARTISANSHIP WITHOUT PUBLIC IDENTIFIERS

Consider the position that campaigns are in when they are operating in states with public records of partisanship. The entire population of registered voters can be segmented into Democrats, Republicans, and independents (i.e., unaffiliated voters). Conditional on a Democrat or a Republican actually showing up to vote, their vote choice for every office on the ballot is predictable with about 90 percent accuracy. This means that a campaign can focus on Get-Out-The-Vote (GOTV) strategies to stimulate turnout among partisans who might not show up at the polls without a push. The campaign can also isolate the independent voters whose past record of turnout suggests they will vote, but who may not be particularly committed to one party. The entire strategy of direct contact can be conditioned on whether or not a voter is registered with a party.

Absent public records of partisanship, what does a campaign do? It must perceive the partisan leanings of voters in some other fashion. The alternatives a campaign uses to perceive its partisan supporters in the absence of party registration data will lead to a different population of *perceived voters* that the campaigns will try to mobilize or persuade.

Consider the main alternative sources of data a campaign will use to perceive supporters. The first is a measure of geography. As discussed in Chapter 3, election administrators publish the outcomes of past elections by precinct. A campaign could perceive its supporters as those who live in predominantly Democratic or predominately Republican precincts. Indeed, campaigns outside of party registration states (and sometimes campaigns inside party registration states) use this method, often focusing on precincts that give more than 65 percent of their vote to one party in past elections. Sixty-five percent is a common threshold for what is known as saturation targeting, wherein all voters in the defined group are mobilized en masse, since the group as a whole leans in one direction.[7]

The trouble with perceiving voter partisanship by using data about precincts is that most voters live in mixed-partisan precincts. A summary view of the perceptions that come from a precinct strategy is shown in Figure 5.2. The figure shows the distribution of two-party support for the presidential contenders in 2008 in more than 120,000 precincts. In this nationwide collection of precinct data, it is clear that most precincts are quite mixed in terms of partisan supporters. Most voters live in neighborhoods that are not lopsidedly partisan. In Figure 5.2, I show a separate density plot for precincts in the states of Michigan, Minnesota, and Wisconsin. These are three of the ten states that report neither party registration data nor party primary data and are also places that are competitive in presidential elections. In these places, *where geographic targeting would be most valuable to campaigns,* the geographic data is especially unhelpful since so many precincts are split evenly between Democratic voters and Republican voters. As an alternative to precinct targeting, campaigns may use coarser geographic measures, such as county election returns, to try to identify areas with supporters. However, as with precincts, most counties are not overwhelmingly partisan.

A campaign in 2012 that looked to precinct returns from 2008 to decide which neighborhoods to mobilize through direct contact would perceive a different sort of electoral coalition than would a campaign that had access to individual-level records of partisanship. To mobilize perceived supporters and minimize the number of non-supporters it contacted, a campaign must restrict itself to the relatively small number of

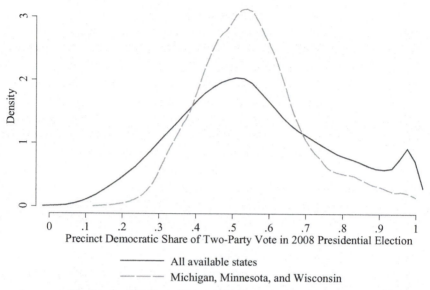

FIGURE 5.2  The Limited Utility of Precinct Targeting: Most Precincts Are Mixed-Partisan.

*Note:* Precinct data from Harvard Election Data Archive. Shown are 123,328 precincts, consisting of all precincts identified in a nationwide data collection. In the states of Michigan, Minnesota, and Wisconsin, there are 9,892 precinct observations. These states are shown separately because they are the traditionally competitive states that do not have any party registration data. It is in these states that precinct targeting would be most beneficial to campaigns, but as shown, there is even less geographic sorting in these states than nationwide.

neighborhoods that overwhelmingly support one side or the other. A campaign might not engage *most* of its supporters simply because they live in mixed-partisan areas. Moreover, the voters who live in homogenous partisan neighborhoods are quite different from the voters who live in heterogenous neighborhoods. For example, in Figure 5.2, there is a small bump on the right side of the graph, indicating a set of precincts in which voters are nearly unanimous supporters of Barack Obama. The bump represents a small set of African-American neighborhoods. A Democratic campaign using a geographic-level strategy might focus its efforts in these neighborhoods not because they contain the only likely Democratic supporters, but because these are the neighborhoods that signal their residents' partisanship most clearly. A geography-based perception of supporters is thus not only less informative of voters' partisanship (because most voters live in mixed precincts) but it is also a perception that is

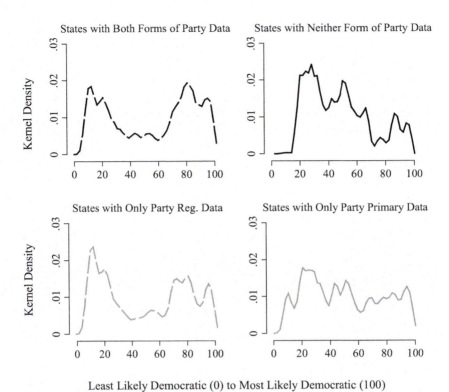

Least Likely Democratic (0) to Most Likely Democratic (100)

FIGURE 5.3 Distribution of Perceived Voters across Partisan Data Environments Using Catalist's Predictive Model of Partisanship.
*Source:* Catalist 1% Analytics Sample from 2010.

distorted, in the sense that supporters who live in homogenous partisan neighborhoods are unlikely to be representative of supporters overall.

A second strategy that campaigns may use to perceive the likely partisan support of voters in the absence of party registration is commercial microtargeting models. As discussed in Chapter 4, Catalist builds one such model that is commonly used across a range of campaigns. A model such as Catalist's uses dozens of variables to predict individual voters' partisanship. It uses demographics and neighborhood characteristics, commercial records of consumer habits, and proprietary records of associational memberships and past records of voter contact. In states where public partisanship records are available, Catalist also incorporates these data into its predictions.

In Figure 5.3, I show Catalist's model of partisanship in four data environments. I cluster the states into groups based on the type of records of partisanship that are available in the voter registration system. Catalist's model runs 0 to 100, where 100 represents voters who are most likely to be Democrats and 0 represents voters who are least likely to be Democrats. Figure 5.3 shows density plots, which means that the higher the vertical peak, the more voters are clustered in that area of the model.

Figure 5.3 is a representation of campaigns' perceptions of voter partisanship, an elite sorting of voters into their likely political camps. This is not the true or self-reported representation of voters' partisanship. Rather, it is the actual sorting that many campaigns use to evaluate which individuals in their electorates are likely supporters (and thus should receive one kind of an appeal), which individuals are independents (and thus should receive another kind of appeal), and which individuals are supporters of the opponent's side (and thus should probably receive no appeal).

The distribution of partisanship clearly looks different across these four groupings of states. The upper-left plot in Figure 5.3 represents states with the most amount of public data. These are the seventeen states that ask voters to register with a party and that record the party of primary elections in which a voter has participated. Notice the line is bimodal; it has a peak on the left that represents voters very likely to be Republican and it has a peak on the right that represents voters very likely to be Democratic. In contrast, consider the upper-right plot in Figure 5.3. This plot represents the ten states that have no party affiliation and do not record party information from primary elections. Instead of a bimodal distribution with clear groupings of Republicans and Democrats, this line indicates that voters appear more spread out and in the middle of the distribution. While some voters appear as likely Democrats, most voters have partisan scores in the 20–70 range.

Figure 5.3 implies that if a campaign lacks party registration and party primary data from the public record, and if it chooses to perceive voters' partisanship by using a predictive model like Catalist's, as many real-world campaigns actually do in the ten states that lack public records of partisanship, then the perceptions of which voters are supporters look much different than in states with public records of partisanship. As I show later, the difference in perceptions across data environments is not a consequence of the voters in these different places having different political preferences; it is merely a consequence of the information resources available to campaigns that inform their perceptions.

Incidentally, Figure 5.3 shows that party registration is more essential to generating distinctive cohorts of predicted Republicans and Democrats than is party primary vote history. The states that have just party registration data but not primary data (lower-left plot) are similar to the states with both forms of party data in exhibiting a bimodal distribution of voters split into distinctive partisan camps. In states with only primary data (lower-right plot), the voters appear more similar to voters in states with no data: mostly spread out over the middle of the partisan distribution.

Party affiliation data is more valuable to campaigns mostly because it has wider coverage. In party registration states, 75 percent of registered voters are listed as Republicans or Democrats in the public records. In the states that collect only party primary indicators, nearly 60 percent of registered voters have never once participated in a primary and so their records offer no signal of their partisan leanings. Because most registered voters choose not to participate in primaries, the public record of past primary participation is less valuable to campaigns than is the record of party registration. As a result of this empirical finding, in most of my analysis that follows, I focus on the differences in strategies in states with party registration versus states without party registration, thus ignoring the nuance of primary data.

Several questions immediately arise upon examining the distributions in Figure 5.3. First, while the distribution of Catalist's scores is different in the states with party registration data from states without party registration, one might wonder whether the scores are equally predictive of vote choice in the different data environments. For example, even though more voters have a score of 60 in data-poor environments, perhaps a score of 60 in those places is as predictive of partisan support as a score of 80 in the data-rich environments. To consider this, I measure the relationship between the partisan support score and vote choice using the 2008 CCES merged with Catalist records. I plot the relationship in Figure 5.4. For voters with a score below 50, voters in party registration states and non–party registration states were about equally likely to report they voted for Obama. But for scores greater than 50 (meaning, Catalist predicted these voters lean Democratic), the scores in party registration states are slightly more predictive of Democratic support than the scores in nonparty registration states. For example, among voters with a score in the 70–80 range, 79 percent of those in party registration states reported voting for Obama, whereas only 70 percent of those in nonparty registration states reported voting for Obama. Thus, not only are many more voters clustered in the middle of the distribution in non–party registration states, but, as evidenced in Figure 5.4, the scores themselves are also slightly less predictive of vote choice in these states.

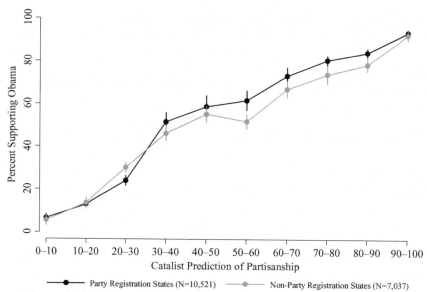

FIGURE 5.4 Relationship between Catalist Microtargeting Score and Self-Reported Vote Choice for Barack Obama.
*Source:* 2008 CCES matched to Catalist records (N = 17,558). Note that not all CCES respondents were able to be matched to Catalist's prediction of voter partisanship.

Next, one may wonder whether the model shown in Figure 5.3, which was developed ahead of the 2008 election, shows the same kind of pattern that one would see using models developed since 2008. In the analysis of Catalist's models, I focus mostly on the 2008 models because I have connected the 2008 version of the Catalist database with survey data in the CCES, which is used, for example, in Figure 5.4. However, in the fall of 2012, I obtained versions of Catalist partisanship model that campaigns utilized in the 2010 and 2012 election cycles. In Figure 5.5, I show four distributions. I show distributions in states with both forms of partisanship data and states with neither form of partisanship data. And I show distributions for each of these state-types using Catalist's 2010 version of its partisanship model and Catalist's 2012 version. Notice that in the data-rich environments, shown in the left-side plots, the 2010 and 2012 models are nearly identical. They are both considerably smoother lines than the lines from the 2008 model, but like the 2008 model, they show clear groupings of Democrats and Republicans. In data-poor states, the 2010 model (upper-right) is much less smooth than the 2012 model

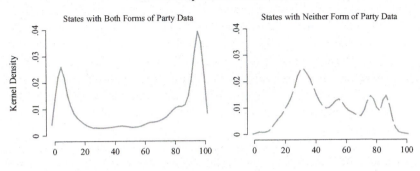

Partisanship Model Used in 2010

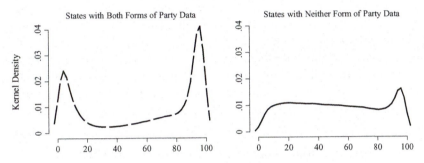

Partisanship Model Used in 2012

Least Likely Democratic (0) to Most Likely Democratic (100)

FIGURE 5.5 Distribution of Perceived Voters across Partisan Data Environments Using 2010 and 2012 Versions of Catatlist's Predictive Model of Partisanship. *Source:* Catalist 1% Analytics Sample from 2012.

(lower-right), but in both years, the model in these states shows voters spread out along the range modeled scores.

In general, the partisanship scores in 2010 and 2012 are smoother than the scores in 2008, which indicates improvements in the model over time as Catalist adds data and nuances to its prediction of partisanship. But the level of smoothness in these models is second order. Quite clearly, the newer models shown in Figure 5.5 exhibit the same dramatic differences across data environments as in 2008. The comparison between Figure 5.3 and Figure 5.5 highlights the year-to-year continuity and change in elite perceptions. Catalist added bells and whistles to its predictive model in 2012 that it did not have in 2008. But the core data that stem from the voter registration system affected campaign perceptions in 2012 about as much as it affected perceptions in 2008. And these data will likely continue to affect perceptions going forward in time, because no statistical trick or new bit of consumer data about voters helps campaigns perceive voters' partisanship as well as public records from the voter registration system. The similarity between the 2008 and 2012 distributions justifies my treatment of these years interchangeably through the analysis here. Between these years, firms like Catalist assimilated new data and techniques into their predictions of partisanship, but the effect of public record availability on those perceptions is nevertheless very apparent across years.

To be clear, the differences in partisanship scores across data environments is not an indictment of Catalist for doing a poor job building models. Catalist's models are cutting-edge in the campaign industry. Voters are perceived differently across data environments *even* in nuanced models like Catalist's because it is plainly difficult to predict voters' partisanship absent personal information in public voter files. Attributes like race, age, gender, neighborhood characteristics, and even proprietary records maintained by political organizations are predictive of partisan support, but not nearly as predictive as the identifiers stored in public registration databases that signal a person's affiliation or primary history.

### Are Perceptions Different Because Voters Are Different?

One plausible, but incorrect, interpretation of Figures 5.3 and 5.5 is that elite perceptions are different in states without party registration data not because it is difficult to perceive voters without public records but because the voters have different partisan dispositions in these places. In states like Wisconsin, Alabama, and Hawaii, which do not collect records of party affiliation or primary participation, perhaps voters themselves are just not as partisan as in other states, and this results in different distributions of *perceived voters* as shown in Figure 5.3.

This line of thinking is consistent with some past scholarship in political science that has studied how the opportunity to register to vote as an affiliated party member may affect a voter's attitudes. Campbell et al. (1960) argue that "community sentiment" in different states generated different election laws, and they hypothesize that once election laws are established, they can have a psychological impact on voters. In this vein, Finkel and Scarrow (1985) and Burden and Greene (2000) suggest that the act of registering with a party can influence one's identity as a partisan.

Without denying the possibility of this psychological impact on voters, I can confirm that the reason the perceived distribution of partisans looks

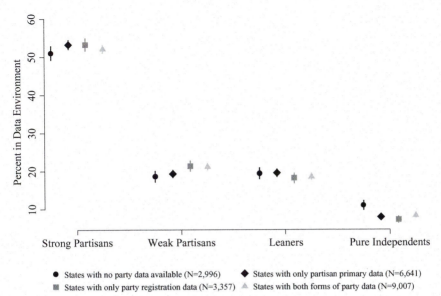

FIGURE 5.6 Partisan Identification across Data Environments.
*Source:* 2008 validated CCES survey.

different across these states is because of the role of public records in shaping elite perceptions, not because voters are different in these states. I do so in two ways. The first, and simpler, way is by measuring the distribution of self-reported party identification across state types. Using the CCES, I show the rate at which voters in each data environment identify as strong partisans, weak partisans, independents who lean toward one party or the other, and "pure" independents. The results are in Figure 5.6.

Figure 5.6 shows that the rate of each type of partisan identifier is similar across data environments. In the CCES survey, about half of the voters in every type of data environment claim to be either Democrats or Republicans, and then when asked if they are strongly or weakly attached to the party, they report they are strong partisans. About 20 percent of respondents in each data environment claim they are weak partisans. Another 20 percent claim they are independent voters but lean toward one of the two major parties. And just under 10 percent claim that they are independents who do not lean toward a party.

Notice that in the states with neither form of public party data (represented by a black circle in Figure 5.6), respondents are slightly more likely to claim they are pure independents and slightly less likely to claim they are strong partisans, compared to other data environments, including

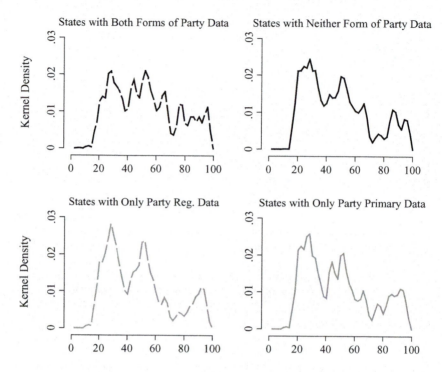

Least Likely Democratic (0) to Most Likely Democratic (100)

FIGURE 5.7 Voters Appear Similar to Campaigns across Data Environments If Campaigns Ignore Party Registration Records.
*Source:* Catalist 1% Analytics Sample from 2010.

the states that collect primary data but not party registration data. These tiny differences in party identification cannot explain the dramatic differences in elite perceptions that emerge in Catalist's predictive models. Voters may have slightly different dispositions toward partisanship in non–party registration states, but the perceptions of elites differ dramatically in these places. Perceptions vary because public information varies, not because voters vary.

An alternative way to show that voters are similar across data environments but that perceptions are different because of public records is by leveraging an altered version of Catalist's partisanship model. The models shown in Figure 5.3 and Figure 5.5 are the models that campaigns employing Catalist actually use in their direct contact efforts. The model shown in Figure 5.7, however, is a separate version of the model that Catalist provides to some of its clients merely for analytic purposes. This analytic model is a prediction of partisanship that is measured consistently across states; it does not treat voters differently depending on whether they are registered with a party or voted in a party primary. For states that do not collect these public data, the model is identical to the model displayed in Figure 5.3. That is, the upper-right plots in the two figures show exactly the same distributions. For these states, the model does not differ since party registration and party primary data cannot be incorporated into the model. For the states that do collect party information, the altered model essentially leaves the registration-based data points out of the prediction. In other words, in Figure 5.7, voter partisanship is predicted in all states based on the same set of explanatory variables. As a result, the model in that figure can be thought of as the counterfactual for how voters would appear in all state environments if all states lacked party signals in the public record.

As is evident in Figure 5.7, the distributions of partisanship across state data environments, as predicted with dozens of demographic, neighborhood, and proprietary data, are very similar. These predictors do not indicate that voters are likely to be more moderate in non–party registration states like Wisconsin and Alabama and more polarized in party registration states like Iowa and Massachusetts, based on demographics, neighborhoods, and other predictors. Voters are only perceived as more polarized in the party registration states and less polarized in the other states because of the public records available to inform campaigns' perceptions. Thus, while data laws might slightly affect a voter's perception of his or her partisan ties, a campaign's perception of voters is different across data environments not because of voters' own attitudes. Rather, the data laws have a direct effect on the way campaigns perceive which voters are likely partisan supporters and which are not.

## 5.3 HOW DO PERCEPTIONS OF PARTISANSHIP AFFECT STRATEGIES?

Political campaigns clearly have an incentive to perceive which voters are likely supporters, likely opponents, or up for grabs. But the ability of campaigns to form perceptions of which voters bear which traits varies by jurisdiction. Because strategic decisions are made based on elite perceptions, the data available for perceiving partisans will yield different strategies across states. I now engage in a cross-state investigation of strategy.

Consider, first, some anecdotal evidence of different strategies employed across data environments. In 2000, Al Gore's presidential campaign was active in Wisconsin, a state that Gore ended up winning by only a quarter of a percentage point. An essential part of Gore's strategy was the direct mobilization of core supporters. In Wisconsin, a state that does not collect public party data, the Gore campaign perceived a core supporter as any registered voter who lived in a precinct in which 65 percent or more of the votes typically go to Democratic candidates. Voters living in such precincts were likely to receive visits at their door, mailers, and phone calls, all urging them to vote. This strategy is not unique to the Gore campaign; many candidates in Wisconsin define their core supporters based on which voters live in highly supportive precincts.

The perceived supporter in Wisconsin is very different than in other states. For example, in Tennessee, where there is no party registration but where the public record indicates past participation in party primaries, consider the campaigns of longtime Congressman Bart Gordon, who retired in 2010. According to Gordon's campaign manager, the Gordon campaign typically defined a base voter as someone who votes regularly in party primaries or who lives in the same house as a voter who shows up regularly in party primaries.

In a third state, Massachusetts, the 2010 Deval Patrick gubernatorial campaign perceived its supporters very differently than did campaigns in Wisconsin or Tennessee. When Governor Patrick was running for reelection, his campaign defined base supporters as registered Democrats who voted in two of the last three important elections in the state. Only this group of voters received direct communications from the campaign. Of course, unlike Tennessee and Wisconsin, Massachusetts provides campaigns with records of party affiliation, thus allowing the Patrick campaign to pursue a strategy in which it restricted contact to known party affiliates.

### Cross-State Strategic Differences

Anecdotal evidence from campaign managers and from strategy documents suggests different approaches to core mobilization across data environments. For a more rigorous approach, I now turn to the survey of campaign workers from the Ground Campaign Project to test whether strategies differ across data environments in ways consistent with my predictions. I focus on the 2012 Obama reelection campaign, and study how strategies varied across the battleground states, based on the data environment of the states.

Nine states were widely considered swing states, or battleground states, in 2012. These states include six party registration states: Colorado, Florida, Iowa, New Hampshire, Nevada, and North Carolina. They also include three non–party registration states: Ohio, Virginia, and Wisconsin. I hypothesize that in party registration states, the direct contacting strategy was more focused on mobilizing voters based on voters' partisanship. I hypothesize that in these states, a campaign will focus less on mobilizing voters in partisan neighborhoods and less on persuading undecided voters, since they have the data resources to focus on individual supporters. Finally, I hypothesize that campaigns in party registration states will make less accidental contact with out-partisans.

On the GCP survey, I asked campaign workers in the 2012 election to "rank the following voter characteristics in order of their importance to strategies in your state." Among the nine choices offered was "Party." This question purposefully did not ask campaign workers to rank the importance of "party registration." Instead, the terminology is ambiguous as to the source of the party information the campaign worker may have in mind. The goal of this question is to see whether party is considered a more important characteristic for voter contact in party registration states, without cuing the respondent to have party registration in mind.

In Figure 5.8, I show the average ranking of party according to Obama campaign workers in states with party registration and in states without party registration (with 95 percent confidence intervals). I also show the means for each of the nine battleground states. Figure 5.8 shows that campaign workers considered party to be a more important characteristic used for direct contact when they were working in party registration states than non–party registration states. On average, workers in party registration states considered party to be a half of a ranking, out of nine rankings, more important – a difference that is statistically significant with a p-value of 0.03. In every swing state with party registration, a voter's partisanship was considered a more important characteristic for direct contact than in any of the non–party registration states.

In Table 5.1, I show additional nuances to the ranking scheme. Party is considered a more important voter attribute in party registration states. Other attributes that can proxy for party thus ought to be more important in non–party registration states. The table indicates that the answer option, "previous precinct results," is ranked a half a ranking higher

in non–party registration states. And "predictions from micro-targeting models" is ranked three fifths of a ranking higher in non–party registration states. Both of these differences are significant and are consistent with the expectations that different perceptions lead to different strategies across data environments.

The results in Figure 5.8 and Table 5.1 conform with the earlier anecdotes that in states like Wisconsin, which do not have party registration, campaigns must target people based on the characteristics of their precincts. Similarly, when campaigns do not have access to party data, they are more reliant on microtargeting models like those developed by Catalist to help them roughly sort voters into probable Democrats and probable Republicans. The absence of party registration forces campaigns to find alternative voter attributes to use as the basis for mobilization. In states without party data, perceived supporters are mobilized to vote based on a different set of criteria than perceived supporters in party registration states.

I hypothesize not only that party will be a more important trait used for mobilizing voters in party registration states than in non–party registration states, but that campaigns will focus more on persuading undecided voters in the absence of party data, since they have less reliable data that predict which voters are supportive. To examine how data availability may lead to a relative focus on persuasion or mobilization, I show results from two analyses.

First, I use Catalist data to simulate a typical campaign's perceptions of base supporters and persuadable voters in each state. Later in this book, in Chapter 7, I discuss in greater detail how I simulate persuadable voter targets and Get-Out-The-Vote targets, but the short version is that I discussed general strategies with campaign experts like Ethan Roeder, who was Obama's data director in 2012, and Hal Malchow, a veteran Democratic microtargeter. Mimicking strategies articulated by Roeder, Malchow, and others, I use Catalist data to measure the ratio of common GOTV targets to persuasion targets in each state. The ratio for each state is plotted in Figure 5.9. GOTV targets consist of voters who live in 65%+ partisan precincts, who are registered as a party affiliate, or who are reported as having voted in past primaries *and* who have a turnout history suggesting they may not vote without an outside push. Persuasion targets consist of voters who live in mixed-partisan precincts, who are not registered with a party and who are not listed as having voted in a partisan primary, and who also have a turnout history suggesting they are likely to vote in a presidential election year.

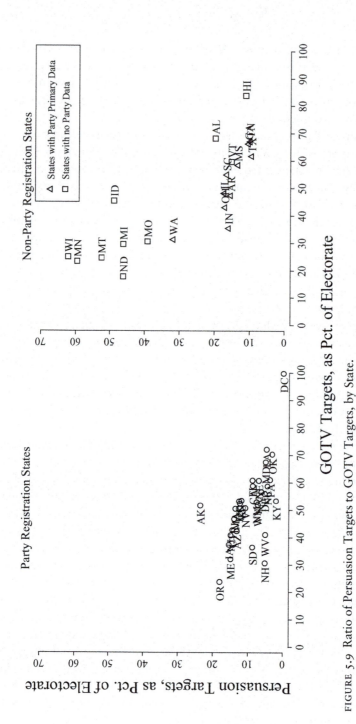

**GOTV Targets, as Pct. of Electorate**

FIGURE 5.9 Ratio of Persuasion Targets to GOTV Targets, by State.

*Note:* These state-level statistics are aggregated from Catalist 1% analytics sample. Targets are constructed based on party registration, party primary, vote history data, as well as precinct-level election returns. The graph demonstrates that the ratio of persuasion targets to GOTV targets is dependent on registration data availability.

In party registration states, shown in the left plot, 30–70 percent of voters appear as targets for mobilization (for both parties combined) and 5–20 percent of voters appear as targets for persuasion. The only outlier here is Washington, DC, where nearly every precinct votes upward of 65 percent Democratic, and so under the scheme in which these precincts are subjected to "saturation" GOTV targeting, just about every voter in the District appears as a GOTV target. States that do not have party registration but do have party primary data (shown in triangles on the right plot) tend to have a higher share of the population appearing as persuasion targets than do party registration states. Because fewer voters turn out for primaries than register with political parties, a greater share of voters in these states appear persuadable.

The most interesting cases, however, are the states that report neither party registration nor party primary data in the public record. In these states, a much higher percentage of voters appear as persuadable. But there are regional differences. In the midwestern states like Wisconsin and Minnesota, not only are there no individual-level signals of partisanship in the voter file, but as I showed in Figure 5.2, very few voters in these states are situated in highly partisan precincts. On the other hand, in states like Vermont and Alabama, many of the voters whose individual records give no signal of partisanship live in precincts that are overwhelmingly partisan.

While some of the differences in Figure 5.9 are attributable to the partisan culture of the states irrespective of the provision of data, clearly the provision of data also plays a role in the ratio of persuasion to mobilization targets. In general, the more individual-level partisanship data that is available in the public record in a state, the more that campaigns are capable of focusing on mobilizing core supporters and the smaller is the proportion of the electorate that appears as persuadable. The implication here is that voter engagement can take on different tones in different jurisdictions not only because local political culture varies across space but because the data that drives political campaigns also varies across space.

Another method to assess the relative importance of persuasion and mobilization in different data environments is to observe responses in the Ground Campaign Project. In Figure 5.10, I summarize the survey question asked to GCP respondents about which strategies they consider to be a main strategy utilized in the area in which they are working. The overwhelming majority of campaign workers (89 percent of Obama workers) thought that in their area, at the time of the interview, the

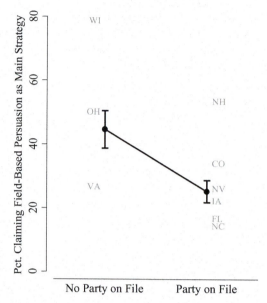

FIGURE 5.10 The Obama Campaign Focused More on Persuasion in Non–Party Registration States.
*Note:* Data from Ground Campaign Project. The difference between respondents in party registration and non–party registration states is statistically significant (p-value < 0.01).

campaign's main focus was on field-based voter engagement (i.e., direct voter contact). Of course, it is not surprising that the workers in the sample, who were engaged in direct contact, thought that the aspect of the campaign in their purview was the main strategy. However, the workers' responses differed in whether the direct contacting efforts in their area were focused on persuasion or on mobilization. As expected from the model, and as reflected in Figure 5.10, respondents in non–party registration states were considerably more likely (20 percentage points) to report that field-based persuasion was a main strategy. Similarly, workers in party registration states were more likely to say that mobilization was the main strategy.

In evaluating the evidence presented from the GCP in this chapter, it is worthwhile to return to the question of whether these low-level staffers and volunteers in the sample know the strategy the Obama campaign was pursuing. At this very basic level of questioning, we can indeed expect them to be aware of the strategy. They should know whether the script they are using in direct contact is a GOTV script (reminding supporters to vote) or whether the script is an attempt to sway undecided voters. They should know whether they are focusing on known partisan supporters or on likely independents. It is reasonable to expect workers engaged with direct contact to know the difference between these aspects of campaigning. Furthermore, the same patterns in Figures 5.8 and 5.10 emerge if the sample is restricted only to full-time paid staffers of the Obama campaign.

One reason that campaign workers in non–party registration states might think that the ground campaign is more geared toward persuasion than toward mobilization is that they have more *accidental* conversations with nonsupportive voters. Even when campaigns are trying to knock on the doors of likely supporters, if they are screening voters based on relatively noisy predictions of partisanship, like geography or microtargeting models rather than party affiliation, workers are going to end up speaking to quite a diverse subset of the electorate. After all, in the campaign that will target geographic areas that are 65 percent Democratic or Republican to mobilize core supporters, up to 35 percent of the doors they knock on will likely be homes of non-supporters.

Hence, persuasion is a bigger part of a campaign's job in a non–party registration state even when the goal of the campaign is simply to mobilize supporters. A campaign focused on mobilization will necessarily encounter more non-supporters, by virtue of having less accurate perceptions. As one political operative in a non–party registration state told me, "You may be contacting people who will never vote for you in a thousand years, but you just don't know."[8] This is much less true in states with party registration, since most voters who are registered with a political party are supportive of candidates affiliated with that party. A mobilization campaign in a party registration state may target affiliated voters and even independents, but the campaign would be able to screen out affiliates of the opposite party.

Because campaign workers in non–party registration states have accidental conversations with non-supporters, these workers have a more difficult task in canvassing voters than do workers in party registration states. Ethan Roeder, data director for the 2012 Obama campaign and national voter file director for Obama's 2008 campaign, suggested that the morale of volunteers working in non–party registration states seems lower to him than in party registration states. Roeder's experience is that volunteers find it draining to have frequent conversations with voters who are not supportive of the candidate they are working for. As much as

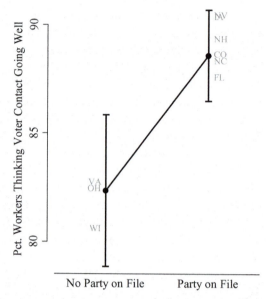

Party Information Available in Public Records

FIGURE 5.11 Success of Voter Contact in Different Data Environments.
*Note:* Data from Ground Campaign Project. The difference between Obama workers in party registration states (885 respondents) and non–party registration states (459 respondents) is statistically significant (p-value < 0.01).

volunteers want to help sway wavering voters, they tend to prefer having pleasant conversations with like-minded supporters than confrontational conversations with voters who oppose their candidate. In party registration states, since volunteers can screen out conversations with affiliated members of the opposite party, confrontational conversations, especially unplanned ones, are much less frequent.

Following on Roeder's observation that campaign workers have a harder time in non–party registration states, I can test his proposition in the GCP. The GCP survey asked campaign workers who were actively engaged in direct contact how well they thought their conversations with these voters were going. The survey used a five-point scale, from voter contact conversations going very well to going very badly. Not surprisingly, an overwhelming majority of respondents thought their conversations were going well. But there was substantial variation in responses across states. As reflected in Figure 5.11, campaign workers and volunteers operating in every party registration state were considerably more positive about the quality of their conversations with voters than those

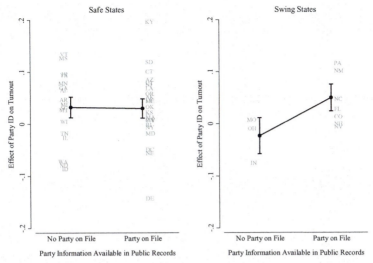

FIGURE 5.12 Relationship between Partisanship and Turnout in Different Data Environments.

*Note:* Using the 2008 validated Cooperative Congressional Election Study, this figure shows OLS regression coefficients from state-by-state models in which validated turnout is predicted with self-reported partisanship. The partisanship measure equals 1 for partisans and 0 for independents. In non-battleground states, there is no difference in the relationship between partisanship and turnout between party registration states and non–party registration states. In the battleground states, however, a substantial difference emerges. In safe non–party registration states, N = 6,590; in safe party registration states, N = 7,787; in swing non–party registration states, N = 2,033; in swing party registration states, N = 4,183.

in non–party registration states. This finding is consistent with Roeder's intuition that campaign volunteers feel more positive when they can avoid accidental conversations with opposing voters, which is easier to do in party registration states.

## 5.4 DOWNSTREAM EFFECTS ON VOTERS

If campaigns in party registration states are more likely to use partisanship as the basis for voter contact, less likely to rely on geographic measures of partisanship, and less likely to engage in persuasion, what are the likely effects of these patterns on voters? In exploring downstream effects on voters, I use data from the 2008 election, when I matched Catalist records and precinct records to respondents from the CCES.

In Figure 5.12, I run a series of OLS regressions in which validated turnout in the 2008 election is the dependent variable and self-reported party identification is the independent variable. The party variable equals 1 for self-reported Democrats and Republicans and equals 0 for independents. Positive values in Figure 5.12 mean that partisans are more likely to vote than are independents. On the left side of the figure I show the pattern for safe states in 2008. As is evident, in the typical party registration state and the typical non–party registration state, partisanship is slightly correlated with turnout, but this relationship does not vary with the data environment. The right side of Figure 5.12 tells a different story. In these states, where the presidential campaigns were active in 2008, there is a noticeable difference in the relationship between partisan identity and turnout depending on whether the state is a party registration state or not. In party registration states, partisans are estimated as 5 percentage points more likely to vote than independents. In non–party registration swing states, partisans are 2 percentage points less likely to vote than independents. This difference is consistent with the evidence presented earlier that campaigns pay more attention to mobilizing partisans in environments in which the public record indicates which voters are affiliated Democrats and Republicans.[9]

While partisans in party registration swing states were more likely to vote than were partisans in non–party registration swing states, the opposite pattern emerges with respect to partisan geographies. Consistent with the expectation that campaigns must focus more on partisan neighborhoods in places that do not record party affiliation, consider the evidence in Figure 5.13. Using the same 2008 CCES survey that I merged not only with Catalist records but also with precinct returns, I show turnout in different kinds of precincts within battleground states.

In the most mixed precincts (defined here as precincts that Obama or McCain won between 45 percent and 55 percent of the vote), turnout was higher in party registration states (difference of means p-value = 0.05). Although these kinds of precincts contain the plurality of voters, campaigns in non–party registration states generally do not approach these precincts in GOTV efforts because they do not know which residents are supporters or not. In party registration states, campaigns can engage voters in these precincts because they do know which voters are partisan affiliates and which are not. The left-most data points are consistent with this story. Moving across the figure to the right, the relationship between precinct-level partisanship and turnout reverses, as expected. In the most partisan precincts, where Obama or McCain won 75 percent or more of the vote, turnout is higher in the non–party registration states

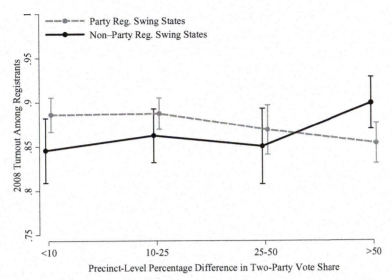

FIGURE 5.13 Relationship between Turnout and Precinct Partisanship in 2008 Swing States.

*Note:* Source is the 2008 validated CCES merged with precinct returns. The x-axis measures the difference in two-party vote share between Obama and McCain in 2008. For example, precincts where Obama garnered 45–55% of the two-party vote are captured in the left-most point in the graph. N = 17,347.

(difference of means p-value = 0.02). In these states, campaigns focus on the homogeneously partisan precincts because campaigns are more reliant on the signal of partisan geography to determine which voters to mobilize.

Past research on campaign effectiveness has demonstrated that campaigns have important and real effects on voter behavior but that their effects are often modest and subtle (see experimental work beginning with Gerber and Green (2000) and observational work such as Holbrook and McClurg (2005) and McGhee and Sides (2011)). Direct voter contact can swing close elections. The patterns I show that distinguish voters in party registration states from non–party registration states are modest but clearly trend in the direction predicted by my theory. In party registration states, turnout is higher among partisans. In non–party registration states, turnout is higher among voters in partisan precincts. These findings make sense in light of the other evidence presented in this chapter that fills out the causal chain. Campaigns have different data resources in party registration states from non–party registration states. As a result, campaigns focus more on voter partisanship in party registration states and more on geography, microtargeting predictions, and persuasion in non–party registration states. In light of this collection of findings from

Catalist and from the GCP survey of campaign workers, I analyzed actual turnout behavior across different data environments and found that the coalitions of voters showing up to the polls are composed more of partisans in party registration states and more of voters living in partisan precincts in non–party registration states.

## 5.5 TESTING THE MODEL WITH A WITHIN-STATE COUNTERFACTUAL

To buttress the findings from the cross-state analysis, I now leverage the two versions of the Catalist model shown in Figures 5.3 and 5.7 to engage in a counterfactual exercise. In this counterfactual, I imagine a party registration state – I use Pennsylvania – that suddenly stops reporting in the public record which voters are Democrats and which voters are Republicans. Imagine a campaign in Pennsylvania suddenly needing to find other ways to mobilize perceived supporters. How would the change in the data environment affect which voters are mobilized?

The logic of the counterfactual is as follows. The Catalist partisanship model is used by many campaigns to perceive which voters are likely supporters. In a state that collects party registration data, such as Pennsylvania, I can compare how voters are sorted by Catalist's actual partisanship model and how they are sorted by a secondary model that is exactly the model a campaign would use if the state abruptly stopped sharing party registration and party primary data with campaigns. I know this because this second model is exactly the model that is used in states that do not collect party information in the public record. In other words, I am taking the microtargeting model of partisanship that is used in states like Wisconsin and applying that model to the voters in Pennsylvania (a state that does collect party information), and I am going to examine how this model would show campaigns a different perception of voters than appear in real-world Pennsylvania.

First, consider the voters of real-world Pennsylvania. Suppose a Democratic campaign in Pennsylvania wants to mobilize core supporters. It might simply mobilize registered Democrats, but it also might use a partisanship model, like one developed by Catalist. Catalist's model in Pennsylvania predicts each voter's partisanship based on party registration, primary voting history, demographics, geographic location, proprietary data, and commercial records. Like in other party registration states, Catalist's prediction of partisanship is largely informed by a voter's party registration status. As a result, Catalist predicts that the Pennsylvania

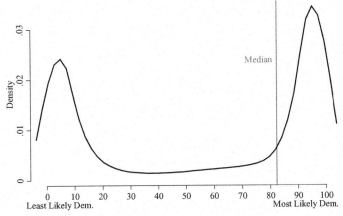

Catalist Prediction of Democratic Support for 2012 Measured with Public Party Data

FIGURE 5.14 Predicted Partisanship of Pennsylvania Registered Voters, Using All Available Data.
*Note:* A random sample of 81,359 registered voters in Pennsylvania is graphed according to Catalist's 2012 partisan support score.

electorate is composed of a group of core Democrats, a group of core Republicans, and very few voters in the middle. Figure 5.14 graphs a random sample of Pennsylvania voters according to Catalist's 2012 support score. Clearly, the electorate is divided into distinct Republican and Democratic camps.

A real-world Democratic campaign using Catalist's model in Pennsylvania might try to build a coalition of supporters by mobilizing the 50 percent of the electorate predicted as most likely to support Democrats. The campaign can simply divide all registered voters in Pennsylvania into two equal camps and mobilize those who are predicted to lean more Democratic. In Figure 5.14, I show the median voter's location on Catalist's Democratic support score. On a scale in which the most Democratic voter has a score of 100 and the least Democratic voter has a score of zero, the median Pennsylvania registered voter has a score of 82. A Democratic campaign might decide to mobilize all voters with at least this score on a model like Catalist's. I call this 50 percent of likely supporters the "perceived Democratic coalition." Of course, this example is a simplification. Real campaigns would not just use a partisan screen like this one, but would also screen voters based on vote history and other measures. Nevertheless, focusing on how a campaign would think about its partisan coalition in the absence of other nuances will be illustrative.

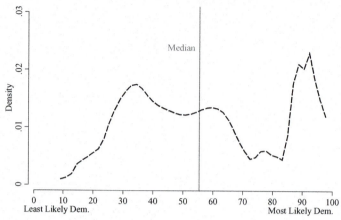

Catalist Prediction of Democratic Support for 2012 Measured without Public Party Data

FIGURE 5.15 Predicted Partisanship of Pennsylvania Registered Voters, without Using Party Registration or Party Primary Data as Predictor Variables.
*Note:* A random sample of 81,359 registered voters in Pennsylvania are graphed according to a version of Catalist's 2012 partisan support score that does not predict partisanship with party registration or primary data.

Now consider counterfactual Pennsylvania, where campaigns do not have access to party registration and partisan primary data. They cannot use these data to build models of support, nor can they use these data directly in mobilization efforts. How would a Democratic campaign figure out which voters are most likely to support its candidates? The campaign might use the version of Catalist's model that Catalist applies to voters in states like Wisconsin, Vermont, Alabama, Hawaii, and all the other states that do not collect partisanship information in the voter registration system. In such a model, Catalist uses all of its predictive variables to estimate partisanship except the records of partisanship that come from the voter files. In Figure 5.15, I plot exactly the same sample of Pennsylvania voters as is plotted in Figure 5.14, but this time I line the voters up on a scale of predictive partisanship that does not use party registration or primary information as predictive variables. In comparison to Figure 5.14, many more of the voters here have predicted scores in the middle of the distribution.

If real-world Pennsylvania, campaigns perceive their likely supporters as those to the left or right of the median in Figure 5.14 and if counterfactual campaigns perceive their likely supporters as those to the left or right of the median in Figure 5.15, how does this change which voters are engaged by the campaign? For one, only 76 percent of the registered voters who are on the Democratic side of the median in the actual distribution of perceived voters are also on the Democratic side in the counterfactual distribution. One-quarter of voters perceived to be supporters in one data environment would be perceived as opponents in another data environment.

Moreover, if I replicate the Pennsylvania analysis using 2008 versions of Catalist's models, I can show how many individuals on each side of the median score voted for Obama. Again, I can make this assessment for 2008 because in 2008 I matched Catalist support scores to respondents in the CCES. According to the CCES data, 82 percent of the actual perceived Democratic coalition in Pennsylvania reported voting for Barack Obama in 2008. But, only 66 percent of the counterfactual perceived Democratic coalition reported voting for Obama. Holding the distribution of actual voters constant, a change in the data environment means not only that a campaign alters its perceptions of who is a supporter, but that its perceptions of supporters also vary considerably in their accuracy. Absent party registration data in Pennsylvania, one out of every three voters perceived through Catalist's data as a likely Democratic supporter actually ended up voting Republican.

In Table 5.2, for each version of the Democratic coalition in Pennsylvania, I show five traits of voters who are predicted to be Democratic supporters. The table simply shows characteristics of voters on the Democratic side of the median in each of the graphs above. In the real world, if a campaign in Pennsylvania were to use Catalist's 2012 model and focus on mobilizing the 50 percent of the electorate that appeared most likely to identify as Democratic, 95 percent of such voters would be registered Democrats. In the counterfactual world, voters who appear most Democratic are only 72 percent likely to be Democratic. That is, if Pennsylvania were not a party registration state, 28 percent of voters who would appear to campaigns as likely Democrats would not themselves register as Democrats if they were given the opportunity. This logic is a bit complicated (as is often true with counterfactuals), but the point is simple: if Pennsylvania lacked party registration data, Democratic campaigns would be engaging with many more independents and Republicans than in the real world, where they can focus almost exclusively on Democrats. Of course, knowing that their mobilization messages would often be received by independents and Republicans, a campaign may alter the tone of communications and may alter the kinds of activities it pursues when contacting voters.

Aside from differences in the party affiliation of voters in the Democratic coalition, Table 5.2 also shows smaller but still important differences between the real-world targeting scenario and the counterfactual

TABLE 5.2 *Comparison of Pennsylvania Targeted Coalitions under Actual Data Conditions (Partisanship Data Available) and Hypothetical Data Conditions (No Partisanship Data Available)*

| Traits | Democratic Coalition | Counterfactual Coalition |
|---|---|---|
| Democratic | 95% | 72% |
| | (40,677) | (40,681) |
| Republican | 0 | 16 |
| | (40,677) | (40,681) |
| Female | 55 | 57 |
| | (39,887) | (39,784) |
| Urban | 34 | 40 |
| | (40,677) | (40,680) |
| Black | 19 | 21 |
| | (40,584) | (40,558) |
| Hispanic | 6 | 8 |
| | (40,584) | (40,558) |

*Note:* Observations are in parentheses. Party and gender originate from official voter registration files. Percent urban comes from the voter file matched to Census block group data. Race comes from Catalist's predictions of racial identity. The Democratic coalition is defined as the 50% of registrants perceived to be most Democratic. All differences of means between these columns are statistically significant with p-values < 0.01.

*Source:* 2012 partisanship models from Catalist 1% Analytics Sample.

scenario. Voters in the actual Democratic coalition include larger proportions of males, rural voters, and white voters than in the counterfactual coalition. This suggests that when voters are sliced differently by the data that parties have at their disposal, demographic groups shift with regard to their position in a campaign's perception of their likely support. Some demographic cohorts, including women, urban dwellers, and racial minorities, tend to lean Democratic. Without public partisanship data, campaigns perceive these groups as more supportive because they lack better alternatives in predicting support. Because voters are difficult to sort along partisan lines in the absence of party registration, campaigns may focus more on mobilizing demographic groups thought to be in their respective camps. Thus, without partisan cues in voter registration records, campaigns must not only contact many more independents and out-party voters than they otherwise would, but key demographic groups shift in their predicted partisanship depending on the availability of party data.

Because the data and models from Catalist are the very data that are commonly used by Democratic campaigns in Pennsylvania and elsewhere, this counterfactual is quite realistic. The provision of public sources of partisanship information affects the kinds of voters that campaigns will engage. To be sure, the data environment is not the only factor that affects strategic choices. The actual distribution of voters in Pennsylvania (e.g., the ratio of self-reported Democrats to Republicans and the particular demographic profiles of voters) will affect strategic decisions as well, and these factors will likely result in different strategies pursued by Republicans than by Democrats. But a set of strategic decisions can be predicted by reflecting on how elite perceptions stem from available data. No matter the distribution of true voters, strategy would shift in the absence of public records in Pennsylvania simply because of the altered perception of which voters are supporters.

## 5.6 SUMMARY

In this chapter, I connected the dots between the public data environment, campaign perceptions, campaign strategies, and voter behavior. I first described how different states collect differing amounts of information in their voter registration records that are indicative of voters' partisan leanings. I then showed how these data affect elite perceptions. When campaigns lack public records that indicate partisanship, the alternative data they use to perceive voters' partisan leanings, such as neighborhood characteristics and commercial microtargeting models, generate a very different perception of which voters appear as likely supporters.

This altered perception results in different strategic choices across U.S. states, as I showed by comparing survey responses of Obama campaign workers operating in different locations. I found that campaign workers in non–party registration states focus less on voters' partisanship in their direct contact strategies. They focus more on persuading undecided voters and on targeting partisan geographies. Consistent with the claim that morale among campaign workers is lower in non–party registration states because of their frequent contact with partisan opponents, I also found that Obama workers in non–party registration states were less likely to think their conversations with voters were going well. In the beginning of the chapter, I showed that voters in party registration states are not notably different from voters in non–party registration states. It does not seem to be the case that campaigns are behaving differently across data environments because of the voters; rather, they are behaving differently because of the available data.

I tested potential downstream effects on voters consistent with patterns of strategy stemming from differences in perceptions. In non–party registration swing states, self-reported party identification is less correlated with turnout, presumably because campaigns are not mobilizing voters based on party in these states. Even though turnout among partisans is lower in these states, turnout in overwhelmingly partisan precincts is higher, presumably because campaigns, lacking partisan information, are more likely to mobilize voters based on neighborhood characteristics rather than individual characteristics.

In a counterfactual analysis in which I kept the voters constant but imagine different types of public records available to campaigns, I have shown that campaigns would mobilize a very different group of likely supporters depending on their data resources. Most importantly, campaigns without individual-level partisanship data interact with far more independents and out-partisan voters than do campaigns where public records of partisanship are available. This counterfactual was based on a comparison of actual models used by campaigns to predict voter partisanship: one model that is typically used in party registration states and another model that is typically used in non–party registration states but that I applied to voters in a party registration state.

In sum, this chapter has shown how public data policies, which vary across states, affect how campaigns perceive their supporters. Perceptions of who a supporter is varies dramatically across the country, because campaigns have different kinds of data in different places that enable them to understand their electorates. The Perceived Voter Model offers predictions about how campaigns interact with voters based on how campaigns perceive voters. I have shown that a voter who identifies as a partisan, lives in a homogenous partisan neighborhood, or bears demographic or neighborhood traits that are predictive of his or her partisan identity will be perceived differently by campaigns in different locations simply because of the information context in which the campaign operates. Whether a campaign focuses on increasing turnout among its known supporters or identifying and persuading undecided voters is a decision influenced, in part, by the campaign's ability to perceive which voters are supportive and which are not.

# 6

# The Public Code of Racialized Electioneering

Just as the provision of partisanship data affects campaigns' perceptions and strategies, so too does the provision of racial data. In this chapter, I explore how the availability of public records about racial identity affects campaign strategy. When public records of race are available to campaigns, campaigns focus more on mobilizing voters because of their racial identity and less on mobilizing voters because they live in racially segregated areas. In this chapter, I first provide some background about state laws regarding the provision of racial data. I then show how perceptions of voters' races, which vary by state, affect campaign strategy. Specifically, I show that campaigns focus more attention on voters' races when public race data are available. Finally, I show how the patterns of voter turnout are consistent with the proposition that campaigns behave differently depending on the public data environment.

## 6.1 PUBLIC RECORDS OF RACIAL IDENTITY

Voter registration databases in eight states, all in the south, contain records of racial identity. In these states, which include Alabama, Florida, Georgia, Louisiana, Mississippi, North Carolina, South Carolina, and Tennessee, the public record lists voters as Caucasian, Black, Hispanic, or by some other racial identifier. When citizens register to vote in these states, they are asked or required to indicate their race, and this designation becomes a public record. Because in the United States racial identity is highly correlated with partisan support, when a voter's race is listed in the public record, campaigns latch onto this data point as a key resource

TABLE 6.1 *Percentage of Registrants Identifying Their Race on Voter Registration Forms*

| State | Race Listed on Voter File | Total Obs. in Sample |
|---|---|---|
| Alabama | 99.0% | 56,176 |
| Florida | 96.7 | 192,856 |
| Georgia | 96.1 | 100,936 |
| Louisiana | 98.1 | 51,789 |
| Mississippi | 38.1 | 37,148 |
| North Carolina | 98.0 | 113,497 |
| South Carolina | 99.7 | 51,033 |
| Tennessee | 67.5 | 71,330 |

*Source:* Two independently drawn Catalist 1% Analytics Samples, combined.

for engaging with voters. Because racial identity is difficult to predict in the absence of public race data, as I show, campaigns have a more difficult time identifying and mobilizing voters by race in places that do not list voters by race in the public record.

In Table 6.1, the percentages of voters listed with a racial identifier in the public voter file in each state are shown. In six of these states (Alabama, Florida, Georgia, Louisiana, North Carolina, and South Carolina), more than 95 percent of registered voters are listed in the public record with a field indicating their racial identity. In Tennessee and Mississippi, indicating one's race on a registration application is optional, and as the table shows, fewer registrants in these states are listed with a racial identifier.

Why in these southern states, but not elsewhere in the country, are voters listed in the public record according to their race? The answer is in state-specific, historical idiosyncrasies. One might incorrectly assume that these data are collected on account of the Voting Rights Act (VRA). Since the passage of the VRA in 1965, racial identifiers in southern states have been used to help gauge discriminatory election practices in "covered jurisdictions" (see Balkin and Siegel, 2005; Cruz and Hayes, 2009). Covered jurisdictions were a set of states and counties that, up until 2013, had to gain approval from the U.S. Department of Justice prior to implementing new election laws in order to guarantee that proposed laws were not discriminatory. Most areas of the south were covered jurisdictions. When a jurisdiction lists voters by race on voter files, it can measure statistics such as differential turnout rates by white registrants and black registrants. These statistics could be useful for analyzing proposed changes to election law.

Even though racial identifiers were used in conjunction with VRA compliance, the identifiers do not exist to facilitate compliance with the VRA. Many areas of North Carolina and Florida are not covered jurisdictions but nevertheless maintain registration records by race, and Virginia is a covered jurisdiction that does not collect these data. Furthermore, racial identifiers on registration applications long predate the VRA. For example, voter registration applications in Alabama asked voters for their race at least as far back as 1922,[1] and registration forms in Louisiana listed race even at the end of the nineteenth century.[2]

Another plausible hypothesis for the existence of racial identifiers in some southern states is that these data were used in conjunction with white-only primaries. White-only primaries were common in the south before they were deemed unconstitutional by the Supreme Court in *Smith v. Allwright* (1944). However, some states that currently collect racial information from voters, namely Tennessee and North Carolina, never had white primaries except in a few counties, and other states in which race data is currently not collected, namely Texas and Arkansas, did hold white primaries (Klarman, 2001). Thus, the administration of white-only primaries does not seem to be the reason why racial identifiers are collected in some states but not others.

Although interesting, the story of why some southern states continue to collect racial information in the public record while others do not is a secondary matter for my purposes. Clearly, politics in the south is more focused on race than politics outside the south, and the south has long tracked the race of residents for an array of administrative uses. However, state-specific explanations are at the root of the question of why the voters in these eight states are listed in the public record with their race while voters in other similar states are not.[3] No matter the origins of these laws, the fact is that some campaigns operate in environments where they have comprehensive lists of voters by racial identity while other campaigns operate in environments where such data are not available. This distinction, I argue, yields differences in strategies for engaging voters.

## 6.2 PERCEIVING RACE WITHOUT PUBLIC IDENTIFIERS

Quite clearly, campaigns would like to know the racial identities of voters. Race is highly predictive of partisan support, especially in the south. The American electorate is sensitive to overt race-focused appeals (Mendelberg, 2001; Valentino, Hutchings, and White, 2002), and so racial identifiers can enable campaigns to use direct contacting strategies to communicate with minority voters separately from white voters. This is particularly important for Democrats, who tend, in recent years anyway, to build coalitions across racial groups. Democratic campaigns want to mobilize African Americans with different kinds of messages than they use to appeal to whites. As a southern Democratic strategist explained to political scientist James Glaser, "you've got to approach the black vote surgically" (Glaser, 1996, p. 75). Some "surgical" approaches leverage segregated media environments, for example, by transmitting appeals to black voters through radio advertisements on stations that have predominantly black audiences. But other surgical approaches involve using canvassers, phone bankers, and mailers to engage different racial groups in different ways.

In the states where 95 percent or more of registered voters are recorded in the public record with their racial identity, it is straightforward for campaigns to consider the race of voters in their direct contacting strategies and to use a surgical approach to target minorities differently than whites. But how do campaigns perceive the race of voters in the absence of individual-level racial data in voter files? One possibility is that campaigns might engage voters based on other characteristics that are correlated with partisan support, turnout likelihood, or persuadability. However, because identity as an African American or Latino is so highly predictive of partisan support, Democratic campaigns in particular do want to focus their direct contacting on minority groups.[4] Absent public records, they must use alternative tools for perceiving race. These tools, I argue, generate different strategies and result in different types of voters being mobilized than if public records of race were available.

Consider three alternatives that campaigns use to perceive voters' races when voters are not listed in public records by race. One alternative method is to use geography as a proxy. In the case of African Americans, a geographical strategy only reaches a portion of black voters, because half of all African Americans live in neighborhoods that are not majority black (Owens and Wright, 1998; Logan, 2001). As Kirk Clay, Director of Civic Engagement for the NAACP, explained to me in an interview, in a segregated black neighborhood a campaign can employ blanket mobilization strategies. In these neighborhoods, campaigns may send "sound trucks" around to broadcast reminders to vote via megaphones. But outside 90-percent-plus areas, campaigns do not use blanket mobilization

TABLE 6.2 *Commercial Predictions of Race are Less Accurate than Public Records of Race*

|  | Commercial Data | | Voter File Data | |
|---|---|---|---|---|
|  | Pct. Correctly Predicted | Obs. | Pct. Correctly Predicted | Obs. |
| Race = White | 90% | 18,528 | 94% | 3,296 |
| Race = Black | 68 | 2,403 | 95 | 841 |
| Race = Hispanic | 73 | 1,898 | 92 | 262 |

*Note:* Data are generated from the 2008 Cooperative Congressional Election Study matched to commercial data by Catalist. Catalist supplies a prediction of race for voters who are not listed in the public record by race. Because most voters do not live in one of the eight states that collect racial data in public records, the sample size for the commercial predictions is much larger than the sample size for the voter file data.

strategies. Such strategies, geared toward black voters, are presumed not to be effective for white voters, and they may even be counterproductive from a campaign's perspective. Consequently, these strategies are not used except in areas that are overwhelmingly black.

A second alternative is to use networks, like churches, to mobilize minority voters. Churches have long been considered a centerpiece of black political mobilization (Harris, 1994; Leighley, 2001). However, as with a geographic strategy, a church-based strategy does not reach nearly as many African Americans as individual-level public records would permit. The political role of churches is somewhat overstated because many African Americans do not attend church, and among those who do, most do not attend the kind of politicized churches that tend to mobilize voters. One estimate suggests that, at most, only a quarter of blacks attend the kinds of politicized churches that increase turnout among attendees.[5]

A third alternative is to employ firms like Catalist to make statistical predictions about voters' races. Using the voter's name and the racial composition of the voter's neighborhood (which Catalist retrieves from the Census), Catalist estimates each voter's race. Table 6.2 shows the accuracy of Catalist's prediction versus the accuracy of the voter file data.

To make this table, I use the CCES survey that was matched to Catalist's records. I consider a record to be accurate if the racial identifier that Catalist retrieves either from the voter file or from a commercial prediction matches the self-reported race of the respondent. This, of course, assumes that survey respondents do not lie about their race. For southern voters listed in the public record with their race, 92–95 percent of them report the same race as is listed in the registration record. Catalist's commercial prediction is nearly this accurate for white voters, who are obviously the largest racial cohort and thus easiest to predict. But among blacks and Hispanics, the prediction is considerably less accurate. Campaigns that use Catalist's model to target Hispanic and black voters can expect that out of every ten targeted voters, three will actually not identify with the racial group that is being targeted. This means that if a campaign uses a commercial prediction of race, their perception of voters' races is considerably noisier than if they had public records.

The evidence in Table 6.2 does not imply that Catalist does a poor job predicting voters' races. Rather, it implies that predicting a voter's race is actually a difficult thing to do. Consider predictions for African Americans. Black names are not generally distinctive from white names, and most African Americans do not live in overwhelmingly African American areas. Thus, the two pieces of information that are used to predict who is African American (names and neighborhood percentage black) are rather limiting.[6] While a commercial prediction is surely more informative than no prediction at all, it is nevertheless difficult for a campaign to perceive voters cleanly as white, black, and Hispanic using tools such as commercial predictions of race.

The obvious takeaway from this discussion is that it is not as easy for campaigns to perceive voters by their racial identity without individual-level public records that are available in only eight states. But there is a more subtle and more important takeaway as well: *The kinds of minority voters who will be mobilized by Democratic campaigns will differ depending on the tools campaigns use to perceive their race.* In the absence of public identifiers, if a campaign focuses its efforts on geographic areas that are homogenously black, then the kind of black person who is contacted by campaigns will be the kind of black person who lives in homogenous black areas. Black voters who live in heterogeneous neighborhoods will be less likely to be contacted. Similarly, if a campaign uses a microtargeting model like Catalist's, it will tend to miss voters whose names and neighborhoods are not predictive of their racial group (e.g., middle-class blacks; Fryer Jr. and Levitt, 2007). If a campaign can use public records, it will be able to mobilize more blacks who live in heterogeneous neighborhoods and have names less distinctive from white names.

A typical model of voter engagement, like the one developed by Rosenstone and Hansen (1993), would predict that because blacks are likely to support Democrats, Democrats will mobilize black voters. The Perceived Voter Model develops a more nuanced prediction. Because of the high level of black support for Democrats, Democrats *want* to mobilize blacks. But which blacks they mobilize, and how they do it, depends on how clearly and through what data they can perceive which voters are black. If they have an individual identifier of race, they have the ability to engage almost any black registrant. If they do not, they might focus just on the 90-percent-plus black neighborhoods or on voters whose names are distinctly black. Or they may focus on networks like churches that will only reach a small portion of black voters. The data environment will affect a campaign's perceptions, the perceptions will affect their strategies, and the strategies will affect which voters are mobilized into the political process.

### 6.3 HOW DO RACIAL PERCEPTIONS AFFECT STRATEGIES?

In the eight states in which they can obtain racially identifying data from the election office, campaigns use these data to engage with voters based on the voters' races. Consider some anecdotal evidence from strategists. One Democratic operative who is involved in multiple southern campaigns explained that every time his campaigns pull lists of voters to contact in states that register voters by race, they screen the lists for race. Sometimes, they gear messages and events to African Americans; other times, they gear them to whites. But race is always part of the decision. Another southern Democratic strategist told me that in his state, "[GOTV] is really easy. You just go after black voters." In a third interview with a Florida-based field organizer from the Obama campaign, the operative told me that the campaign's goal was for voters who were listed on the registration rolls as African American to receive three in-person contacts from the Obama campaign. Three in-person visits to a voter is an aggressive use of resources, but because African Americans were leaning so strongly toward Obama *and because* nearly all registered voters in Florida are listed by race, the campaign deemed this strategy worthwhile.

On the Republican side, the efficient strategy in most southern elections is to ignore voters listed as African American, just as campaigns might ignore members of the opposite party in favor of focusing on independents and members of their own party. Efficiency simply means campaigns spend less time interacting with citizens whose votes they have little chance of winning. Given that black voters are upward of 90 percent likely to vote for Democrats, Republican campaigns can best employ their resources by focusing on white voters – deleting voters listed as black from their contact lists. While no Republican campaigner described this practice to me directly (no doubt owing to the sensitivity of the question), this use of race data is an entirely obvious and straightforward strategy for Republican campaigns. Data are not only useful to decide which voters to engage with; they are just as useful to decide which voters to ignore. Both parties use data in this way. A Democratic campaign manager told me that he uses public records about hunters and gun owners simply to exclude these voters from his contacting efforts, because gun owners lean Republican. Republican campaigns can be expected to use this same strategy with respect to racial identifiers.

Given that race data are a valuable resource for mobilization, what statistical evidence is there that the provision of public racial identifiers affects the way campaigns engage voters? In the Ground Campaign Project, I asked Obama campaign workers in 2012 to rank voter attributes in terms of their importance to the campaign's contacting strategies. Among the nine attributes offered was race. The other attributes, as discussed in Chapter 4, included party, gender, age, income, and other such options. The survey question did not cue campaign workers to think about racial registration data in particular, but simply asked them to think about the voter characteristics that are used in contacting voters, whatever the source of those characteristics.

The results are shown in Figure 6.1. The two 2012 swing states with racial registration data are North Carolina and Florida. In the swing states of North Carolina and Florida, campaign workers reported that race was a much more important voter characteristic than did campaign workers in other states. The average ranking for North Carolina and Florida is a point and a half higher than in the other states.

As I argued in Chapter 4, the low-level staffers and volunteers engaging with voters on behalf of the Obama campaign do not need to know the details of the campaign strategy to discern that their daily efforts are focused more on one or another kind of voter. Evidently, workers in Florida and North Carolina recognized that they were engaging with voters more based on their race than did workers in other states. This suggests that the strategy was indeed different in these two states than elsewhere. Figure 6.1 implies that the public data environment causes campaigns to pay more attention to race-based canvassing than campaign would in the absence of public race records.

To develop this argument, consider the state of Virginia in Figure 6.1. Campaign workers in Virginia reported that race was as strategically important as did campaign workers in other nonracial registration states.

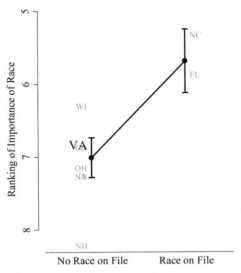

FIGURE 6.1 Importance of Voters' Race to Campaign Mobilizers in Different Data Environments.
*Note:* Data from Ground Campaign Project. Data generated from 187 campaign workers in states with racial registration and 344 respondents in states without racial registration. The difference of means between campaigners in racial registration and non-racial registration states is statistically significant (p-value < 0.01). Virginia's position is emphasized to show its contrasting position to other southern states.

But Virginia is a southern state, a VRA state with a history of racialized politics, much like its neighbor North Carolina. Virginia was also a battleground state in 2012; the Obama campaign exerted a similar effort in Virginia and North Carolina, in terms of expenditures. Virginia and North Carolina are also similar in the percentage of their populations that are African American; both are approximately 20 percent black. But Virginia is very different from North Carolina in the importance of race to direct contacting strategies. Figure 6.1 shows that only campaigners in states with race data, and not similar states like Virginia, considered race to be a particularly important informational resource for direct contact. Likewise, Ohio, a northern swing states with large pockets of African-American voters, does not show an unusually strong focus on race in campaign efforts. The unusual position is reserved for the two states in the data in which voters are listed in the public record with their racial identities.

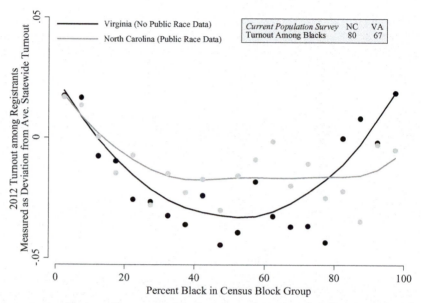

FIGURE 6.2 Turnout in 2012 by Block Group Percentage Black in Virginia and North Carolina.

*Note:* Data are from the Catalist Q Tool. Each dot represents a 5-percentage-point range of block-group percentage black, from 0–5% black to 95–100% black. The full population of registered voters is observed, including 5,233,943 registrants in Virginia and 6,433,168 registrants in North Carolina. The dot representing the fewest number of registrants represents 19,948 registrants.

*CPS data source:* United States Census Bureau, Current Population Survey, "Table 4b: Reported Voting and Registration, by Sex, Race and Hispanic Origin, for States: November 2012." Turnout for CPS is calculated based on citizens. If calculated based on reported registrants, turnout is 94.1% in North Carolina and 92.6% in Virginia.

## 6.4 DOWNSTREAM EFFECTS ON VOTERS

Because of the similarities between North Carolina and Virginia in terms of region, battleground-state status, and percentage black, I focus more on the comparison between these two states. If the Obama campaign in 2012 was active in both these states but had to engage voters differently in each state on account of the data environment, what evidence is there that different perceptions of blacks in these two states resulted in differential effects on the electorate?

Consider Figure 6.2. In the upper-right of this figure, I note that according to the Census's Current Population Survey, turnout among blacks in North Carolina was higher than turnout among blacks in Virginia. Of course, citizens often lie about whether or not they voted, but I want only to draw attention to the *relative* turnout between these two states: turnout for blacks appears to have been higher in North Carolina than in Virginia. As indicated in the figure's note, this is true whether turnout is calculated based on the citizen population or the registered population. Given that the campaigns could target individual black voters in North Carolina but not Virginia, I expect this higher rate of turnout among blacks in North Carolina.

The main plot in Figure 6.2 shows an unusual pattern. Using data on all registered voters acquired from the states and supplied by Catalist, the plot estimates turnout among registered voters of all races by the kind of neighborhood in which they are registered. Turnout for each kind of neighborhood is subtracted from the overall turnout rate in the state. Turnout is measured this way to easily compare the neighborhood patterns across two states that had slightly different overall turnout rates. As an example, the interpretation of the leftmost dots is that in both Virginia and North Carolina, turnout in the neighborhoods with the lowest black population was about two percentage points higher than the statewide turnout rates in those states. The aspect of the graph to pay particular attention to is the slopes of the two lines. Notice that in Virginia, the relationship between neighborhood percentage black and turnout is much more pronounced. Neighborhoods that are more than 80 percent black have turnout approximately five points higher than neighborhoods that are 40–80 percent black. In contrast, North Carolina neighborhoods that are anywhere from 30 percent black to 100 percent black have similar rates of turnout.

This pattern is exactly what one would predict if Democratic campaigns target black individuals more in North Carolina (where racial data exists) but target black neighborhoods more in Virginia (where racial data does not exist). In the environment that lacks public records of race, turnout among blacks is not only lower; it is also *geographically contingent*. This suggests that the kind of black registrant who votes in Virginia is different from the kind who votes in North Carolina on account of campaigns' differential ability to perceive voters in each state. Black *perceived voters* in North Carolina are similar to the actual black electorate (since nearly all black voters are listed with their race in the public record), but black *perceived voters* in Virginia are a distorted version of the black electorate: they are blacks who live in black neighborhoods or who have racially distinct names and therefore can be identified as black in the absence of public records.

Two further aspects of this graph are worth noting. First, in a graph from Catalist data such as this, which is calculated based on the full population of registered voters, statistical measures of uncertainty are not visible because of the large number of voters under investigation. The dot in Figure 6.2 that represents the *smallest* number of people represents nearly 20,000 individuals. Data from more than 11 million Americans are used to calculate Figure 6.2. Given this, analysts are free to focus on substantive differences rather than statistically significant differences. Put another way, any substantive difference that one perceives in this graph is also statistically significant. Second, note that the similarity of the slope in the homogenously white areas of Virginia and North Carolina is consistent with the notion that racial data does not serve the same role for white voters as it does for black voters. Turnout is higher in white block groups in both these states, but the data environment does not make as much of a difference for white voters.

## Turnout Effects within Racial Identifying States

Another opportunity to explore the effects of data laws on the turnout patterns of racial groups is to observe the eight states that list voters by racial group, focusing attention on the small number of voters in these states who are not listed in the public record by race. Notice in Table 6.1 that even in the states that require voters to list their races on their voter registration application, about 5 percent of voters do not list a race. States generally process registration applications even if the race field has been left blank. And in the states of Mississippi and Tennessee, a much greater share of registered voters do not list their race. In all these states, I expect campaigns to put more emphasis on the voters whom they know more about and less emphasis on voters who are listed without a racial identifier. Indeed, one southern strategist told me that since he always screens voters based on their racial identity, voters who are not listed by race in southern states will never receive mail, door-knockers, or telephone calls from his campaigns. It should be noted that even though the presidential campaign is not active in every southern state, all of these states have active congressional and state campaigns that utilize direct forms of contact that take racial identifiers into account.

In Figure 6.3, I show that voters who are listed in the public record with their race are significantly more likely to vote than voters who are not listed with their race. The figure is generated from Catalist data acquired in 2010. Turnout among 2010 registered voters is shown for the 2008,

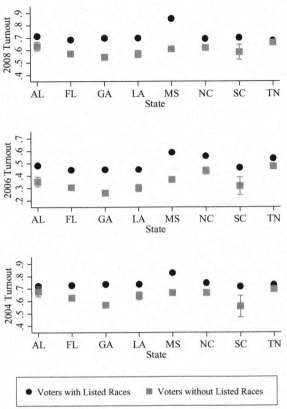

FIGURE 6.3 Turnout in 2008, 2006, and 2004 for Voters Listed in the Public Record with Their Race and Voters Not Listed with Their Race.

*Note:* Data from two combined 1% analytics samples downloaded in the spring of 2010 from Catalist. Mean values are shown along with 95% confidence intervals; however, the confidence intervals are mostly too small to see. Note that the y-axis scale is shifted downward in the 2006 election to accommodate overall lower turnout in the midterm election. The graph shows that in nearly all states and election years, turnout is substantially lower for voters not listed with racial identifiers in the public record.

2006, and 2004 general elections. The difference between voters listed with their race and those listed without their race is quite stable across these eight states and across the three election years that are observed. I focus on these election years because, later in the chapter, I use a set of data I was able to acquire in 2010 to assess the pattern I observe. Analysis of these earlier election years supplement the analysis of the 2012 election shown in Figures 6.1 and 6.2.

Figure 6.3 raises a question: Why is turnout lower among voters not listed with a race in the public record? The reason I have suggested is that campaigns ignore these voters in their appeals, leading to lower turnout levels, but there are other plausible explanations. I now try to exclude those other explanations. It might be the case that voters who opt to omit their race from voter registration applications are, in some important way, different from voters who do list their race. Perhaps they are lower on the socioeconomic scale and are not as adept at filling out forms, or perhaps they have more introverted personalities and prefer not to share personal information. If these sorts of differences are correlated with turnout, and if they are also correlated with a voter's decision to list his race on the public record, then the result in Figure 6.3 may be attributable to one of these factors and not to campaigns.

To engage with one alternative hypothesis, I look at socioeconomic attributes of voters who do and do not list their race in the public record. Consider the income and education levels of the Census block group (i.e., neighborhood) of each voter. It turns out that voters who do not list their race on the voter file tend to live in slightly *more* educated and wealthier neighborhoods. These socioeconomic traits are typically correlated with higher levels of turnout, but as shown in Figure 6.3, voters without listed races are actually less likely to vote.

To test a second alternative hypothesis, consider some personality traits. In general, personality traits have not been found to have notable effects on turnout (Mondak et al., 2010; Gerber et al., 2009). Even so, are people who fill out their race distinct in personality? The 2009 Cooperative Congressional Election Study, which Stephen Ansolabehere and I matched into the Catalist database, asked respondents how much they agree or disagree with characterizations of themselves on ten personality traits. Of these ten traits, three seem relevant to filling out race on a registration form: extroversion, openness, and being conventional. On the first two of these traits, extroversion and openness, southern respondents who did not list their race on the voter registration application were just as likely to define themselves as extroverted and open as those who did list their race. However, whereas 21 percent (N = 1,873) of voters listing their race considered themselves conventional, notably fewer registrants (10 percent [N = 98]) who did not list their race considered themselves conventional. This seems reasonable given that more conventional types might be more willing to provide information requested of them. However, the validated turnout rates of respondents who said they were conventional and those who said they were unconventional were identical:

83 percent turnout in 2008. Thus, it would not be expected that the higher rate of turnout among those who listed their race is attributable to this personality trait.

To test a third alternative hypothesis, I observe the reported turnout rates of respondents to the November 2008 Current Population Survey (CPS) who refused, did not know, or left blank the race item on the survey. A simple regression model that controls for socio-economic status shows that individuals who left their race off the CPS were no less likely to report voting than those who identified their race. This suggests that something about racial identification on the voter file might have a distinct effect on turnout, namely that campaigns use the voter file as the basis of voter mobilization.

To test a fourth alternative hypothesis, I take a more sophisticated approach. I use a technique called matching to try to limit the chance that confounding factors are influencing the result. In a matching technique, I compare turnout rates of voters listed with their race and without their race, but I restrict the analysis to voters who are identical on a number of other characteristics. I look at voters who are of the same age group, gender, party affiliation (in the three southern states that register voters by party), who first registered to vote at about the same time, and who are in the same state. Furthermore, I look at voters whose Census block groups share a common character as measured by their percentage black, percentage with a college degree, and median household income. I also look within groups of voters who, according to commercial records, share certain behavioral characteristics. Namely, Catalist lists which voters have in the past responded to commercial mail advertisements, subscribed to magazines, and made mail-order purchases. These variables signal a voter is willing to sign up for products and provide information about themselves. These variables might indicate a voter who has a "form-filler-outer" tendency. If the form-filler-outer tendency is captured by these commercial variables, then these variables help confront the alternative hypothesis that voters with form-filler-outer tendencies are more likely to vote in the absence of any campaign appeals and are also more likely to provide their race on a voter registration application. (Although, I have just reviewed other evidence inconsistent with the form-filler-outer hypothesis in the 2009 validated survey of personality traits.)

In this matching analysis, unlike in Figure 6.3, I look at white voters and black voters separately. Given that a voter is black or white, what is the relationship between their decision to list their race on their registration application and their subsequent decision to vote? I separately estimate the effect for white and black voters because the effect should be much more potent for black voters, given that their racial identity is a particularly strong signal of partisanship and therefore particularly valuable to campaigns. That is, listing one's race on a voter registration application should increase turnout more for blacks than for whites.

To compare voters who are listed in the public record according to their race with voters who are not, I need to determine the race of voters who are not publicly listed by race. To do this, I use Catalist's commercial prediction of voters' race, which Catalist only provides for those not listed by race in the public record. I restrict my use of commercial predictions to voters for whom Catalist is most confident about the accuracy of its prediction. In validating Catalist's model with the 2008 CCES, 93 percent of voters predicted as white or black for whom Catalist is highly confident in its prediction report in a survey that they are of the same race that is predicted. This high level of accuracy is different from the results displayed back in Table 6.2 because the data here are restricted only to Catalist's highest-quality predictions. Thus, I compare turnout rates of voters who are listed as black or white with voters who are not listed with any race but whose race is predicted with high confidence, after first matching these voters on all the demographic, Census, and commercial behavior variables just described.[7] I use a technique called coarsened exact matching (Blackwell et al., 2009); the particulars of the procedure are described in Appendix C.

In Table 6.3, I compare the turnout rates of the matched groups in the 2004, 2006, and 2008 elections.[8] Voters listed as black in the public record voted at a rate 3–6 percentage points higher than their comparison group – voters who have the same characteristics except their race is not listed on the registration file. Those listed as white voted at a rate of 1–2 percentage points higher. The magnitude of the effect is quite reasonable in light of findings from mobilization field experiments (e.g., Gerber, Green, and Larimer, 2008).

All of this effort in describing the matching technique used in Table 6.3, as well as the other tests, such as the analysis of personality traits in the 2009 CCES, serve one purpose: they help assess potential reasons for why voters whose races are listed in the public record consistently vote at higher rates than voters whose races are not listed in the public record. I have one clear causal story. From theory, anecdotes, and evidence in Figure 6.1, it seems that campaigns working in states with racial registration are more focused on race as a tool for voter contact and latch onto individually identifying race data as a key informational resource. From a vast literature on campaign effectiveness, it is clear that campaign appeals

TABLE 6.3 *Difference in Voting Rates between Treatment Group (Race Listed on Voter File) and Control Group (Race Not Listed on Voter File)*

| Voter Turnout | Race Listed on Voter File | Race Not Listed on Voter File | Dif. Of Means p-Value |
|---|---|---|---|
| **Blacks** | | | |
| 2008 General | 76% | 72 | 0.00 |
| | (8,887) | (2,903) | |
| 2006 General | 50 | 44 | 0.00 |
| | (7,124) | (2,219) | |
| 2004 General | 75 | 72 | 0.02 |
| | (6,411) | (1,992) | |
| **Whites** | | | |
| 2008 General | 81 | 79 | 0.00 |
| | (128,812) | (34,745) | |
| 2006 General | 62 | 60 | 0.00 |
| | (119,583) | (21,502) | |
| 2004 General | 84 | 83 | 0.00 |
| | (112,973) | (20,562) | |

*Note:* Observations are in parentheses. Comparison is between matched groups.

to targeted voters can generate increases in turnout. I have shown that voters listed with their races are both the target of appeals in the south and vote at higher rates compared to voters who do not disclose their race. Can I entirely exclude other explanations for why voters with listed races vote more than those without listed races? No, but I have made several attempts to account for any connection between listing one's race on the voter file and other confounding correlates with turnout, such as demographics and personality traits. To the extent that I can measure those correlates, they fail to explain why voters listed on registration files by race turn out at higher rates than similar voters who do not list their race. This arguably leaves campaign engagement based on available information as the most plausible explanation for why turnout is higher among listed black and white voters in the southern states.

## 6.5 SUMMARY

In this chapter, I first examined the variation in the public data environment with respect to individual-level racial identifiers. In eight states of the U.S. south, campaigns can perceive voters' races in public records. Absent these records, campaigns must find other resources to perceive race, such as a voter's neighborhood or a predictive model that estimates race using characteristics like a voter's name and Census block. I have argued that these different data tools generate different perceptions of racial cohorts and result in different strategies.

As evidence of differential strategies resultant from the data environment, I have shown that 2012 campaign workers in states that collect racial data considered race to be a more important characteristic in their voter engagement strategies than did campaign workers elsewhere in the country. Racial groups are targeted differently in the southern swing states of Florida and North Carolina than in states that are otherwise similar, like Virginia. When campaigns can perceive voters' races in public records, the evidence from the Ground Campaign Project suggests that they pay more attention to race in voter contact strategies as a result.

I have shown two downstream consequences of the racial data environment on voter turnout. Comparing North Carolina and Virginia, two states that have much in common except for that North Carolina collects racial data and Virginia does not, I have shown that 2012 turnout among blacks in North Carolina was higher and that turnout in Virginia was more geographically contingent. This evidence is consistent with the theory that campaigns direct more attention to black voters in the state where they have public data, and otherwise they use tools like geography to perceive blacks, which results in a different cohort of voters being engaged.

As my second examination of downstream consequences, I showed that registrants in states that commonly list voters by race but who are not themselves listed by race vote at lower rates than voters who are listed by race. Differences in these voters' socioeconomic statuses, observable personality traits, and demographics do not account for their differential turnout. However, as articulated by the campaign strategists with whom I spoke, it appears that voters who either accidentally or purposefully register to vote without listing their race in the southern states are much less likely to be engaged by campaigns. Because of the racialized nature of politics in the south, which is enabled in part by the availability of public records that allow campaigns to easily segment voters by race, voters whose races are ambiguous to campaigns are less likely to be contacted and, it appears, less likely to vote.

# 7

# Persuadable Voters in the Eyes of the Persuaders

In crafting their direct contacting strategies, campaigns generally take a two-pronged approach: they seek to mobilize their base and to persuade voters who are persuadable. But there is an interesting asymmetry in a campaign's ability to perceive these two target audiences. Whereas some public records in some states reveal to campaigns which voters are likely to be base supporters, there is essentially no data available anywhere in public records, or in commercial records, or in party records, that reveal to campaigns which voters are persuadable. Persuadability is a disposition that scholars of political psychology have explored by analyzing public opinion surveys. These scholars focus on voters' level of political awareness, knowledge of political information, cross-cutting positions on issues, and value systems as dispositions that indicate one's latent persuadability or fickleness of opinion. The trouble is that no information that campaigns have about voters allows them to connect with voters who are persuadable as measured in these ways.

The asymmetry between data resources predictive of voters' partisanship and predictive of voters' persuadability squares with research findings about the effectiveness of direct voter contact. Scholars and political practitioners who have measured the effectiveness of voter contact have established a clear set of best practices for get-out-the-vote (GOTV) efforts (Green and Gerber, 2008). Collectively, ground campaign experts know a lot about how to increase turnout among known supporters.[1] In sharp contrast, there are no equivalent best practices for persuading voters. Experimental studies on persuasion show these efforts are often ineffective and sometimes even counterproductive (Bailey, Hopkins, and Rogers, 2013). In part this is because it is easier to measure the effectiveness of GOTV efforts than persuasion efforts: turnout is a public record; vote choice is not. Here, I point to a different reason why persuasion efforts are difficult. In campaign databases, there is no identifiable group of voters who are predictably and consistently persuadable. In other words, persuadable *perceived voters* are a very noisy approximation of actual persuadable voters.

Unlike the previous two chapters that show how perceptions vary across jurisdictions according to the provision of data, this chapter shows that across all jurisdictions, perceived persuadable voters are not actually persuadable. I demonstrate that common methods used to perceive persuadable voters do not allow campaigns to connect with actual persuadable voters. Campaigns tend to converge on a few subsets of the electorate whom they target at the individual level with persuasion messages. Campaigns essentially gear persuasion messages in the ground campaign to voters whom they think will vote but for whom the public record does not indicate a clear signal of partisanship. Using Catalist's database of voters, I reconstruct these common "persuasion targets." Then, utilizing the CCES survey that has been merged with Catalist records, I reconstruct categories of voters who are often classified in public opinion research as persuadable or fickle. I compare the campaign targets and the survey-based constructions in terms of their ideological composition, their undecidedness, and their propensity to shift support from one candidate to another over the course of a campaign.

This exercise serves to show how difficult it is for politicians to connect with persuadable voters on account of the data that inform their perceptions. A theoretical model of campaign strategy that is inattentive to perceptual biases might posit that campaigns pursue voters who are persuadable in their opinions about issues and candidates. The Perceived Voter Model posits that to understand campaign strategies it is necessary to focus on the perceptions that campaigns have of voters. Campaign decisions are constrained by the limits of their perceptions. While campaigns have a clear strategic goal to target persuadable voters, their actual choices suggest they do not often succeed.

Incidentally, the findings in this chapter offer a new perspective on a normative question that has been considered by political scientists for decades. Undergirding a literature in public opinion research about low-information voters (e.g., Converse, 1964; Zaller, 1992; Bartels, 1996; Lenz, 2009; Bullock, 2011), there is a worry that because so many voters are uninformed and willing to alter their opinions in the face of elite messages, political elites may be able to prime, persuade, or even trick voters into thinking one way or another. The present chapter shows that the data and strategies that real-world elites use to find persuadable voters do not enable them to connect with voters who are most susceptible to elite influence. Concerns about the vulnerability of the democratic process to undue elite influence ought to be tempered by the finding that elites cannot easily target fickle voters on an individual basis.

## 7.1 PERSUADABLE VOTERS

Survey research on the movement of voter opinion presents a range of findings about which types of voters are swayed by elite messages. Zaller (1992) argues that opinion change is a function of political awareness, predispositions, and the intensity of message campaigns. Ansolabehere and Iyengar (1995) find that responsiveness to television advertisements is a function of partisanship, with uninformed partisans most affected by negative ads and independents not at all affected. In reviewing research on framing, Chong and Druckman (2007) describe that people with strong values are less susceptible to opinion change. Lenz (2009) shows that movement of opinions in response to campaign stimuli is concentrated among those who did not know the positions of the competing sides prior to the start of the campaign.

In campaign studies, scholars have similarly focused on which voters are most apt to change their behavior or opinion in light of different campaign environments and messages. Key (1966) investigates the "party-switchers" and "standpatters" in presidential elections, with a focus on whether the switchers appeared to be making reasoned decisions. In other classic works, Campbell (1960) and DeNardo (1980) investigate the "peripheral" voters who show up in high-intensity surge elections but otherwise do not vote, and they explore the durability of their partisan allegiances. More recent work has homed in on the types of individuals whose votes are up for grabs and who therefore may be responsive to persuasion messages. To pollsters like Gallup and Pew, a so-called swing voter is someone who responds on a survey that they are undecided or may change their mind (Jones, 2008; Dimock, Clark, and Horowitz, 2008). To Mayer (2007), a swing voter is a person who likes or dislikes the opposing candidates in a race at similar levels. To Campbell (2008), a swing voter must lack attachments to the political parties. To Hillygus and Shields (2008), persuadable voters are those who are cross-pressured on issues.[2]

Whether a person is defined to be independent, undecided, party-switching, swing voting, or cross-pressured matters mainly for two reasons: (a) we are interested in which voters campaigns pay attention to, and (b) we are interested in which voters shift in response to elite-driven stimuli and thus alter political outcomes. The second rationale seems more important, but it is actually dependent on the first rationale, in the following sense: if campaigns cannot identify voters who are swayable, then the fact that some particular subset of the electorate *is* swayable matters less. In other words, one's concern about the capriciousness of voters should be conditioned on the extent to which persuaders can target the capricious ones. This is especially true in an era in which campaigns individually target voters whom they believe will be receptive to their appeals.

Political science conceptualizations of persuadable voters like the ones just described do not typically reflect the on-the-ground targets of direct contacting campaigns. There are two reasons for this disconnect, one theoretical and one practical. The theoretical reason is that social scientists may be interested in the segment of the population most susceptible to changes in attitudes rather than in the segment that is targeted with real-world stimuli. The practical reason is the data that campaigns use in direct contacting strategies is fundamentally different from the data political scientists typically study. Campaigns, facing full populations of registered voters, rarely have access to survey items about issue positions, partisan loyalties, or measures of undecidedness, and when they access surveys, they usually only have responses from a small fraction of their electorates. Campaigns rely predominantly on data taken from public records and on commercial models that are built from public records. Political scientists typically rely on opinion surveys but rarely have information emanating from survey respondents' public records.

The difference in data resources between campaigns and researchers is the difference between studying elite persuasion from the voter's-eye-view and studying elite persuasion from the campaign's-eye-view. Extant models of elite communications, focused as they are on the voter's-eye-view, have not appreciated the uncertainty politicians have about who their supporters, opponents, and swing voters are. When campaigns canvass by house visits, phone banks, mail, and e-mail, they simply cannot target the voters they would ideally like to reach if only they had survey responses for every voter.

It is important to emphasize that campaigns fail to target voters whom political scientists might think of as persuadable, not because the campaigns themselves are unsophisticated, but because of the very nature of their task. Sophisticated campaigns can employ well-trained social scientists to conduct surveys and inform the canvassing strategy; the trouble they have is applying the results of their surveys to the canvassing plan. Even in a sophisticated campaign database, virtually nothing accurately predicts psychological or attitudinal traits that show up on surveys. And because some campaigns seek to contact hundreds of thousands of voters, they simply cannot survey every person. It is this disconnect between survey data and voter file-based data rather than unsophisticated campaigns that is at the root of the campaigns' uncertainty about who the persuadable voters are.

Before turning to strategies that campaigns use for targeting persuasion messages, it is worth noting that prior studies of persuasion have focused primarily on how voters are affected by untargeted television programming, not messages targeted to voters through mail, phone, and canvassing campaigns (e.g., Zaller, 1992; Mendelberg, 2001; Mutz, Sniderman, and Brody, 1996; Gerber et al., 2011; Huber and Arceneaux, 2007). These works have typically set aside the portion of elite persuasion that happens through individual-level contact. The focus here on targeted persuasion messages is important in light of the growing prominence of direct contact in campaign politics. Furthermore, unlike research based on TV ads, research about direct contact applies to a wide range of subnational campaigns that are priced out of broadcast advertisements and that conduct most of their persuasion efforts through strategies of direct contact.

## 7.2 PERSUADABLE PERCEIVED VOTERS: A SIMULATION

Who are the voters that campaigns target as persuadable? The first step in the empirical investigation of this chapter is to simulate how the typical campaign decides which voters to treat as the audience for their direct persuasive appeals. Mimicking the conventional uses of campaign data is a complicated undertaking. Electoral politics in the United States is decentralized, and in every election cycle there are hundreds of campaign strategists independently deciding which voters to mobilize and which to persuade. However, when speaking with strategists and seeing their data, it is clear that campaigns generally use a common set of data resources and strategic choices to define their universe of persuasion targets.

Over the course of sixteen months, more than a dozen strategists, including high-ranking and low-ranking campaigners, veterans and newcomers, reviewing the strategies used in many campaigns, guided me through their own conventions for engaging with voters. Perhaps more uniquely, strategists *showed me* how they work with voter data from

Catalist and from their own campaign databases. From their explanations, I attempt a recreation, or a simulation, of a conventional approach to segmenting the electorate in order to find the types of voters who generally receive persuasion messages. I do so from the perspective of a large-scale campaign (e.g., presidential, gubernatorial, senatorial, or congressional), just prior to a presidential general election. I simulate targets both from the perspective of a 2008 campaign and a 2012 campaign, but I compare my simulated target groups with survey data from 2008. This is because the survey that I have merged with Catalist records that best allows me to compare survey versions of persuadable voters with campaign versions of persuadable *perceived voters* was fielded in 2008. As discussed earlier, while campaign targeters have added new bells and whistles to their predictive models since 2008, much about campaign perceptions remains the same. Thus, the results here are applicable not just in 2008; they continue to be applicable today.

## Common Persuasion and GOTV Targets

At the most basic level, campaigns look at their electorate and first decide which voters need their attention at all. In a general election campaign, this often means ignoring citizens who are not registered or have voted very infrequently in the past. In addition, campaigns often decide not to contact voters who never miss an election and are known partisans. These individuals may be called upon for donations or volunteer support, but campaigns often treat their regular-voting supporters as known entities. This leaves two groups that attract most of a campaign's attention: (1) voters thought to be supportive but who may not show up to vote without reminders, and (2) likely voters who may be undecided about which candidate to support. The latter group is my focus here, but I review common implementations of both groups.

The conventional approach to identifying persuasion and mobilization targets in a campaign is to use signals in the public record that the voter is affiliated or unaffiliated with a political party, combined with data on the voter's history of past election participation. There are three standard conventions that campaigns use for predicting voters' likely partisanship. In party registration states, they focus on registered voters who are or are not enrolled with a party. In states that track the party of each primary in which a voter has participated, they focus on voters who do or do not have a record of previous participation in either party's primaries. And in all states, they can look at geographic-level election returns to see, for example, which precincts have a significant number of votes going to either one or to both parties' candidates.

Campaigns can alternatively perceive a voter's partisanship through commercial targeting models like those supplied by Catalist. For example, they could define someone as plausibly unaligned with a party if the person receives a partisan support score of 30–70 on a 0–100 scale. However, as I have shown, public records like party registration and party primary data do much of the work in sorting voters into likely supporters and likely opponents in a commercial model of partisanship. Here, I first focus on a non-model-based approach to estimating partisanship, defining independents as those who are registered independent, and/or are not listed as having voted in partisan primaries, and/or live in mixed-partisan precincts. I compare these registration-based segments to segments of voters that would be targeted using more sophisticated microtargeting models.

Campaigns typically combine registration-based, precinct-based, or model-based signals of partisanship with vote history data in order to isolate segments of the electorate to whom they will direct their attention. Their highest priority for persuasion is typically *regular-voter targets*, who nearly always show up to vote but whose partisan leanings are undetermined or independent. Ethan Roeder, Obama's data director, calls these voters the "high-turnout persuasion universe." Hal Malchow, a veteran microtargeting consultant, suggests that these individuals are often identified as registrants who have participated in 70 percent or more of eligible elections. This is a common campaign implementation and the one I use here. Campaigns focus on regular-voter targets because if they can convince them to their side, the voters' history of participation suggests they will actually contribute their vote to the candidate.[3]

A second group commonly subjected to persuasion messages is *surge targets*, also known as sporadic-voter targets. For targeting surge persuasion voters, campaigns often focus on voters who give an independent or undetermined partisan signal but who vote only in presidential years. Mimicking a 2012 campaign, for example, I implement this as registrants eligible since 2008, who voted in 2008 but not in the 2010 general election. This is a common implementation. Consider a confidential memo written by Catalist about their 2008 election efforts that was leaked on the Internet.[4] In this memo (p. 25), sporadic voters were defined precisely:

> The term 'sporadic voters' refers to people who voted in the most recent presidential election but who did not vote in the mid-term elections. In

this case, the term refers to people who voted in the 2004 presidential election but who did not vote in the 2006 mid-term elections. From a campaign's perspective, these voters fit into one of two general profiles. They either (a) tend to be less polarized and somewhat more moderate then [sic] people who voted in both elections, but can be counted on to vote in the current election; or (b) they are highly partisan but require outside efforts to galvanize them to vote on election day. Consequently, sporadic voters are crucial targets of any campaign, as they match the audience profile of persuasion and GOTV activities.

As further evidence of the use of this implementation of "sporadic" voting is a memo by liberal activist group the New Organizing Institute that defines sporadic in exactly this same way.[5] Of course, this definition is also found in political science work aimed at explaining the surge of voters that come into the electorate during presidential years but not during congressional years (Campbell, 1960).

Surge, or sporadic, voters, when they do have a signal of partisanship in a campaign database, are the primary targets for GOTV. This is reflected in the leaked Catalist memo. In presidential years, campaigns tend to focus on known partisans who failed to vote in the midterm general election. It is also common for GOTV strategies to focus on known partisans whose vote history generally shows an unreliable record of turnout. Malchow (2008) suggests that campaign focus on known base supporters who have a 30–70 percent turnout rate, which can be implemented as the rate of past behavior in eligible elections.[6]

A final group of voters that receive attention from campaigns both in persuasion and GOTV strategies is *new-voter targets*. In the case of 2012, those who registered between January 2011 and November 2012 fit this criterion. These voters may have joined the rolls because of a particular interest in the current race, and so campaigns may attend to them. New registrants who have not signaled an affiliation with a party might be subjected to persuasion messages, while those new registrants who registered with a party or live in very partisan areas might be subjected to GOTV messages. New registrants, it should be noted, are not merely those who come of age during the year or two prior to an election, but also other adults who because of a move or a prior lack of interest were not previously registered at their current home address. (See Hanmer, 2009 on the mobilization of new registrants.)

To recap, I have defined three groups of voters who, based only on registration data, would be commonly targeted by campaigns in persuasion efforts. These voters include: (1) *regular-voter targets*, who voted in 70+ percent of previous eligible elections; (2) *surge targets*, who voted in the last presidential contest but not the last midterm; and (3) *new-voter targets* who registered in the current election cycle. These groups are restricted to those who are not registered with a party and are not known to have voted in a particular party's primary.

Before taking into account geographic-level election returns, if I just characterize voters based on their party and vote history, *regular-voter targets*, *surge targets*, and *new-voter targets* in 2008 include 11 percent, 7 percent and 7 percent of all registered voters, respectively. This is as measured based on a random sample of 1,825,215 U.S. registrants from Catalist's records, from the perspective of a 2008 campaign. In Catalist's 2012 records, *regular-voter targets* compose 10 percent of the registered voter population and *surge targets* compose 9 percent of the population, similar as in 2008. However, *new-voter targets* only make up 3 percent of the registered voters, a smaller share than in 2008, reflecting a lower incidence of new registrations in 2012 from 2008.

The next step in my simulation is to account for the geography of partisanship. To incorporate geographic targeting into this scheme, I consider all voters who live in overwhelmingly Democratic or Republican areas to be targets of mobilization. This includes voters who would otherwise be listed as persuasion targets or who would not be targeted at all. An overwhelmingly partisan area can be estimated by precincts that give more than 65 percent of their vote to one party in the past elections. Again, 65 percent is a common threshold for what is known as saturation targeting.[7] If I define persuadable targets based both on registration data and on precinct data, *regular-voter targets* compose 8 percent of the registered population, *surge targets* compose 5 percent of the population, and *new-voter targets* compose 4 percent of the population. This is based on a 2008-era simulation. I was not able to match the 2012 data to precinct returns in a similar fashion owing to a more limited set of data I obtained from Catalist in 2012.

Note that in addition to the persuasion targets I generated, I have similarly crafted three simulated groups of voters who would be commonly targeted by campaigns in get-out-the-vote efforts. These include: (1) surge targets, who voted in the last presidential but not the last midterm; (2) sporadic targets, who voted in 30–70 percent of past eligible elections; and (3) new voter targets, who registered to vote in the current election cycle. These groups are restricted to those who are either registered with a party or are known to have voted in a particular party's primary. I also consider a GOTV target to be any voter living in a highly partisan precinct. I used the 2008 simulated definitions of persuasion and GOTV targets to generate Figure 5.9 back in Chapter 5. I now use these

TABLE 7.1 *Definitions of Voters Simulated as Targets for Persuasion Efforts*

| Name | Definition |
| --- | --- |
| *Regular Voter Targets* | Voted in 70%+ of eligible elections |
| *Surge Targets* | Voted in last Presidential year, but not last midterm |
| *New Voter Targets* | Registered in current cycle |

**Conditions for All Target Groups**
1. Not registered with a party
2. Not listed as voting in party primaries
3. Registered in a mixed-partisan precinct

definitions to compare common targets of persuasion messages to survey-based definitions of persuadable voters.

The definitions of my targeting simulation are summarized in Table 7.1. This targeting scheme I have constructed based on registration and precinct data will not, of course, resemble the precise persuasion strategy used for canvassing in every campaign. Still, it should appear uncontroversial to those familiar with campaign strategy that the general conventions I have simulated here closely resemble how campaigns decide to whom they will direct such messages. The lesson to draw from the sketch of campaign targeting strategy is that when campaigns are looking at voter databases, they see nothing of issue positions, psychology, or political knowledge. They see a basic set of partisanship cues, geographic references, and vote history records, and from these they identify broad segments of the public that may be generally amenable to persuasion. If I were to make slightly different choices in how I simulate a typical campaign targeting scheme, such as by adjusting the cutoffs for "saturation" targeting, or by considering a "regular voter" to be someone who voted in 80 percent of past elections rather than 70 percent, these tweaks would not affect the basic point made in the analysis, which is that very little about a voter's public data profile proxies for, or correlates with, attitudes and dispositions relevant to persuadability.

When one begins to think through the kinds of targeting choices campaigns make in defining their persuasion universes, it is clear that the voters that campaigns target are more aptly characterized not as actual persuadable voters but rather as voters who are likely to vote but whose vote choice is a mystery to the campaigns. To put it another way, since campaigns in recent years know that voters affiliated with a political party are very unlikely to defect (about 90 percent of voters registered with a party vote for that party's candidates), campaigns believe that the persuadable voters are contained in this large subset of the electorate whose partisanship is unknown and who are likely to vote. Campaigns can focus on driving up turnout among their known base, but often they will need votes from this mysterious group of seemingly independent voters who are likely to turn out. They interact with these voters to try to secure the percentage of the vote they need among non-base supporters.

## Targeting Scheme in Sophisticated Campaigns

It may strike a reader that the targeting scheme I have recreated seems more applicable to down-ballot campaigns than to sophisticated, well-financed presidential races. To some extent, that is true. Presidential campaigns invest in microtargeting data and hire professional social scientists to devise more fine-grained plans. On the other hand, even presidential campaigns rely on voter file data to craft their persuasion strategies. This happens because consumer data is not generally predictive of political outcomes, as I discuss in the next chapter. Reliance on voter file data even in modern presidential campaigns was confirmed when I reviewed a set of confidential field plans from the 2008 Obama campaign. In one swing state, the Obama campaign's strategy document reads: "Our plan is to target our persuasion universe based on vote history." Another state's plan sought to explain why more than 40 percent of the state's electorate was going to be treated as swing voters: "due in part to the lack of party registration on the file." In 2008, the Obama campaign was considered the most sophisticated campaign in history and its use of high-tech models and consumer data was widely discussed. However, from its own strategy documents, it is clear that while the campaign used some additional bells and whistles to find persuadable voters, its strategies too were mostly a function of voter file records.

In 2012, the Obama campaign moved persuasion targeting a step forward. As Sides and Vavreck as well as Issenberg have discussed, the 2012 campaign used an experiment-informed model of persuadability.[8] In February 2012, the Obama campaign called 500,000 voters as part of an experiment in which some voters were given a persuasion message while others were not. The campaign mined the resultant data to find the correlates of persuadability. The campaign then used these correlates to build a model for future persuasion-oriented targeting. Sides and Vavreck report that the persuasion message from the initial phone call increased support for Obama by four percentage points.

In thinking about the 2012 Obama efforts, three points are worth considering. First, an experiment involving 500,000 households that are randomized to receive a persuasion message from volunteers is a strategy that is out of reach to all but the most well-resourced presidential campaign. Accordingly, it will be difficult for most campaigns to replicate this aspect of the Obama strategy. Second, it is hard to say whether lessons from the 2012 experiment will be applicable in the future. For example, Issenberg reports that the Obama campaign discovered that volunteers whose home state is California tended to be most effective in persuading voters. Does this mean that future campaigns should try to employ Californians? Probably not. Without any convincing theory that explains why Californians would be particularly adept at persuasion, this finding is likely an odd and random result discovered through data mining that bears no long-lasting connection to persuasion.

The third and most important point to keep in mind about advanced models that predict characteristics like persuadability is that any attribute that is being predicted is modeled only based on variables that are available for the full population of registrants. These variables tend not to be very predictive of nuanced psychological traits. Well-financed campaigns are increasingly building models that predict persuadability, positions on specific issues, and support for specific candidates. In these models, the outcome that is predicted is a survey response (e.g., a survey question soliciting the strength of support for one candidate versus the other). But the variables used to predict the outcome do not come from survey responses; they must come from population data, such as registration and Census statistics. Otherwise, the model could not be used for canvassing voters who were not part of the survey sample. In a confidential memo I obtained that assessed dozens of commercial models like these, it was reported that the following variables contain nearly all of the predictive power in all targeting models: vote history, party registration, gender, age, geography, race, marital status, presence of children, Census measures (like percent urban, percent black), and precinct data. The difference between one model and the next is often just the weight given to these predictor measures. For example, in a model that predicts support for Barack Obama, the relative youth of the voter may be given more weight than it is given in a model that predicts general support for Democrats.

The point is that while predictive models are common, and while experiment-informed models are increasingly common, these models are all dependent on public records, and they are only as good as the public records at predicting the outcomes of interest. When the outcome of interest is a complex disposition like persuadability, these basic public records will not be very highly predictive of the outcome. For this reason, while strategies like the Obama experiment are certainly more sophisticated than targeting persuasion messages based on simple registration and geographic data, they are nevertheless going to succumb to the same biases in perceiving persuadable voters as the basic strategies I simulate here.

As an illustration, consider an approach to persuasion targeting that one might implement using models from Catalist. The most typical way to use models in finding persuadable voters is not to build custom persuasion models, as the Obama campaign did, but to focus on voters who are moderately to highly likely to vote and who appear neither strongly Democratic nor strongly Republican. Recall the contact data from the 2008 Obama campaign in Figure 4.2, showing that the campaign focused on voters who were scored middle-to-high on the turnout model and who scored in the middle on the partisanship model. This is the most common model-based version of the discrete implementation that I simulate here.

If a campaign was to target voters who score middle-to-high on a turnout model and middle on a partisanship model, it would essentially be targeting the same individuals whom I suggest are common targets of persuasive messages based on raw registration data and precinct data. To show this, I turn to the Catalist database, and I construct my simulated persuasion targets using both 2008 and 2012 data. I then observe the distribution of my target groups on Catalist's 2008 and 2012 partisanship and turnout microtargeting models. The analysis is in Figure 7.1.

The x-axis and y-axis in each of the subplots in Figure 7.1 represent Catalist's micro-targeting models for predicted turnout and predicted partisanship. Higher points on the vertical axis mean that Catalist predicts a voter was more likely to vote in 2008 or 2012 elections. The x-axis shows how likely a voter is predicted to be a Democratic supporter. Points to the right indicate voters who are predicted as more likely Democratic. In each subplot, I show the median partisanship score and median turnout score for each of the three types of persuasion targets I simulated. The 'X' marks the overall medians for all persuasion targets. The lines emanating from each point show the interquartile range of scores for the target group. Looking at the black square on the right plot, the interpretation is as follows. For simulated *regular-voter targets* in 2012, the typical voter had a partisanship score of 42 and a turnout score of 91. Fifty percent of *regular-voter targets* had partisanship scores between 21 and 70 and had turnout scores between 85 and 94.

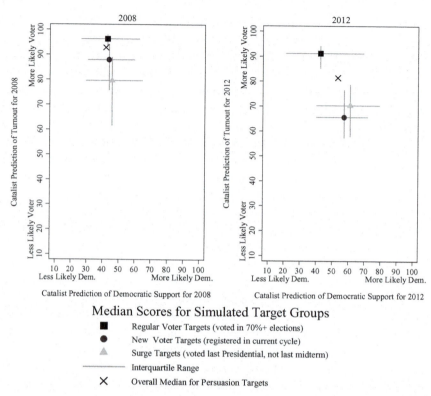

**Median Scores for Simulated Target Groups**

■     Regular Voter Targets (voted in 70%+ elections)

●     New Voter Targets (registered in current cycle)

▲     Surge Targets (voted last Presidential, not last midterm)

—————     Interquartile Range

✕     Overall Median for Persuasion Targets

FIGURE 7.1 Relationship between Registration-Based Persuasion Targets and Microtargeting Model-Based Persuasion Targets.
*Note:* For each simulated target group for persuasion messages, I show the Catalist's median partisanship score and median turnout propensity score. The 'x' indicates the overall median. Gray lines indicate the interquartile range of each target group on the two targeting scores. For 2008 data, N = 450,924. For 2012 data, N = 374,353.
*Source:* Catalist 1% Analytics samples. Note that this graph does not account for precinct-based definitions of persuadable voters.

Though the points vary somewhat between 2008 and 2012 in Figure 7.1, the general placement of the dots in each year indicate that the common persuasion targets I defined using public records are highly concentrated in the region of the models that suggests the voters are moderately to highly likely to vote and are neither strong Democrats nor strong Republicans. These plots show that the persuasion targets constructed based on the simple voter registration data and precinct data are clustered in the areas that would be targeted by a campaign if the campaign was to use a more sophisticated model. In addition to showing the close relationship between a typical registration-based approach and typical model-based approach to targeting persuadable voters, Figure 7.1 also confirms that the targeted groups constructed from the common practices described to me by campaign operatives are consistent with targeting choices of real-world campaigns. After all, the propensity scores shown in the plots are the same ones used by many real campaigns as the basis for targeting.

Note that Figure 7.1 does not account for voters' precincts. In the rest of the analysis, I only consider voters to be persuasion targets if they live in precincts in which 35–65 percent of the two-party vote went to Barack Obama in 2008. While I can connect precinct returns to the 2008 Catalist data, I cannot connect them to 2012 Catalist data. To show comparable plots between the two years in Figure 7.1, I leave out precinct definitions from both plots. However, the left subplot looks practically identical if I accounted for precinct returns in the 2008 targets.

## 7.3 PERSUADABLE VOTERS AND PERCEIVED VOTERS COMPARED

Having constructed a conventional typology of persuasion targets, I now turn to the main task of comparing the kinds of people who are subjected to persuasive messages (as identified by the simulation) with some of the most prominent conceptualizations of persuadability utilized in survey-based political science. To do this, I utilize the 2008 Cooperative Congressional Election Study (CCES) matched to the Catalist database.

The three groups of persuasion targets that I constructed (regular-voter targets, surge targets, and new-voter targets) will be compared with four definitions of persuadable voters commonly operationalized by political scientists. The comparison groups are as follows: (1) *pure independents*, defined as independents who do not lean toward either major party; (2) *uninformed voters*, defined as those who incorrectly answer factual questions about politics; (3) *independent cross-pressured voters*, defined as independents (including independent voters who lean toward a party) who agree with more than two Republican issue positions and more than two Democratic issue positions; and (4) *partisan cross-pressured voters*, defined as partisans who agree with the opposite party on more than two issues.

These definitions merit further explanation. It is common for political surveys that ask voters about their party identification to ask a follow-up question: voters who report on surveys that they are independent are asked whether they lean toward one party or the other. Those who not only report that they are independent but also claim that they do not lean one way or another are referred to as *pure independents*.

*Uninformed* respondents are those who lack knowledge or awareness about politics. Zaller (1992) finds that political awareness is an essential moderator of opinion change. In a high-intensity environment like a presidential general election campaign, it is the least aware voters who are most susceptible to persuasion. I measure political awareness as Zaller does, with a battery of factual questions about the political world. The measure includes indicators for whether the respondent correctly identified the Democratic Party as more liberal than the Republican Party and Barack Obama as more liberal than John McCain. The measure also includes indicators of whether the respondent correctly identified the party of his or her state's governor, two senators, and his or her representative. Lastly, the measure includes indicators of whether the respondent knew which party held the majority in the U.S. Senate and House of Representatives, as well as the upper and lower chambers of his or her own state's legislature. In total, there are ten individual awareness items that are additively combined and divided by the total number answered by each respondent. I consider someone uninformed if, of the questions they answered, more than half are incorrect.[9]

The classifications of *independent cross-pressured* and *partisan cross-pressured* voters are modeled after those developed by Hillygus and Shields (2008). Cross-pressured voters, Hillygus and Shields find, are persuadable and amenable to appeals from both political parties. Hillygus and Shields define persuadable partisans to be those who disagree with their party on two or more issues, agree with the other party on those issues, and believe the issues to be important. I cannot use exactly the same definition because the 2008 CCES does not ask voters about the importance of particular issues, and the issues covered in the CCES are different than in the surveys used by Hillygus and Shields. Without access to the issue importance questions, I opted to raise the number of issues for which one has to agree with the opposite party from two to three in order to count a respondent as a persuadable voter. Using this strategy, 46 percent of the sample is considered cross-pressured, exactly the same percentage as Hillygus and Shields consider to be cross-pressured under their alternative measurement strategy. The cross-pressure measures are constructed from twelve issue questions. Coding details are included in Appendix D.

TABLE 7.2 *Sample Sizes of Targeted Groups in CCES-Catalist Matched Sample*

|  | Proportion of Sample |
|---|---|
| *Registration-Based Targets* | |
| Regular-Voter Targets | 0.07 |
| Surge Targets | 0.02 |
| New-Voter Targets | 0.03 |
| All Targets | 0.11 |
| *Survey-Based Targets* | |
| Partisan Cross-Pressured | 0.40 |
| Independent Cross-Pressured | 0.06 |
| Uninformed | 0.21 |
| Pure Independent | 0.12 |

*Note:* The sample consists of 25,666 CCES survey respondents who were matched into Catalist records as being currently or formerly registered to vote.

## Basic Comparison

The comparison between campaign targets of persuasive appeals and survey-based persuadable voters begins in Table 7.2. Here, I simply show the proportion of the CCES sample of registered voters associated with each group. *Regular-voter targets* compose 7 percent of the sample, *surge targets* compose 2 percent, and *new-voter targets* compose 3 percent. Table 7.2 also shows the percentage of the CCES registered voter sample that is cross-pressured, uninformed, and pure independent. As in the Hillygus and Shields's analysis, a substantial minority of voters are considered to be cross-pressured, with many more partisan cross-pressured voters than independent cross-pressured ones. Uninformed voters compose 21 percent of the sample and pure independent voters make up 12 percent of the sample.

In the analysis, I define persuasion targets based on registration and precinct data; however, it must be acknowledged that out of 25,666 registered voters in the CCES sample, only 17,347 (68 percent) were able to be matched to their precinct returns. The missing data is attributable to the need to locate precinct returns based on nine-digit ZIP codes (Catalist did not provide me with the voting precinct of respondents in the sample), and ZIP-9 data that were matchable to precinct returns were not available for all voters. The nature of missingness in the precinct data merged with the CCES is unknown. The analysis that follows does not markedly change if I opted not to use the precinct screen. Nor does it change if I use a different geographic measure and remove from the persuasion target groups voters who live in highly partisan counties instead of precincts. (Nearly all respondents can be matched to county-level data.) Geographic screens have a limited impact on the analysis because, as I have shown, most voters do not live in highly partisan geographies. Further, and as importantly, precinct-based strategies are no more able than registration-based strategies to pinpoint psychological or attitudinal characteristics that hint at persuadability. Nothing about a voter's precinct, like nothing about a voter's registration record, allows a campaign to find voters who are actually persuadable. Indeed, that is the lesson of this chapter. Nevertheless, because the most realistic simulation does screen by precinct, this is the variant of the analysis I opt to show here, even though not all CCES respondents can be matched to their precinct returns.

To begin to compare campaign targets of persuasion with survey-based constructions of persuadable voters, I simply estimate how predictive each campaign target group is of the survey-based dispositions. Consider the upper-left plot in Figure 7.2. As this plot indicates, 40 percent of the overall sample is defined as partisan cross-pressured. This means that if a campaign were to contact voters at random (i.e., not targeted), 40 percent of the people it would encounter would bear the traits of partisan cross-pressured voters. Do the segments of voters who are commonly targeted with persuasion messages contain a more concentrated group of partisan cross-pressured voters? It depends on the group. Among the largest group of persuasion targets – the regular voters who are not identifiable with a party affiliation – only 35 percent are partisan cross-pressured. The other two groups of targets contain a slightly higher concentration of partisan cross-pressured voters than the population at large. However, among all target groups together (shown in the top dot), there are actually fewer partisan cross-pressured voters, as a percentage, than in the population at large. Figure 7.2 shows that among target groups, there are only slightly higher percentages of independent cross-pressured voters, uninformed voters, and pure independents compared to the population at large. *Surge targets* and *new-voter targets* do contain somewhat concentrated groups of uninformed and pure independent voters, but overall the persuasion targets are not strong signals of the survey-based dispositions.

If a campaign wanted to isolate a group of voters who are presumed to be persuadable owing to their dispositions as recorded in surveys, and if a campaign attempted to interact with these voters based on common

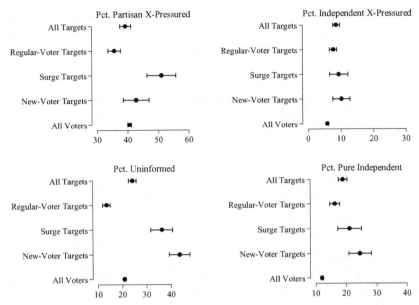

FIGURE 7.2 Relationship between Campaign Persuasion Targets and Survey-Based Persuadable Voters.

*Note:* For each type of campaign target, this figure shows the percent of respondents among the targeted who fall into the survey-based classifications of being cross-pressured, pure independent and uninformed. At the bottom of each subplot, the percentage of overall voters classified as each survey type is shown. 95% confidence intervals are shown around the means.

*Source:* 2008 CCES survey matched to Catalist

strategies used to perceive targets of persuasion messages, the targeting scheme would not enable campaigns to connect with a concentrated group of persuadable voters. Put differently, the propensity to be persuadable according to survey-based definitions and the propensity to be targeted by a campaign as a persuadable voter are only mildly correlated. One reason for this is that the largest cohort of persuasion targets – the regular voters – are particularly unlikely to bear the characteristics of persuadability. They are quite informed about politics and not very likely to be cross-pressured or purely independent. But because much of a campaign's persuasion efforts are geared to individuals who vote regularly but whose partisan ties are not predictable based on public records, the people who campaigns try to persuade do not bear the traits commonly thought to be associated with persuadability.

It should be noted that the patterns in Figure 7.2 are not an artifact of differing kinds of party registration data being available in the various states. Recall, for example, that Midwestern states that do not collect party registration or party primary data have an unusually high number of voters who may be treated as persuasion targets (see Figure 5.9). Thus, there may be a concern that this compositional effect is driving the results in Figures 7.2 and the analysis throughout this chapter. In consideration of this point, I have replicated the entire analysis of this chapter only in party registration states, and the substantive disconnect between persuadable *perceived voters* and survey-based definitions of persuadability is as apparent as it is here, when voters in all data environments are combined.

### Differences in Attitudes and Behaviors

When campaigns target independents who vote frequently in elections, who vote in presidential years but not midterm years, or who have recently joined the ranks of registered voters, how can one characterize the political dispositions of these voters? I now explore the ideological dispositions, the degree of undecidedness, and the willingness to change support for candidates among voters who are commonly targeted with persuasion messages. I compare these traits to voters whom survey measures suggest might be actually persuadable.

Figure 7.3 shows the ideological positions of the different groups. Respondents were asked whether they consider themselves moderate, liberal, conservative, very liberal, or very conservative. The figure shows the proportion responding that they are moderate (upper plot) and the proportion responding as very liberal or very conservative (lower plot). The registration-based groups are all considerably more ideological than the survey-based respondents are. Whether survey respondents are considered persuadable because they have cross-cutting issue positions, are independent, or are uninformed, these groups are all more moderate than the campaign targets. No matter whether campaigns focus persuasive messages on surge voters, new-registrant independents, or regular-voter independents, only about a third of the targets will be moderates. Unfortunately for campaigns, prior to making contact, they have a hard time knowing whether they are interacting with conservatives, liberals, or moderates.

Next, I observe respondents who changed their preference for a presidential candidate from a pre-election survey to a post-election survey. This included respondents who stated a preference for either John McCain or Barack Obama during the pre-election (October) CCES survey and then reported in the post-election survey that they voted for the other

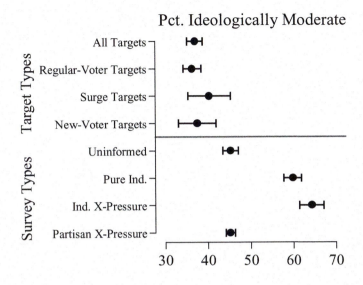

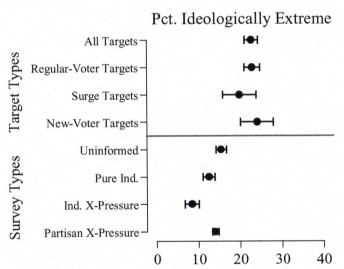

FIGURE 7.3 Ideological Disposition of Campaign Persuasion Targets and Survey-Based Persuadables.
*Note:* 95% confidence intervals are shown.

candidate. It also includes respondents who claimed to be undecided in the pre-election survey and then reported they voted for one of the major candidates in the post-election survey. The results are displayed in Figure 7.4. Apart from cross-pressured partisans, the other three

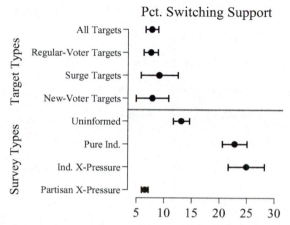

FIGURE 7.4 Percent of Persuasion Targets and Survey-Based Persuadable Voters Reporting Vote Choice Reversals from Pre-Election Preference.
*Note:* 95% confidence intervals are shown. Switchers also include respondents who reported being undecided in the pre-election survey and then reported voting for a candidate in the post-election survey.

survey-based groups – especially the pure independents and independent cross-pressured groups – reported switching preferences at a significantly higher rates than did any of the campaign target groups. Among the registration-based campaign targets of persuadable voters, very few changed their preference. Note that the same pattern holds if I exclude pre-election undecided voters from the analysis here.

The evidence in Figure 7.4, it should be noted, is susceptible to a form of "post-treatment bias." The measure is meant to demonstrate the kinds of voters who are fickle in their opinions, and thus potentially persuadable. However, between the time when the pre-election survey was fielded and the post-election survey was fielded, campaigns might have been actively trying to persuade voters in some of these groups but not others. Thus, one might ask: Is the evidence in Figure 7.4 showing the kinds of voters who are fickle or the ones who were actually influenced by real-world campaigns? The response to this point is that there is very little movement in the groups that could actually be targeted by campaigns through direct appeals. Only the survey-based groups changed their opinion. The survey-defined voters might have changed their mind about candidates because of other campaign stimuli, like television advertisements, but they were not targeted by campaigns on account of being cross-pressured independents, pure independents, or uninformed voters.

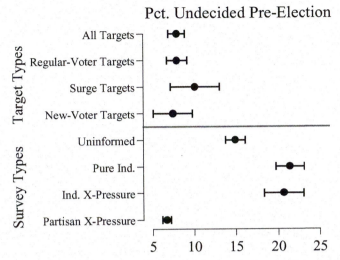

FIGURE 7.5 Percent of Persuasion Targets and Survey-Based Persuadable Voters Reporting They Are Undecided in Pre-Election Survey.
*Note:* 95% confidence intervals are shown.

Campaigns do not know the typical voter's knowledge of political trivia or positions on the issues. Thus, whether the higher rate of switching among survey-based persuadable voters is an indication that these voters responded to non-targeted appeals or else that they are just fickle in their opinions regardless of campaign stimuli, it is doubtless that these are exactly the kinds of voters campaigns would like to approach with persuasive appeals. But campaigns have trouble finding these voters at the individual level.

Finally, Figure 7.5 shows the proportion of voters in each group who said that they were undecided in the pre-election survey. The CCES pre-election poll was conducted in October 2008, at a very active time in the campaign season. Of the campaign persuasion targets, 5–10 percent reported that they were undecided about which candidate they would vote for. In comparison, there is much more variability in the survey-based persuadable voter groups. Only 7 percent of cross-pressured partisans reported being undecided, but more than 20 percent of cross-pressured independents and pure independents were undecided, and 15 percent of low-information voters were undecided.

As with the previous figure, it is not clear whether the reported levels of undecidedness displayed in Figure 7.5 are affected by campaigns trying to persuade voters during the election cycle. However, the fact remains that voters who were yet undecided in October 2008 were concentrated among cohorts of voters that the campaigns could not interact with through direct contacting strategies. No campaign data very accurately identifies voters according to these kinds of political attitudes.

### Predicting Survey Measures with Campaign Data

Suppose a campaign decided to use a microtargeting model to target persuadable voters, but instead of targeting voters who appear in the middle of the distribution on a prediction of partisanship, the campaign decided to generate a new kind of model that predicts the kinds of voters who are likely to be cross-pressured, uninformed, or pure independents. A campaign could conduct a survey on a sample of voters, use registration-based predictors to model answers to questions related to persuadability, and then generate predicted values for all voters in the electorate. In other words, a campaign could predict an attribute such as cross-pressure just as it predicts partisanship in common microtargeting models. Campaigns can pursue this strategy, but it is of limited value for the simple reason that data available to campaigns for the full population of voters does not predict well dispositions like political independence or cross-pressure. Registration data and Census data are only modestly predictive of attributes like cross-pressure, and so microtargeting models predicting such dispositions will not enable campaigns to isolate groups of persuadable voters.

To confirm this is the case, I generated a series of models in which the predicted variables are equal to one if the respondent is uninformed, pure independent, cross-pressured partisan, or cross-pressured independent, respectively. I predict each one of these identities with data from the campaign voter file: age, gender, race, party affiliation, registration date, Census block-group measures of income, urbanicity, homeownership, race, and education, participation in prior general elections, precinct partisanship, and state of residence. I run the models on voters who have voted in at least 30 percent of the general elections for which they were eligible, given that campaigns tend not to focus on individuals whom they suspect will not vote. A prediction of a survey-based persuasion target, even with all of these explanatory variables, is very noisy. A campaign that composes a list of people who are predicted as pure independents or cross-pressured independents cannot do better than a list in which well more than half of the people modeled to have these traits actually do not have them. In other words, if one were to create a model of pure independence or cross-pressured independence and target as persuadable the voters who score high on the model, most of the targeted voters would actually not be pure independent or cross-pressured independent voters.

Cross-pressured partisan voters and uninformed voters could be targeted better than the other groups, in that it is possible to use predicted values to create a target list in which most of the recipients of contact would be true positives on the defined trait. As of this writing, models of partisan cross-pressure and low information are not something I have encountered campaigns or firms like Catalist using. However, future campaigns will no doubt try to do better at developing models predictive of attributes like these. Of course, their efforts will only take them so far; as long as the root population data come from public records, campaigns will only be able to stretch these data so far in forming predictions of attributes like the propensity to be uninformed about political issues.

## 7.4 SUMMARY

This chapter described a simulation exercise in which I analyzed groups of voters commonly targeted with persuasive appeals. Just as registered party affiliates are often targeted with mobilization appeals, registrants who turn out regularly in elections and are not known to be partisans are typically targeted with persuasive messages. Using data from Catalist, I recreated three common groups of voters who tend to receive persuasive appeals. Linking these records to a public opinion survey, I conducted a comparison of the simulated persuasion targets whom campaigns typically approach at the individual level with survey-based measures of persuadability. I explored the relationship between campaign targets and measures of cross-pressure, pure independence, and low information.

The key finding in this comparison is that voters who are targets for campaign persuasion are quite unlike voters who appear on surveys to be susceptible to persuasion. The group of campaign targets is dominated by registrants who have no signal of partisanship in their public record but who vote with regularity. Regular voters tend to be ideologically committed. On the other hand, voters who are cross-pressured, pure independents, and especially voters who have low awareness about politics tend to be ideologically moderate. Voters who, by survey measures, appear potentially persuadable are much more likely to be undecided about their vote choice and also more likely to change their vote choice over the course of the campaign season as compared to voters who, by campaign measures, are subjected to persuasion.

Ahead of an election, campaigns seek to convince persuadable voters to support their candidate. Given their data resources, campaigns cannot target voters whom survey researchers might indicate are fickle. Fickle voters are out there, but campaigns do not know how to find them. Instead, campaigns focus on registered voters who are likely to vote (as measured by their history of past voting) and for whom no record exists that indicates that they are partisans. Are these targeted voters persuadable? Based on a comparison with survey-based indicators of persuadability, the targeting strategies campaigns typically use provide them with very noisy estimates of the voters who are actually persuadable.

Campaigns have a clear incentive to interact with persuadable voters. A model of campaign strategy conceived of from the voter's-eye-view might hypothesize that campaigns seek to persuade voters who are cross-pressured on issues, pure independents, or who are uninformed. But a model of campaign strategy from the campaign's-eye-view predicts otherwise. The information that campaigns have to estimate which voters are persuadable offers only the noisiest approximation. Campaigns have trouble figuring out which voters are persuadable, not because strategists are unsophisticated, but because the information they have about the electorate cannot provide them with sharp estimates of persuadable voters. Campaigns target persuadable *perceived voters*, and persuadable *perceived voters* are not voters whom a survey researcher would define as persuadable.

The result holds some important lessons for understanding campaign strategies. First, it is clear that campaign databases can offer much clearer signals of partisanship than of persuadability. In data environments in which voters are listed with their party or their race and in the few places where partisans are geographically clustered, campaigns essentially know which voters are their base supporters; there is little difference between the true base supporters and the base *perceived voters* that campaigns can estimate with data. But no record in a campaign database comes close to providing as clear a signal about persuadability. As a result, for campaigns in states with party registration or racial registration, we can expect a greater focus on mobilization than persuasion. The opposite ought to be the case in states without public signals strongly correlated with partisanship. This is consistent with evidence presented in Chapter 5, such as the Pennsylvania counterfactual and Figure 5.10.

Given the noisy approximations that campaigns make of persuadable voters, another implication is that voters who are actually persuadable, including voters who do not know a lot about politics and voters who are cross-pressured because they support positions on both sides of the political divide, will not be pinpointed by campaigns. These voters might benefit from interacting with representatives of opposing campaigns. They, more than their peers, might be helped to reach voting conclusions by hearing messages from both sides on the key issues of the campaign. However, while these voters might receive generic, non-targeted appeals, campaigns will not target them specifically with persuasive messages. Campaigns do not know that these voters are persuadable. Thus, not only does information affect the campaign's decision to focus on mobilization or persuasion, but a lack of information that signals which voters are persuadable means that voters who actually are persuadable will have trouble being persuaded.

# 8

# Voters Perceived in Social Networks
# and Consumer Files

In the previous three chapters, I have shown that campaigns behave in predictable ways based on the kinds of data available to them. Public records in some places provide clear signals of voters' partisan and racial identities; therefore, campaigns in such places focus more on mobilizing partisans and racial minorities than they otherwise would. Public records do not correlate well with voters' degree of persuadability in any place; therefore, campaigns often fail to connect with persuadable voters and prefer a strategy of mobilization. In this chapter, I provide some additional evidence to explain why public records have this strong effect on campaigns. Given the conventional wisdom that contemporary campaigns have highly advanced technology, it might be hard to believe that the availability of just a few public records predicts so much about how campaigns behave. This chapter attempts to explain further why access to public records so deeply affects campaigns.

In Chapters 2 and 3, I offered three explanations for why public records in the voter registration system ought to influence elite perceptions so much that their differential availability across jurisdictions results in different strategies pursued by campaigns. First, public records, such as party affiliation and racial registration, are highly correlated with attributes that campaigns care about. I have shown this to be the case in Chapters 5 and 6. Second, public record laws can be designed to be valuable to campaigns because politicians consider the political uses of the information when making laws about the collection of personal data. This I have shown to be the case in Chapter 3.

Third, alternative sources of information, like consumer data and social networks, are not as effective tools for perceiving voters' political attributes as public records are. I have evaluated this claim briefly in each of the previous three chapters. However, in this chapter, I add some additional clarity to this claim. The commercial data, proprietary data, and social network data that campaigns have utilized in the last few election cycles do not allow campaigns to perceive voters in the same way that public records allow. For example, if a campaign lacks party registration data, it will typically not be able to perceive accurately which voters are partisan supporters, even if the campaign has hundreds of consumer variables, an organized social network of locally situated supporters, and individual-level records from past campaigns about expressed voter preferences.

I show evidence that consumer variables are not as accurate as public records, that consumer records and proprietary party records are not as predictive of voters' political attributes as public records, and that social network–based contacting strategies have not been able to reach the voters that campaigns most want to target. By showing evidence in support of these claims, I do not argue that campaigns never do, never can, or never should utilize consumer data, proprietary party records, or social networks. In certain circumstances, these sources of data can offer campaigns much clearer perceptions of voters than they could otherwise obtain. I aim only to build the intuition for the findings of the previous three chapters by demonstrating that these alternative sources of data cannot fully compensate for the limits of perceptions that stem from the absence of public records. Campaigns perceive voters differently in different contexts because when they use alternative data sources in places where they lack key public records, these alternatives are imperfect substitutes. This leads to a different class of *perceived voters* who are engaged by campaigns.

## 8.1 COMMERCIAL DATA AND PROPRIETARY PARTY RECORDS

Popular writers on campaign technology often emphasize that campaigns have become adept at linking voter records to consumer information. Indeed, in Catalist's large voter database, every voter is listed with more than 700 descriptive fields, and of these fields almost half come from commercial sources. Catalist includes predictions such as whether a voter has a dog or cat, takes expensive vacations, and is an arts-and-crafts hobbyist. The very fact that voter registration records have been linked to consumer preferences like these may be an intriguing news story, but it may not be all that important to our understanding of how elites perceive the electorate in ways that affect their strategic choices.

To understand the limits of consumer data in allowing campaigns to perceive voter preferences, it is useful to distinguish two ways these sorts of data can be used. First, they can be used directly. For example, a campaign can acquire a list of voters who are predicted to own cats, and it can transmit a political message geared toward cat owners. Alternatively, campaigns can use commercial variables indirectly, by employing them as inputs to targeting models, like the partisanship and turnout models I discussed in earlier chapters. If cat ownership is predictive of a political trait like partisanship, then it can serve as one of dozens of explanatory variables in a generic targeting model. I first discuss the limits of direct uses of consumer data. Then, I discuss the limits of indirect uses of the data.

## Direct Use of Commercial Microtargeting Data

According to targeting experts I interviewed and campaign documents I reviewed, campaigns rarely use consumer data directly, and there are several reasons for this. One is simply that most campaigns do not have the resources to buy commercial data and link it to their voter file. Even though Catalist has records such as cat ownership, it uses these fields in analytics work and does not let its campaign clients compose contact lists of cat owners. Second, even in well-financed campaigns, there is rarely an interest among campaign strategists to send fifty different messages to fifty different segments of voters.[1] Campaigns tend to focus on just a few differentiated messages. The targets for these messages are important demographic subgroups such as women, racial groups, or age cohorts, not consumer segments like cat owners. More often, campaigns only care about targeting messages to the broadest classes of the electorate: persuadable voters and core supporters.

The 2012 Obama campaign may initially seem like an exception to this tendency. For example, it was widely reported that the 2012 Obama campaign experimented with many variants of e-mail messages to its supporters. This practice was documented by ProPublica's project, Message Machine. The differentiated messages with which the Obama campaign experimented had slight variations in language and subject lines, designed to gauge how to pique people's interest and inspire them to open an e-mail or make a donation. The variants used by the Obama campaign were not divergent messages that solicited niche audiences in clearly distinguishable ways.

But even campaigns that have an interest in microtargeting voters based on consumer attributes face more serious limitations that prevent these variables from having much use. Commercial variables are often inaccurate and not highly correlated with politically relevant outcomes. Why are commercial records typically inaccurate? The first reason is that there is a lag in their accuracy. As one high-ranking strategist told me, "cat owners have cats that die; people with loans pay down their loans. The merging and updating of the commercial and political files generates a lag." Suppose a person fills out a consumer survey and indicates a particular hobby or consumer preference. By the time this attribute is merged with a voter file, the voter might have different preferences. Until the voter fills out a new consumer survey or has taken an action that is somehow logged in his or her digital paper trail, the original preference will stick with them. Because of this lag, some strategists shy away from commercial data even when they have the resources to pay for them.

A second reason why commercial data fields are inaccurate is that they tend to offer very rough predictions of true attributes. Often, marketing aggregators do not *know* whether a person owns an SUV, enjoys camping, buys and sells stock, or has a life insurance policy. Rather, they have a model and they predict the probability that voters have these attributes based on what they do know about them. For some tiny fraction of the population, aggregators might know who owns an SUV or has some other trait. But, for the rest of the population, they create a standard predictive model to find people who are similar to the ones with SUVs. Then they list every person in their database with an "SUV score," say 0 to 100, estimating their probability of owning an SUV. This is the same method that firms like Catalist use when building a partisanship score or another microtargeting score. This form of prediction creates a problem for targeters who want to engage voters based on a particular trait. As microtargeting consultant Hal Malchow told me, "You assign people probabilities and confidence scores, but at the end of the day, you need a yes-no answer." Malchow points out that if a campaign is going to use these commercial predictions directly in contacting strategies (e.g., by targeting cat owners or SUV owners), it needs to determine a cutoff point on a probability scale. It cannot target cat owners; it can only target people who are X percent likely to be cat owners. As Malchow explained, campaign strategists often avoid this kind of strategy because there is no straightforward way to select an appropriate cutoff point without up-front and expensive validation exercises.

TABLE 8.1 *Accuracy of Commercial Microtargeting Predictions of Religion and Marriage*

|  | Pct. Correctly Predicted | Observations |
|---|---|---|
| Predicted Married > 0.5 | 89 | 13,029 |
| Religion = Catholic | 38 | 6,061 |
| Religion = Jewish | 25 | 566 |
| Religion = Protestant | 39 | 10,232 |

Data are generated from the 2008 Cooperative Congressional Election Study matched to commercial data from Catalist. CCES sampling weights are employed.

All the campaign strategists I spoke with seemed to intuit the general inaccuracy of commercial predictions. However, for a few commercial predictions found in the Catalist database, I can actually estimate their accuracy by comparing how individual voters described themselves in the CCES survey with how some of Catalist's commercial records described these voters. Back in Chapter 6, I showed that commercial predictions are quite noisy for estimates of minority racial identity. Of those listed as black or Hispanic in commercial records, only 68 percent and 73 percent, respectively, claim that racial identity. In Table 8.1, I show two additional commercial predictions found in Catalist's database that are regularly used by campaigns, and I estimate their accuracy by comparing them to survey self-reports.

First, I show Catalist's model of marital status. This model provides a fairly accurate picture of marriage. The model ranges 0 to 1, and each voter in Catalist's database is given a score in that range estimating the likelihood they are married. If a campaign uses the halfway point as a cutoff and focuses on voters with a marriage score of 0.5 or higher, 89 percent of its audience will be people who report being married. The main reason for this high level of accuracy is that public records that contribute to the commercial marriage model are highly predictive of martial status. If a voter is registered at an address at which there is another registered voter about the same age, same last name, and opposite gender, chances are that person is married. Indeed, if I predict self-reported marital status among CCES respondents based *only* on this information from the voter file, I am able to isolate a group in which 83 percent of people are self-reported as married. Thus, almost all the lift for the marriage prediction comes from public records, not commercial records.

In contrast, Table 8.1 also shows the accuracy of predictions of religious affiliation, which is considerably less accurate than the marriage prediction is. Given that someone is predicted as Catholic, Protestant, or Jewish, only 38 percent, 39 percent, and 25 percent, of voters respectively report they adhere to that religion. There are a couple of reasons for these lower accuracy rates for religion. One is that the commercial predictions do not segment voters into categories like "atheist," "agnostic," or "no religion." Some survey respondents who were incorrectly predicted by Catalist claimed to be in one of these categories. But just as often, respondents who are predicted as one religion actually report adhering to another religion.

From one perspective, Catalist's predictions of religion are actually quite good. Suppose a national campaign wants to communicate with Jewish voters. If it sends a Jewish-focused message to the full population of voters, 2 percent of the recipients will be Jews and 98 percent of the recipients will not be Jews, since Jews compose about 2 percent of the population. In comparison, if the campaign uses Catalist's model and only sends the message to voters predicted to be Jewish, then 25 percent of recipients will be Jewish and 75 percent will not be. Compared to the non-targeted strategy, campaigns will have a much higher success rate when using the model.

But from another perspective, a 25 percent success rate is not very good. If a campaign transmits a Jewish-oriented message, and 75 percent of individuals who receive the message are not Jews, then the targeting strategy may not help the campaign. If the false-positives (non-Jews predicted to be Jewish) react negatively to the Jewish-focused message, then the campaign may do itself more harm than good in targeting these voters. This is what Brian Schaffner and I (2013) found with respect to Hispanic targeting. In a series of survey experiments, we created a fictitious candidate who transmitted Hispanic-targeted appeals to non-Hispanics. We found that non-Hispanic voters penalized the candidate who sent such messages to them. Considering that one in every four voters typically predicted by campaigns to be Hispanic do not identify as Hispanic, this rate of back-fire can render targeted appeals ineffective.

The Catalist variables can only be validated if survey respondents are asked about a trait that is also captured by the matched Catalist records. Apart from race, religion, and marriage, further validations were not possible in the CCES. However, it is fairly uncontroversial to assume that attributes like race and religion are easier to predict than attributes such as most personal hobbies, consumer preferences, and issue positions. Compared to those traits, race and religion ought to be more stable and more easily measured. In that sense, it is probably fair to assert

TABLE 8.2 *Data from Public Records Are Less Noisy*

| Traits | Pct. Correctly Predicted | Observations |
|---|---|---|
| Race = White | 94 | 3,296 |
| Race = Black | 95 | 841 |
| Race = Hispanic | 92 | 262 |
| Age = Correct ± 3 yr | 95 | 25,381 |
| Gender = Correct | 99 | 25,381 |
| Party = Democratic | 95 | 5,101 |
| Party = Republican | 94 | 3,907 |

Data are generated from the 2008 Cooperative Congressional Election Study matched to voter file data from Catalist. CCES sampling weights are employed.

that commercial predictions of hobbies, consumer preferences, and issue positions are even noisier than the predictions of race and religion are.

Predictions like religion that are in Catalist's database are inaccurate not because the statisticians who generate them are incompetent. Religion is simply hard to predict. A voter's name and geography and other public records do not provide very good hints about a person's religion. And, of course, people change their religious affiliations over the course of their lives. Campaign vendors argue that though the estimates may be noisy, they are better than no estimates at all. However, campaigns do not often validate their models to determine whether potential negative reactions of the false-positives negate the potential positive reactions of true-positives, as Schaffner and I have begun to study.

By way of comparison to Table 8.1, Table 8.2 shows a set of data fields that stem not from commercial records but directly from voter registration records. On all these measures, public records indicate the same attributes as survey respondents describe about themselves in about 95 percent of cases. Clearly, part of the reason that campaigns are so reliant on public records in their contacting efforts is that public records enable campaigns to target voters accurately on politically relevant traits whereas commercial records do not offer such accurate predictions.

Even if the commercial predictions are not entirely accurate, campaigns may want to use them to target voters if they are correlated with quantities campaigns care about, like partisanship and turnout. The trouble is that except for predictions of attributes such as race and religion, commercial variables are not typically correlated with these politically relevant quantities. Consider Table 8.3. The table reports a list of some of the commercial characteristics that are available in the Catalist database. These

TABLE 8.3 *Differences in Partisanship and Turnout among Middle-Class White Men with and without Selected Consumer Traits*

| Consumer Traits | Pct. Democratic | | Pct. 2008 Turnout | |
|---|---|---|---|---|
| | For Voters *with* Trait | For Voters *without* Trait | For Voters *with* Trait | For Voters *without* Trait |
| Interest in Fashion and Jewerly | 41 | 40 | 83 | 77 |
| Boat Owner | 41 | 40 | 82 | 79 |
| Car/Automotive Enthusiast | 41 | 40 | 82 | 77 |
| Cat Owner | 41 | 41 | 81 | 79 |
| Interest in Crafts, Sewing, or Needlework | 41 | 39 | 82 | 77 |
| Dog Owner | 41 | 40 | 80 | 79 |
| Interest in Food and Wine | 41 | 39 | 84 | 77 |
| Interest in Golf | 41 | 38 | 82 | 78 |
| Mail Order Buyer | 42 | 38 | 83 | 76 |
| Uses Retail Store Credit Card | 41 | 40 | 85 | 77 |
| Military Veteran in Household | 41 | 41 | 82 | 79 |
| Gambling/Sweepstakes Interest | 40 | 42 | 81 | 78 |
| Interest in Photography/ Videography | 41 | 41 | 83 | 78 |
| Interest in Gardening/ Outdoors | 43 | 38 | 82 | 76 |
| Magazine Subscriber | 42 | 39 | 83 | 74 |
| Grandparent Living in House | 41 | 41 | 79 | 79 |
| Total Observations | 49,966 | | 109,416 | |

*Note:* This table reports statistics for U.S. registered voters who are suburban white males, ages 35–55, who live in Census block groups in which the median household income is between $50,000 and $100,000. The Democratic percentage is based on voters registered as either Democratic or Republican. Only registered voters for whom any commercial data is available are included. Overall, 86% of registered voters have commercial data available.

*Data source:* Catalist 1% Analytics sample.

are the kinds of traits that extend beyond race, religion, and marriage – traits known to be politically salient – to the more intriguing consumer habits and hobbies that populate commercial microtargeting databases. For each trait, Table 8.3 lists the percentage of Democrats among registered voters with the trait and the percentage of Democrats among registered voters who do not have the trait. The table also lists the percent of registered voters who voted in 2008 who bear each trait and the percent voting who lack each trait. Importantly, the table is restricted to a universe of suburban white males, ages thirty-five to fifty-five, whose

Census block group median income is between $50,000 and $100,000. By restricting the universe in this way, I am, in essence, controlling for some characteristics that I know are actually relevant to political outcomes, including age, gender, race, urbanicity, and income, but that can be estimated through Census and voter registration records rather than consumer records.

When one accounts for simple demographics from public records, commercial variables explain very little about what distinguishes Democrats from Republicans. This should not be particularly shocking. Most consumer habits and lifestyle choices are politically irrelevant. Political fissures are not defined by these sorts of things. Surely owning a boat is correlated with income and income is correlated with partisanship. But once accounting for characteristics such as the wealth of one's neighborhood, boat ownership does not distinguish Democrats from Republicans.[2] Databases composed by consumer aggregators are geared toward commercial clients that seek to sell products. For those clients, information about habits, hobbies, and preferences shown in Table 8.3 may have some value. But these sorts of variables do not predict levels of partisan support and turnout. Thus, the use of commercial databases in campaigns is limited. That stated, in Table 8.3, there are some variables that are noticeably correlated with turnout. The strongest effect is for magazine subscribers, who are nearly nine percentage points more likely to vote than non–magazine subscribers who otherwise share demographic attributes. In the following section, I discuss how variables like this can be incorporated indirectly into a campaign's perceptions, through their use in targeting models.

### A Challenge to Hillygus and Shields (2008)?

If commercial variables are (a) often out of date, (b) measured with substantial error, and (c) not typically predictive of traits that campaigns care about, how can one explain the view of modern campaigns in which commercial microtargeting data play a large role? In political science research, this view of campaigns is most prominently associated with the work of Hillygus and Shields (2008). The argument about microtargeting offered by Hillygus and Shields and the argument about microtargeting offered here are actually easy to square with one another. Their apparent difference results from two different evidentiary bases. Hillygus and Shields present evidence of the outputs of strategic choices. For example, they show an array of issue-based messages that were transmitted by campaigns in 2004. In that election, campaigns sent direct mail messages highlighting issues like abortion, gay rights, minimum wage, health care, and terrorism. While Hillygus and Shields gather data on the kinds of messages transmitted, they do not offer as much evidence about how campaigns decided to send certain issue-based messages to certain segments of the population. They also did not measure whether the recipients of issue-specific mailers held views on the issues that were presumed to be the basis for targeting them.

In contrast, the evidence I have collected for the analysis in this book is not evidence of campaign outputs – the content of targeted messages; rather it is evidence of campaign inputs – the informational roots of strategic targeting. Data from Catalist and NGP VAN do not tell me what messages were contained in direct mail or canvassing scripts; rather, they tell me how voters are perceived in a wide array of campaigns. These data lead me to conclude that although campaigns transmit issue-specific messages, they do not perceive audiences with sufficient granularity to pinpoint issue messages to just the voters who will be receptive to such messages. I would posit, for example, that when one sees a candidate send a message with a pro-life issue position, it is not likely that this message was surgically targeted to a subset of the electorate that is actually pro-life. Instead, it may have been targeted using a rough approximation of pro-life *perceived voters*. For example, voters who live in conservative and religious neighborhoods populated by family households may be the kinds of voters perceived to be responsive to pro-life messages. Of course, the pro-life *perceived voters* may not actually be a very good approximation of pro-life voters in reality. Precision targeting is highly prone to error, even when based on simple characteristics like religious affiliation; it is likely even more prone to error when based on approximations of voters' issue positions.

My argument helps build upon the story that Hillygus and Shields began telling by focusing on the informational roots of targeting. My addendum to their argument is that the choices campaigns make and the perceptions they form about voter attitudes are largely a function of public records. Campaigns may have hundreds of commercial variables in their databases, but when campaigns perceive voters' politically relevant attributes, these variables are only marginally useful. When campaigns have accurate records of attributes like a voter's party, age, gender, race, and neighborhood characteristics, or when they have licensing records such as records of hunting and fishing licensees from state agencies, campaigns can use these data to perceive voter attitudes and then microtarget messages. But for attributes of voters that cannot be so easily perceived from public records, like most issue positions, campaigns cannot target voters narrowly based on these traits. Their perceptions simply are not sufficiently clear.

## Indirect Use of Commercial Data

Even if commercial variables are often inaccurate, and even if they are predictive of consumer preferences that are mostly unrelated to politics, campaigns can, and do, still use these variables *indirectly* by including them as explanatory variables in targeting models. If a combination of commercial variables can help distinguish a few more partisans from non-partisans or voters from nonvoters, then it might be worth the investment to incorporate these variables into targeting models. If, after accounting for basic demographics, knowing that someone has an interest in gambling tells a data miner that this person is two percentage points more likely to be a Republican than a Democrat and three percentage points more likely to be a voter than a nonvoter, then this is helpful to campaigns. Commercial data are not useless; they just have much less predictive value than public records do. Consequently, absent public records, the perceptions garnered from commercial data alone are different and less accurate than the perceptions garnered from public records.

When I now quantify the nature of the supporting role that commercial data plays in targeting models, I simultaneously examine the role of proprietary party data in shaping campaign perceptions. I examine commercial and proprietary party data together as they contribute to the predictive model of partisanship that Catalist uses to perceive voters' likely Democratic support. Recall that Catalist's partisanship model is a representation of a campaign's best guess at voters' actual partisan identities, based not only on public records but on dozens of commercial and proprietary records as well. The question I can ask is: How much more information about partisanship is contained in the commercial and proprietary data than in the public record of party registration alone?

To answer this question, I return to a comparison between two versions of Catalist's partisanship model. The first is the model that is used by real-world campaigns and that incorporates party registration and party primary data in places where such data are available. The second model is essentially the same model except that it does not incorporate the party registration and party primary data as predictors of partisanship. This latter model predicts voters' partisanship using approximately 150 other variables, including data about consumer habits as well as proprietary data like field IDs from earlier campaigns. (Recall, a field ID is an indicator

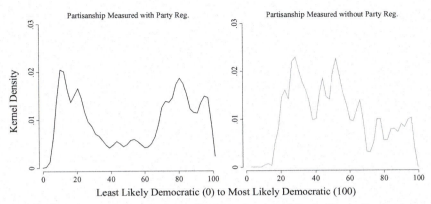

FIGURE 8.1 Catalist's Prediction of Voter Partisanship in Party Registration States, Modeled with and without Using Party Registration as an Input Variable.
*Note:* Catalist's 2008 partisanship models are observed for a random sample of 1,044,503 voters in party registration states.
*Source:* Catalist 1% Analytics Sample.

in a voter's electronic profile created when a prior campaign logged an interaction with the voter.)

Consider the difference between the model measured with party registration data and the model measured without it, just in the party registration states. Figure 8.1 shows the density plots. Like the counterfactual exercise with Pennsylvania voters back in Chapter 5, this graph shows the distribution of exactly the same voters, but whose partisanship is predicted based on two different versions of the partisanship model. When party registration data are used to predict partisanship (left plot), two groups of voters emerge: voters predicted as very likely to be Republican and voters predicted as very likely to be Democratic. When party registration data are not used (right plot), voters appear more spread out across the range of values in the model.

In interpreting Figure 8.1, it is important to keep two points in mind. First, voters actually look like the left plot – the perception as generated by the model that incorporates party registration data. As noted back in Chapter 5 (see Figure 5.6), voters in party registration states overwhelmingly identify as strong partisans. Just over 50 percent consider themselves either strong Democrats or strong Republicans. The remaining 50 percent are distributed across five categories of weak Democrats and weak Republicans, independents who lean Democratic and lean Republican, and pure independents. Simply put, based on how voters self-identify, the left plot in Figure 8.1 is a much more accurate representation of voters' partisanship. Second, it is also important to keep in mind that the specific values on these two versions of the partisanship model have similar substantive meanings, insomuch as a score of X on one model is about as predictive of partisan support as the same score on the other model. According to CCES respondents matched to Catalist scores, respondents who were listed with any given score on the Catalist model measured with party data voted for Barack Obama at approximately the same rate as did respondents who were listed with the same score on the model not measured with party data.

The difference between the two perceptions shown in Figure 8.1 is that when partisanship is predicted without party registration data, nearly 60 percent of voters are scored with values in the 30–70 range. These voters had essentially a 50/50 chance of supporting Barack Obama. In contrast, when campaigns incorporate party registration data, only 22 percent of the population of registered voters have scores in the 30–70 range. These are the same voters, but when campaigns perceive them without party registration data, their perceptions about which voters are supporters are much less clear.

If the nonpublic data sources were collectively predictive of partisanship, then the right plot in Figure 8.1 would show two groupings of strong Democrats and strong Republicans, consistent with the reality of how voters identify. Even sophisticated organizations like Catalist have difficulty figuring out which voters are strong Democrats or Republicans without the use of party registration data. If Catalist lacked party registration data, but still had all their forms of commercial and proprietary data, they would only be able to predict partisan identification as well as is displayed in the right plot in Figure 8.1. As I discussed back in Chapter 5 (Figure 5.5), Catalist's model in 2012 did somewhat better in distinguishing likely supporters from likely opponents than did Catalist's 2008 model. But even in 2012, in the absence of party registration data, most voters have scores indicating substantial uncertainty of their likely partisan support.

In a sense, this result is mundane. Party registration is a much better predictor of self-reported partisanship and presidential vote choice than any other measure is. What makes the evidence surprising is that the perception of partisanship explored here is not a measure concocted by a political scientist, but one built by national political campaigns that leverages actual contact data and proprietary records of Democratic Party organizations, as well as data from dozens of campaigns, unions, and interest groups. Even with millions of records of prior campaign contact, 150 predictors of partisanship, advanced statistics, and decades of experience with voters, campaigns and parties using Catalist's state-of-the-art partisanship model depend on public records to estimate voter partisanship. Campaign resources such as group membership lists, field ID data, and commercial variables barely sort voters at all in comparison to the simple public record of party registration.

The limited value of field ID data is particularly intriguing. If a campaign sends volunteers to visit voters' homes or to call voters on the telephone, and if the volunteers ask voters which party or candidate they are supporting, why does the data generated from these field IDs have limited predictive value? When I put this question to campaign strategists, they explained that volunteers and staffers are often overly ptimistic about their interactions with voters. Voters often lie about their level of support in order to end the conversation, and canvassers often believe that their appeals to voters were more positively received that they actually were. This is consistent with evidence from the GCP survey. Most canvassers who were interviewed in the GCP survey claimed that their interactions with voters were going well (see Figure 5.11). The rosy picture painted by the canvassers seems overly optimistic. When canvassers write down that a person they contacted was sure to vote for their candidate, the result is that this field ID may not be particularly predictive of future behavior of the voters.[3]

I emphasize, once again, that the limits of Catalist's predictive models of partisanship are not attributable to any inadequacies on the part of Catalist, but simply reflect the data that Catalist must use as its inputs. In fact, the value of Catalist models to campaigns is precisely in the regions of the country where campaigns cannot obtain clear signals of voter attributes from public records. Campaigns rely on Catalist especially when no public sources of data allow them to distinguish likely supporters from likely opponents. Consider the Catalist model that does not incorporate party registration as a predictor variable. While this model does not sort voters as well as a model that could incorporate party registration data, it is far better than having no model at all. Prior to firms like Catalist developing models like this, campaigns had essentially no way to sort voters into likely supporters and likely opponents, apart from using precinct data. Thus, from the perspective of campaigns, in places that lack party registration data, the Catalist models are a vast improvement in perceiving voters over the prior status quo. In places with robust public records of partisanship, the models provide less added value.

The purpose for demonstrating that commercial variables are inaccurate and not especially predictive of political attributes is to help explain the results of the previous chapters. I found that campaigns perceive voters quite differently across jurisdictions as a result of the provision of public records, and consequently they engage with voters differently in their direct contacting strategies. I also found that campaigns in no jurisdictions are able to target persuadable voters successfully. The key to understanding these empirical findings is that the alternative sources of data that campaigns use – commercial records and proprietary party lists of field IDs – are no substitute for public records in enabling campaigns to perceive voter attributes. If the alternative data sources were as informative of voter attributes as public records are then it would be difficult to explain why campaigns and voters seem to behave differently depending on the public data environment. Because it is now clear how perceptions vary depending on the informational inputs that elites use, the findings about strategy and voting behavior are more understandable.

### Future Uses of Consumer Data and Proprietary Data

Looking into the future, it is useful to speculate about the kinds of commercial records and proprietary party records that might do a better job of helping campaigns perceive voters. With respect to commercial records, campaigns would most benefit from records that cover a large segment of the electorate, that are accurate, and that are politically relevant. What kinds of data bear these traits? Self-reported information that appears on Facebook profiles is a good example. Many Facebook users identify their political views in their profile. Facebook allows advertisers to target user accounts based on profile segments, but the company does not allow clients to extract lists of users identified by name and by traits like self-reported ideology. If they did, this data field would be of substantial use to campaigns, allowing them to perceive the self-reported ideological disposition of millions of Americans. Campaigns could then engage voters in direct contacting strategies based on these perceptions. This is the kind of commercial data field that exists but has so far not been shared with or sold to campaigns.

Another commercial data source that is increasingly being used by campaigns (but probably will not add much precision to their perceptions) is variants on targeting models. Microtargeting consultants can build an array of models that score voters not just on their likely partisanship but on their likely support of niche issues and candidates. These models can be built by taking a poll of voters and asking them a question – for example, what their position on immigration is. The consultant would then predict a yes or no answer to this question with data available for the full population of registered voters. Since the kinds of data available about the full population – vote history, party registration, gender, and age from the voter file, Census neighborhood data, and so forth – are not likely to be especially predictive of nuanced issue positions, these models cannot add much value above and beyond what a standard model of partisanship would provide for campaigns. Of course, the exception would be a model predicting a trait that is closely correlated with some demographic or neighborhood variable that is available in the public record.

With regard to proprietary party data, there are several kinds of data that may be of greater use in the future in helping campaigns perceive voters' attributes. The first is self-reported data provided by campaign supporters directly to campaigns. For example, the Obama campaigns collected data from supporters by asking them to sign up on a campaign website. Supporters were invited to provide contact information, identify their group associations, and describe the issues they cared about. This form of proprietary data can be useful to campaigns in a number of different ways. For example, it can be used in targeted volunteer recruitment. If a campaign knows that there are a thousand people who are willing to volunteer and who, for example, identified as military veterans when they signed up on a website, then the campaign might use these volunteers to try to mobilize other military veterans in the future.

This form of user-generated proprietary data does have some limitations. Very few campaigns other than presidential campaigns have the resources or activist support to obtain data like these. Even if a presidential campaign like Obama's shared its user-generated IDs with other campaigns, those other campaigns might find that the data provided by enthusiastic volunteers might only be relevant to the specific candidate who garnered that enthusiasm in the first place. Also, these data come from a narrow slice of activists who are already committed voters. They do not come from everyday voters. While the data can be used for volunteer recruitment, the data cannot easily be used for direct, strategic voter contact. Nonetheless, it is possible for user-generated ID data to claim a larger role in future campaign perceptions and strategies.

Another kind of proprietary data that might be of more use to campaigns in the future is professional telephone identifications of supporters. Earlier, I discussed why volunteer-based IDs may be of limited predictive value. An alternative way to identify voters' likely support is to use a professional survey firm to solicit information from voters. In 2008 and especially in 2012, the Obama campaign called large numbers of voters through professional polling firms. These responses may be useful for future campaigns that might like to know the candidates who voters claimed to have supported in the past.

The usefulness of such proprietary data relies on prior campaigns sharing their data with future campaigns. In the past, candidate-centered campaigns, even for the presidency, evaporated following their election, and the next campaign started anew. If campaigns within each partisan camp can coordinate and share data more than in the past, then records of professional phone contacts, like those generated by the Obama campaign, will help future campaigns perceive voters. Of course, the usefulness of these data also depends on the strength of the relationship between voters' support for one candidate and support for the next candidate.

## 8.2 SOCIAL NETWORKS

Another way for campaigns to perceive voter dispositions is by leveraging social networks. Network-based targeting can happen offline, through neighborhoods and community organizations. Social network targeting can also happen online, through websites like Facebook. So far, social networks have not provided campaigns with clear perceptions of voter attitudes such that campaigns can compensate for the limits of public records. Again, my argument is not that network-based targeting is of no use to campaigns. I merely seek to establish more intuition for why campaign strategy, even in 2012, was so affected by the provision of public records. Why could campaigns not generate clear perceptions about voter attitudes through social networks? And from such perceptions, why could they not devise direct contacting strategies? To answer this question, I first discuss case studies of campaigns that tried to engage with social network targeting but largely failed. I discuss two offline network-based approaches and then discuss a Facebook approach pioneered by the 2012 Obama campaign. Then, I show evidence from NGP VAN about the limited use of social network targeting. Finally, I discuss future uses of network-based contacting.

### Case Studies in the Limits of Network-Based Targeting

Consider the campaign organization of Deval Patrick, elected Governor of Massachusetts in 2006 and 2010. In the 2006 campaign, Patrick was an underdog and an outsider. He had a passionate following, but as a first-time candidate, he lacked the infrastructure and broad party support available to his main rival, then–Attorney General Tom Reilly. "By philosophy and necessity," Patrick was fond of saying, "we were a grassroots campaign."[4] Patrick's 2006 campaign manager, John Walsh, who later became chair of the Massachusetts Democratic Party, was interested in experimenting with social network mobilization. Walsh has been a firm believer that campaigns are not won with TV ads or media endorsements, but through direct contact. But Walsh saw how common it had become for voters to avoid phone calls from campaigns and to throw out mail without opening it, and so the campaign tried something new. "We need people to talk to their friends," Walsh told me in an interview. Instead of hosting traditional phone banks in which volunteers call through lists of voters provided to them by the campaign, Walsh wanted people to call contacts through their mobile phone address books and message their Facebook friends.

In 2010, when the campaign faced a tough reelection battle, the campaign decided to invest more formally in a network-based strategy. The campaign asked volunteer "organizers" to recruit fifty of their acquaintances to commit to voting for Governor Patrick. The organizers were then asked to do two things: (1) send the list of "supporters" back to the campaign and (2) take responsibility for ensuring their supporters showed up to the polls on Election Day. When they got data back from organizers, the campaign linked personal identifiers to their database, and they then removed the identified supporters from the standard forms of direct mobilization outreach. The campaign left the organizers fully responsible for the recruits they had identified through their personal networks. The Patrick campaign invested resources into the network recruitment program, dedicating a full-time staff person to the endeavor.

This strategy harkens back to the precinct-captain model of campaign mobilization from an earlier era, when parties relied on local activists to take responsibility for mobilizing the voters in their area. But in contemporary campaign politics, this strategy was very unusual; it was a major departure from standard list-based voter contact. To be safe, the network strategy was accompanied by a standard list-based strategy as well: the campaign sought to mobilize registered Democrats who voted in one or two of the following three elections: the 2006 general, the 2010 general, and the 2010 special election for U.S. Senate. This kind of targeting of "sporadic" partisans is common in midterm election years. For these voters, the campaign utilized door-to-door canvassing and phone-banking tools.

How did Walsh's alternative strategies turn out? The 2010 campaign was successful insomuch as the candidate won the election. But the network-based approach turned out to be problematic, for three reasons. First, many core volunteers did not like recruiting voters on their own. They did not like sitting at their home computers and messaging Facebook friends; they did not like going to their neighbors' houses by themselves. People who volunteer for campaigns tend to enjoy the social aspects of campaign volunteering (e.g., meeting other volunteers in call centers, being paired up with a stranger to knock on other strangers' doors); confining themselves to their own networks proved less enjoyable for many of the volunteers.

Second, the network approach did not reach very many people. By October 17, two weeks before Election Day, when the campaign switched over from recruitment to get-out-the-vote efforts, the year-long program produced 40,000 identified supporters, or roughly 1 percent of registered voters in the state of Massachusetts. This number actually exaggerates the count of supporters in the system because it double-counts supporters who were recruited by multiple organizers. (I could not discern the exact number of double-counted voters from the data I retrieved.) In comparison, the list-based target universe of "sporadic" Democrats consisted of 13 percent of all registered voters. The point is that the campaign dedicated substantial resources to the network-based recruitment, and through the program it reached a very small fraction of voters. If the goal is to achieve a plurality of voters in a large electorate, 1 percent of registered voters is a drop in a bucket.

Third, the social networks in which campaign organizers are embedded are filled with people who are already politically active. John Walsh is well aware of the "silo" effect of network approaches. Too many acquaintances of politically active volunteers are themselves politically active. Walsh says that this is a big problem for campaigns. Many of the people listed as supporters were already very likely to vote, and to vote for Deval Patrick, without the prodding of the campaign's volunteer organizers. Thus, the 1 percent slice of voters engaged through the network approach massively *over*states the success of the program. Unlike the sporadic targets of the list-based mobilization, who have a clear sign in the public record that they only sometimes vote, the network recruits were composed of people who were already likely to vote and to vote for Deval Patrick.

From the perspective of John Walsh, network-based strategies are the future. He is well aware of the shortcomings just described, but he thinks campaigns need to push further in the direction of network approaches anyway. The same sentiment is shared by Josh Hendler, a leader in the Democratic Party's "neighbor-to-neighbor" program, a tool developed during the 2008 election cycle that aimed to help volunteers canvass their neighbors by themselves. In an insightful history of the program's development, Hendler (2012) admits that the multiple iterations of the program proved largely unsuccessful. Volunteers prefer not to go it alone and target their own networks without working under the direction of a campaign's field office.

It is worth reflecting on the lessons of Patrick's 2010 effort and Obama's 2008 effort at mobilizing through networks. The first lesson is that network-based approaches to contact are rare. The Democrats' neighbor-to-neighbor program and Patrick's strategies are the exceptions, not the rule. Even in the modern era, strategic campaign contact looks a lot more like the Patrick campaign's list-based, "sporadic" voter targeting than it looks like network-based contact. The second lesson is the intuition about *why* network-based recruitment is so hard: (1) volunteers often prefer talking to campaign-targeted voters rather than their own networks; (2) volunteers' own networks are not nearly expansive enough to engage as many voters as a campaign needs to reach; (3) volunteers' personal networks are composed of politically active voters so the campaign has difficulty reaching "sporadic" or "treatment-responsive" voters through networks – the people who are disconnected from political conversation may never hear about campaigns from social-network engagement; and (4) campaigns do not know how to target networks on their own.

This last point merits additional explanation. When reflecting about what political parties know about voters, one might think that the stable parties in American politics possess careful records about voters and communities. One might think that they *know* which voters are central nodes in social networks. But consider that the sitting governor of Massachusetts, armed with the resources of an overwhelmingly dominant and historically powerful Democratic party, does not *know* how to target networks; the best his campaign can do is ask organizers who in turn are only able to reach 1 percent of voters through their networks. The campaign's data can help target people who look like sporadic Democratic voters, based on their party registration and voter history, but the campaign does not know very much at all about personal networks. This is why list-based contact has been, and continues to be, the dominant form of strategic voter recruitment efforts.

In 2012, the Obama campaign tried a network-based approach through leveraging Facebook connections. Jonathan Alter, in his retrospective of the Obama campaign, described the Obama Facebook strategy as follows:

> If an Obama supporter had, say, one thousand Facebook friends, the campaign could determine that nine hundred of them were already for Obama, focus on one hundred who were persuadable, and ideally zero in on six or so who lived in battleground states and were in regular enough contact to be considered real friends, not just Facebook friends. When those potential Obama voters were identified, their friend (the active Obama supporter) would be notified. He or she could then send them Obama's position on issues and urge them to register and eventually to vote.

The actual process of linking names of Facebook users to voter registration files is not very easy, as Alter goes on to explain. But setting aside the logistics of linking databases, the limits of this style of targeting are straightforward to see in light of the examples discussed above. First, as Alter suggests, the vast majority of voters who are in the social network of Obama campaign volunteers are themselves likely to be sure Obama voters. Second, even if the Obama campaign can locate a voter in a swing state that the volunteer seems well-suited to target, the campaign may have a very poor estimate of whether this voter is persuadable. As I have shown, a voter perceived by a campaign as persuadable is unlikely to actually be persuadable. Third, applying the lessons from the 2008 neighbor-to-neighbor strategy and the 2010 Deval Patrick strategy, a 2012 Obama volunteer may much prefer to persuade strangers than to actually engage her friends and family members in a discussion of politics.

By articulating the limits of network-based strategies, I do not at all mean to claim that these strategies can never be useful to campaigns in the future. Rather, I only intend to show why they do not dramatically alter the role of public records in shaping the perceptions of campaigns that translate into direct contacting strategies.

### Evidence from NGP VAN Data on Social Networking Strategies

Beyond these cases, what other evidence is there that campaigns perceive or do not perceive voters through the lens of social networks? Consider a voter database like Catalist's. Nowhere in Catalist's database are there indicators of how one voter is connected to another voter (other than by household and neighborhood). There are no columns connecting voters to their workplace, to their friends, or to their membership organizations. If Catalist has records of these kinds, it uses them for modeling its scores, but campaigns do not have access to such records to query lists of voters.

Of course, some elements of network-based targeting are themselves pursued by means of public records. To the extent that a voter's most important social network is his or her household, public records allow for network-based targeting, because registered voters can be identified by their household in voter files. To the extent that social networks are geographically based, public records also define for campaigns the boundaries of precincts, wards, and other neighborhood demarcators. But when thinking of network-based contact, one might think of church members, union members, workplace cohorts, and friends and neighbors of a campaign's activists. At least in Catalist's records, voters are not listed according to these networks.

Still, campaigns might have their own lists of networked voters to whom they reach out. I can estimate the prevalence of such lists in two ways. First, in the GCP survey, we asked 2012 election campaign workers what they thought was the main strategy their campaign was pursuing in their area at that time. We gave volunteers a list of eight options. (Options and question wording are in Chapter 4). One of these options was that the campaign was mainly pursuing a social network–based strategy. The question here is: What percent of campaign workers chose this option?

Table 8.4 has the results. To make this table, I restrict the sample only to those campaign workers who chose no more than three options. Even though we asked campaign workers to "characterize the campaign's *main* strategy," we did allow them to choose as many of the eight options as they liked. Of respondents who answered this question, 81 percent chose one, two, or three options. The remaining 19 percent choose four to eight options. It is sensible to restrict the responses to those who did think truly about main strategies. However, the substantive point remains unchanged if I analyze the data differently.

Table 8.4 shows that, overwhelmingly, most campaign staffers in our sample considered the main strategy of their campaigns to be volunteer-based field mobilization. The next most popular option was volunteer-based field persuasion. Recruitment through social networks was one of these least popular options. Indeed, 95 percent of respondents in our sample did not select this as a main strategy. Because of the sampling design, the people in our sample are those who are most active in ground campaign strategies. This might explain why so few thought paid ads

TABLE 8.4 *Democratic Campaign Workers' Opinion of the Main Strategies Pursued in Their Campaign*

| Response Options | Percent |
|---|---|
| Volunteer Field Contact for Mobilization | 67 |
| Volunteer Field Contact for Persuasion | 49 |
| Registering Voters | 28 |
| Paid Ads for Persuasion | 10 |
| Building Party Support | 8 |
| Other | 5 |
| **Recruiting Voters through Social Networks** | 5 |
| Paid Ads for Mobilization | 3 |
| *Observations* | 2,759 |

*Note:* Data source is the Ground Campaign Project. Percentages add up to greater than 100% because respondents could choose multiple options. In this table, I restrict the analysis to respondents who selected up to three strategies as the campaign's "main" strategy. The table demonstrates that social network–based recruiting was not seen as a main strategy by 95% of campaign workers in the sample.

were the main strategy being pursued, but it does not explain why so few thought network-based strategies were being pursued. Indeed, these would be the very workers pursuing such a strategy.

Note that the substantive result in Table 8.4 does not change if I restrict the sample to paid staffers and exclude volunteers, under the assumption that volunteers may know less about strategic choices. The result also does not change if I distinguish campaign workers on the Obama campaign versus campaign workers in local contests who responded to the GCP survey, under the assumption that the Obama campaign championed social network approaches.

Another way to examine the role played by social network data in direct contact is to look at the NGP VAN query project I conducted with Brian Schaffner. Recall that for a number of campaigns in a single state, we collected the query definitions of all voter contact lists composed during the 2010 campaign season. Table 8.5 shows the percentage of general election lists that queried voters based on each variable that was available to the campaigns.

Most of the variables that we classified in Table 8.5 are self-explanatory variables that stem from public records, commercial predictions, or some combination of the two. The relevance of Table 8.5 here, however, is in the final grouping of queries, labeled as "custom list queries." In these queries, campaigns are not using canned variables

TABLE 8.5 *Democratic Campaign Workers' Use of Variables in Building Voter Contact Lists*

| Pct. of Lists Querying Trait | |
| --- | --- |
| *Party Queries* | |
| Strong Democrats | 20.5% |
| Lean Democrats | 17.4 |
| Independents | 12.7 |
| Lean Republicans | 4.4 |
| Strong Republicans | 2.7 |
| *Vote History Queries* | |
| General Election Vote History | 7.0 |
| Primary Election Vote History | 3.0 |
| *Geographic Queries* | |
| City | 0.0 |
| Ward | 0.2 |
| Precinct | 33.7 |
| ZIP code | 0.6 |
| Street | 2.9 |
| Media Market | 1.3 |
| *Geographic Context Queries* | |
| Precinct Dem. Performance | 0.0 |
| Census variables | 0.0 |
| *Demographic Queries* | |
| African Americans | 1.6 |
| Hispanic | 0.0 |
| Women | 0.5 |
| Men | 0.1 |
| Age | 4.6 |
| Registration Date | 0.9 |
| *Custom List Queries* | |
| Target List | 20.9 |
| Canvass List | 4.9 |
| Turf List | 10.5 |
| **Activist List** | 4.7 |
| N (Lists) | 2,511 |
| N (Candidates) | 21 |

*Note:* Data source is the VAN query project done in conjunction with Brian Schaffner. Percentages add up to greater than 100% because lists were queried on multiple variables. The table considers all unique lists composed by twenty-one general election campaigns in an anonymous state.

made available through the national Democratic Party; rather they are imputing their own records into the computer system. There are several types of custom lists that Schaffner and I identified among the thousands of list queries in this state.

"Target lists" incorporate voters who were modeled as having some characteristic, like voters with candidate-specific support scores. "Canvass lists" indicate voters who are screened based on whether they had previously been canvassed by the campaign. "Turf lists" are campaign-defined lists of voters within a geography that will be used for telephone or door-to-door appeals. For example, a volunteer might be sent to canvass all the houses on a block. Those houses might be a "turf" within a precinct. Finally, there are "activist lists." These are lists of voters who requested yard signs, people who attended particular events, people who are family or friends of candidates or of campaigns staffers. This category also includes specific group lists such as Shriners, police officers, and women's rights activists. This is the only subset of campaign contact lists that would reasonably be considered as targeted based on social networks.

The values in Table 8.5 indicate the percentage of general election campaign lists that use each of the various query options. Campaigns in this sample, which include campaigns for statewide, congressional, and state house races, often contacted voters based on partisanship, and they regularly selected voters based on the precinct in which they lived. Some forms of custom lists were used with regularity, but only 5 percent of the 2,511 voter contact lists in this sample include "activist" screens, indicative of network-based targeting. Incidentally, 5 percent is the same value as is found in Table 8.4 indicating the percentage of campaign workers who considered network-based approaches to be their campaign's main strategy. The upshot: although campaigns may use social networking strategies in their contacting efforts, these strategies are secondary to the simple reliance on public records.

### Future Uses of Social Network Data

Given the increasing role of online social networks in public discourse, campaigns will obviously continue to leverage these networks in their voter engagement strategies. But there are two factors that could limit the use of social network data in future election campaigns. The first is a technical factor. It is plainly difficult to describe voters as nodes situated in social networks and to link network data to voter files. At least on the Democratic side, the 2012 Obama campaign began to work through these technical issues, and both parties will no doubt continue on this path in the future.

However, the second factor limiting the use of social network data may be more challenging than the technical issues are. It relates to the disposition of the supporters who campaigns would depend on to carry messages through social networks. As was discussed with respect to the Barack Obama and Deval Patrick campaigns, even if a campaign has supporters for whom friends or family members can be identified who are good targets, it is unclear whether these supporters want to engage their acquaintances in political discourse. As political scientist Diana Mutz (2002) has written, people with diverse political networks tend to be less engaged in politics, and in part this is because "the inherently controversial nature of politics is perceived to pose threats to the harmony of social relationships." Campaign volunteers seem much more willing to engage with strangers than with people with whom they plan on having repeated interaction. Thus, for campaigns to capitalize on the power of social networks to mobilize and persuade voters, they will need to find strategies to ease the burden on the volunteers on whom they will depend to carry messages. Overcoming this challenge is not necessarily insurmountable, and surely campaigns in the future will continue to try.

## 8.3 SUMMARY

In this chapter, I sought to paint a clearer picture of why the perceptions that translate into strategies are so affected by the provision of public records. A large part of the reason why public data matters so much is that other sources of data that could inform elite perceptions are only marginally helpful to campaigns. Campaigns collect commercial records from data aggregators, they utilize records such as field IDs from prior campaigns, and they perceive voters through social networks. But none of these alternative sources of data affect their perceptions as much as public records do.

Dating back to 1972, and probably earlier, media commentators have drawn attention to the technological sophistication of campaigns, especially presidential campaigns.[5] This chapter attempted to push back on claims that oversell the value of nonpublic sources of data in contacting efforts, both past and present. As for future campaigns, it is quite hard to know if the overwhelming reliance on public records will continue indefinitely into the future. It is conceivable that campaigns will be able to inexpensively obtain commercial records that are more accurate, have wider coverage, and capture more politically relevant voter attributes than today's commercial records can. It is also possible that Web-based social networking data will eventually become more useful and that political parties will be able to do a better job learning about individual voters' political dispositions over time. On all of these fronts, campaigns have made great strides in the last two decades. However, at least up to the present, when a campaign perceives voters, its perceptions vary dramatically according to the public data environment. This happens because the nonpublic data has not been a sufficient substitute such that campaigns can become less reliant on the basic public records.

Perhaps the most likely prediction about future campaigns is that they will continue to benefit from new sources of *public* data. In Chapter 3, I briefly reviewed the kinds of data that campaigns get from state and federal Freedom of Information Act (FOIA) requests. In many jurisdictions, campaigns obtain lists of hunters and fishers, school teachers and medical workers and farmers. Into the future, campaigns will continue to request data from governments that contain new kinds of politically relevant information about individual voters.

Consider that in Wisconsin, in 2012, approximately 1 million voters signed a petition calling for a recall election of Governor Scott Walker. Wisconsin is a state that does not collect party registration or party primary indicators from voters, so this list of voters, which is a public record and which has already been merged with campaign databases, provides campaigns with a new signal of partisanship for a large group of individuals. As another example, while exploring materials from the 2008 Obama presidential election campaign, I found a list of more than 14,000 households in one state that were flagged for receiving low-income housing subsidies. This list was then merged by the campaign with the voter registration file. A subset of households in which residents were not registered to vote was listed separately, presumably to be used in a mobilization effort.

Both governments and private firms are increasingly collecting personal data about citizens. Much of the government data that is being collected is a matter of public record. Except for data that is considered sensitive or privileged, campaigns will leverage open records laws to obtain lists and use them to perceive the political dispositions of voters. Thus, to the extent that elite perceptions may change in the future by campaigns finding new sources of data, elite perceptions may especially change by campaigns finding new kinds of public records that help them strategize in direct voter contact.

# 9

# Conclusion

Having investigated how the provision of public records affects elite perceptions, and how the perceptions, in turn, affect campaigns and voters, I now consider the normative questions that often motivate discussions of campaign data and strategy. As discussed in the introductory chapter, public discourse about campaign targeting can be framed as a debate between those who see value in campaigns using data to better understand their constituents and those who believe that microtargeting may lead to strategies that are harmful to democratic representation.

How does one make sense of this debate in light of the findings that campaigns are highly reliant on public records, such as voter registration records, to inform their perceptions? The findings influences the normative debate in two important ways. First, the findings draw attention to a new ethical concern about microtargeting, quite distinct from the question of whether the use of data in targeting is good or bad for democracy. The new concern is that the process by which campaigns acquire personal information – by leveraging administrative data – presents a conflict of interest that is susceptible to abuse. The conflict of interest results from a tension between politicians' political interests on the one hand and their administrative interests on the other hand.

Second, the findings serve to define the existing debate about political targeting and democratic representation as a debate over public policy. Whether one evaluates targeting strategies pursued by contemporary campaigns as good or bad for democracy, what I have shown is that campaigns' uses of these strategies are at the mercy of public policies which are always subject to reform. Debunking the myth of the secretive campaigns that use vast databases to pinpoint the preferences of every American citizen, it is clear that what campaigns are doing is not so much a product of technological innovation as of government regulations. Campaigns rely on voter registration laws and open records laws to perceive voters' political dispositions. These laws are levers. They can be dialed up or down in ways that will have clear ramifications for campaign behavior. A normative discussion about microtargeting need not take the form of vague laments or hopes about the inevitable uses of personal data in politics; rather it can take the form of a clear set of expectations about how specific policies lead to one or another form of campaigning. This frame of reference promotes a more thoughtful discussion about the benefits and drawbacks of targeting.

In this chapter, I discuss these two normative topics in turn. I first examine the conflict of interest inherent in campaigns making use of government data or governments making use of campaign data. I offer recommendations for avoiding unseemly political and governmental uses of personal data. Second, I articulate the two sides of the debate about the value of microtargeting for facilitating democratic relationships. I show how arguments made by participants in this debate may be cast in terms of public policy. I also offer a policy recommendation that can help facilitate a resolution to this debate. After discussing these two normative angles of the Perceived Voter Model, I conclude by offering an overall summary of the book's contributions.

## 9.1 CAMPAIGN DATA AS A CONFLICT OF INTEREST

It is uncontroversial to assert that elected leaders and their subordinates often have political considerations in mind when carrying out their official duties. Mayhew (1974), for example, highlights features of the legislative branch that seem to be designed to facilitate the reelection of members of Congress. The tension between administrative duties and political incentives is quite apparent in public records laws. When generating a system to collect, and then disseminate, public records that contain personal information of citizens, politicians are likely to consider the political uses of these data.

There are two aspects of the political repurposing of public records that seem troubling and that merit remedial attention. The first involves government data either being collected or utilized inappropriately for campaign purposes. The second, and more troubling, aspect involves campaign data being used inappropriately to facilitate targeting in the conduct of official government business.

## Using Official Data for Campaign Purposes

When do campaigns utilize government data inappropriately? In Chapter 3, I reviewed examples of lawmakers seeming to propose to collect data from voters merely because political parties have an interest in using the data for direct voter contact. I also reviewed examples of lawmakers rejecting proposals to restrict data from being used for political purposes on the grounds that campaigns rely on such data for targeting voters. These examples highlight the political considerations that often underly policies about data collection.

Just because politicians consider the value of data for direct voter contact when passing laws about public records does not make their behavior necessarily inappropriate or corrupt. But there are problematic features of this practice. The political uses of public records are not always obvious or presented transparently. Legislation about voter registration or about open records regulations can appear to be policies simply aimed at making elections run more smoothly or facilitating government disclosure. It may not register with the public that these data policies could primarily serve political interests rather than administrative ones. Relatedly, state-level data policies are typically not at the top of the agenda for media outlets and public interest groups, which means that these laws are debated and passed with very little public awareness. Thus, what is problematic with the laws in this domain is not that politicians have political interests, but that politicians can often change laws and further those interests without much public scrutiny.

When new laws are proposed about collecting personal data, it is important for the public to learn why a government seeks to collect the information. The rationales for collecting data should be transparent, especially given historical precedents of data misuse.[1] In the instances I uncovered in Chapter 3 of recent legislative activities that have clearly been motivated by political considerations of legislators, I found scant public reporting of the legislation in question. In every statehouse, lawmakers frequently engage with proposals that bear on how political parties and campaigns will engage with voters in direct contact efforts. For example, according to the National Conference of State Legislatures, between 2011 and 2014, state legislators across the country voted on more than 420 bills that dealt with the content of voter registration applications, the maintenance of centralized voter lists, or the sale, distribution, and use of voter registration lists. As I have shown, these policies can affect the strategies that campaigns use and the voters with whom they decide to engage. Thus, these sorts of policies need more public review.

There is a more specific and unambiguously problematic way that public data is sometimes used for campaigning. Politicians can sometimes leverage their special access to administrative data in order to give their campaigns an advantage. For example, in the summer of 2012, Washington, DC mayor Vincent Gray became the subject of a federal investigation because, among other charges, his election campaign appears to have misused government data that had been collected about public housing residents. The *Washington Post* discovered that Gray's campaign had incorporated public housing residents' identifiers into its databases, data that it may have retrieved from one or more of Gray's deputies who worked in the housing authority, and that was then linked with other campaign records.

At first glance, this conduct does not seem to be much different than campaigns incorporating other forms of public records into databases, such as voter registration records. But the concerns here are, first, that this use of data may have been illegal; second, that Gray seems to have had special access to the data that other politicians did not share; and third, that the housing data identifies a particular subset of the population that is especially dependent on government resources, and so if the campaign contacts them because they use a service over which the politician is directly responsible, the voters may feel as though they are being coerced or that their political behavior is being monitored.[2]

There are two remedies to problematic uses of data like this. The first is for media outlets and concerned parties to audit the contents of campaign lists. As in the case of Mayor Gray's database, this can happen by whistle-blowing campaign workers anonymously leaking database files. But given that campaign workers will be more inclined to protect their candidate than to leak damaging information, this remedy will not be sufficient. Consequently, it is also important for local authorities involved in database management to have sufficiently strong protocol to limit the chance that personal data end up being used for political purposes. Agencies responsible for data management often have systems in place for ensuring that personal data are not compromised in general, but they should be particularly attentive to the possibility that public servants with access to the data may have political interests and may be able to use databases of personal information for political ends.

In sum, to the extent that politicians can leverage special access to personal records and use these records for the benefit of their campaigns, data administrators should ensure that their databases are not vulnerable to such illegal political uses. To the extent that data policies are often passed by legislatures with little public discussion or public awareness of how such data will be used, media outlets ought to do more to spotlight and scrutinize legislation about data collections that may have uses beyond the stated intentions of legislators. Heightened public awareness about the political uses of administrative data will help ensure that when governmental data is repurposed by campaigns, the political uses of the data are at least transparent.

## Using Campaign Data for Official Purposes

Just as some political uses of administrative data may raise concerns of misconduct, there are ways that campaign records are being used in official government business that raise red flags as well. As I have shown, political data vendors have assembled large databases composed mostly of linked public records. Once campaigns have generated clean lists that profile each voter, the lists also end up having some uses in official government business. One of the reasons to pay attention to individually identifying campaign databases is that these databases are increasingly informing official government perceptions of voters, not just campaign perceptions.

Consider that campaign databases are now widely used to facilitate targeted responses to constituent service requests in congressional offices. Legislators dedicate substantial staff resources to responding to constituents who need help or want to weigh in on legislative debates. To help their offices process constituent communications and respond to specific constituents, members of Congress typically contract with outside data vendors. Among the big players in this business are Lockheed Martin, Fireside21, iConstituent, and Catalist. Constituent service vendors offer data and computer interfaces for staffers to send e-mail and mail newsletters to voters as well as to respond to constituents' service requests. One of the key services these companies provide is linking information sent by constituents to the constituents' voter registration records and other public and commercial records. The vendors connect the constituent who contacted the Congress member to database fields that look very similar to campaign database records and that enable the congressional office to respond to constituent requests with the benefit of microtargeting strategies.

When, for example, voters visit the website of a member of Congress in order to send the legislator an e-mail, they may be asked to provide information like their nine-digit zip-code, name, and street address. The information that constituents are required to fill out in order to send an e-mail is sufficient to identify a specific voter. The vendors use this information to link the record of contact to a database containing voter registration data and other descriptive information. Thereby, when congressional offices respond to communications from constituents, they can "create and filter audiences . . . based on user fields, affiliations, address information, correspondence history and . . . issue fields," as Fireside21, one of the major vendors, advertises.[3]

In providing this service, the data vendors are helping clients by linking two forms of data that the legislators are legally permitted to use: voter registration databases and constituent service databases. For example, if a constituent contacts a legislator, depending on the state of residence, the vendors can show the legislative office whether the voter participated in a recent Democratic or Republican primary. Or, a legislator who received mail from constituents both in favor and opposed to health care reform can sort the two groups into camps and send different official correspondences to the two different groups. In short, vendors merge constituent information with the kinds of data found in campaign databases so that the offices can microtarget responses.

The use of commercial segmentation strategies in constituent communications and especially in casework may seem inappropriate. When *campaigns* use databases of linked public records to target segments of the electorate or to estimate which voters are supporters, this is a less objectionable behavior than when similar strategies are used in official responses to constituent requests. The latter behavior seems ripe for a kind of abuse by which government officials treat perceived supporters differently than perceived opponents. When I asked Fireside21 CEO Ken Ward about this concern, this is what he said:

> If an office wants to use these tools and this means that they are excluding people from their engagement, is that good? Probably not, but if you do that sort of thing, you probably won't get re-elected.[4]

In other words, Ward argues that if Congress members use segmentation tools in their casework, they will eventually be penalized by the electorate. If voters feel that their elected leader is not responsive, they will vote him or her out of office. Of course, if the point of the segmentation is to pay less attention to voters who are expected not to be supporters, then these voters' protests may not appear as a threat to the legislator.

To better understand the permissible use of campaign-related data for official business, it is helpful to reflect on the stated policy. Here is the policy for the U.S. House of Representatives, according to that body's Ethics Manual:

> The *Members' Handbook* issued by the Committee on House Administration provides that official funds may be used to purchase and produce mailing lists, provided that, among other things, 'the list does not contain any campaign, campaign related, or political party information.' The *Handbook* further provides that a Member may not use official funds to purchase mailing lists from the Member's campaign 'unless the lists are available on the same terms to other entities through an arms length marketplace transaction.' (Note that subject to the same conditions, a Member also has the option of purchasing a mailing list from his or her campaign with personal funds and then making that list available for use by the congressional office.)
>
> The *Members' Handbook* also provides that, '[o]fficial mailing lists may not be shared with a Member's campaign committee, any other campaign entity, or otherwise be used for campaign purposes.'

Two features of this policy are particularly noteworthy. First, there is an explicit prohibition on the use of "political party information" in Congress members' official lists of constituents. Note that this does not extend to Congress members' inclusion of primary election vote history in their databases, which is an excellent predictor of congressional vote choice for approximately 40 percent of the electorate. Second, there is an explicit prohibition against purchasing lists with "campaign" or "campaign-related" information. This would include, for example, records of donors, records from canvassing activities, and records of constituents who have requested yard signs. But public records such as registration data, public license data, and Census data are not prohibited, and neither are commercial data (such as commercial predictions of race and ethnicity) that can be purchased on the open market. These data are, of course, "campaign related" in the sense that campaigns rely on these data to communicate with voters, but they are not "campaign related" in the sense covered by the ethics policy. In short, there is sufficient wiggle room for a legislative office to buy or access data that looks very similar to the data used in campaign efforts. And these data are precisely what legislative offices are getting from their vendors.

While many forms of data that appear in campaign databases are permitted to be used for official House business, there are, of course, general restrictions against House members favoring supporters or ignoring opponents in their constituent case work. As the Ethics Manual states,

> A Member's responsibility in this area is to all his constituents equally and should be pursued with diligence irrespective of political or other considerations.[5]

The problem is that incorporating public records, such as registration data, into constituent services databases makes it all too easy for legislative offices to violate this ethical standard. Before helping a constituent, a caseworker can use a database like Catalist's to check information such as the constituent's race, precinct, history of participation in party primaries, likely religion, and so forth. As I have shown, some of these data, particularly data stemming from commercial sources, may not be accurate, but that does not mean the data are not put to use. The way congressional offices respond to constituent requests is not policed; it remains up to each congressional office to ensure that they are acting appropriately. But consider the temptation. A constituent calls his or her member of Congress asking for help. The staffer who answers the call pulls up on his computer screen the constituent's information. Depending on the vendor the office is using, the staffer might be able to see the voter's race, age, gender, voting history, neighborhood, licensing information, and so forth. Will the staffer respond to the constituent "irrespective of political or other considerations," as their ethics manual requires? The data displayed on that screen make it easy for the staffer to put politics before public service.

In other areas of constituent services, Congress has created systems of oversight. For example, Congress members can use their franking privilege to send mass mailers to their constituents at the public's expense. However, to ensure that these mailers are not outright campaign advertisements but instead serve some official function, congressional offices must submit them for review to an internal Franking Commission that determines whether mailers are over the line into political marketing.

With campaign-like databases in congressional offices, the oversight is trickier than in franked mail. It is not necessarily the content of communications that is problematic but the process of targeting communications. Content is easier to monitor than the data that feeds into strategic targeting decisions. Communications are targeted when voters receive different mailers from their member of Congress depending on their personal characteristics that are displayed in public records. Communications are also targeted when a caseworker reviews politically relevant personal information about constituents before responding to requests for assistance. The mere availability of data that are used as the basis for constituent communication does not necessary leave a paper trail that can reveal whether an office is acting improperly.

As legislative offices contract with data vendors that supply them with ready access to demographic and political profiles of their constituents, there is a need for greater oversight. This issue is especially concerning for groups whose political leanings can be predicted by attributes listed in public records or by models built from those attributes. In experimental work, Butler and Broockman (2011) have shown that legislators discriminate in their willingness to help constituents by racial profiling of voters based on voters' names. This form of discrimination is all the more likely given that voters' personal characteristics are increasingly listed outright in constituent service databases.

The strongest policy response would be to restrict the set of information that congressional offices can incorporate into their constituent databases and official communication decisions. It is not enough to restrict offices from using political party affiliation and campaign data such as donor lists. Congressional offices should probably be restricted from using other records, like vote history, predictions of race, ethnicity, religion, and licensing data. A weaker but still meaningful policy response is to require vendors to collect, and make available to an internal commission or to the public, data on the fields each office is using in their search queries and targeting queries. In other words, the firms would need to share log files that show how offices are using personal information about constituents when processing constituent communications. Congressional offices must balance their legitimate interest in gathering data about their constituents so that they can better serve them with the public's interest in not having congressional offices inform their casework and communications decisions with data that are too closely connected with political outcomes. Just as Congress created the Franking Commission to police its use of taxpayer-funded mailers, Congress should police its use of public and commercial records that allow their offices to so easily check citizens' politically relevant demographic traits before offering them assistance.

When voters register as Democrats or Republicans or participate in a Democratic or Republican primary, they are unlikely to fully understand the ramifications for how elected public servants will interact with them as a result. When primary voters ask their Congress member for help, they should increasingly expect the congressional staff to check out which party's primaries they are voting in before responding. This is part of the bargain when a voter decides to participate in elections. But it is a bargain that most voters know little about and that is permitted because of loose standards for how taxpayer-funded data are collected and used. To prevent abuse, it is necessary for Congress to ensure that microtargeting strategies that are accepted as common practice in campaigns are not used in congressional offices to favor supporters and punish opponents.

## 9.2 CAMPAIGN TARGETING AND DEMOCRATIC REPRESENTATION

Entirely separable from the tension between political and administrative uses of data is the question of whether targeting voters based on attributes captured in campaign databases furthers or hinders democratic representation. Many of the arguments offered about the virtues or drawbacks of targeting are still relevant even after learning that most of what campaigns do in microtargeting strategies is utilize public records to perceive voters' political dispositions. The opportunity for campaigns to use data through firms like NGP VAN and Catalist still presents campaigns with a different set of strategic options than if campaigns were only using broadcast strategies. The question is: Are these strategies good or bad for our democratic system? Here I seek to articulate the two sides of the targeting debate in light of the Perceived Voter Model, and then to describe a research agenda and a policy proposal that may help resolve the debate.

### Argument in Favor of Microtargeting

The best argument in favor of the use of individual-level data in campaign targeting stems from the realization that actually perceiving voters' attitudes and interests is quite difficult in large electorates. Politicians on the campaign trail want to perceive whether voters are supporters or opponents, but they also want to develop an intuition for what voters care about so that they can select policies that suit the needs of their voters. Perceiving the will of the people is not easy, and data can help. Politicians, of course, can take polls to perceive where voters stand, but individual-level databases like those used in campaign targeting and constituent services allow politicians to form clearer perceptions of voters than they could form absent these resources.

Consider an example of how publicly available targeting data might help a politician perceive and represent his or her constituents. Imagine a politician running for office who thinks the most important issue facing society is environmental conservation. Imagine also that there is a coalition of voters in the electorate who would support this politician because they too are motivated primarily by environmental concerns. But can this politician find those voters? Can he knock on their doors and ask them for their vote? Can he appeal to them for financial and volunteer support? The struggle for politicians to connect can be remedied with data. If the politician has data that identifies which voters are concerned with conservation issues, he might just be able to mobilize the inactive but supportive constituency that is out there.

As organizers from a national environmental organization explained, conservation-oriented campaigns can obtain documentation from federal records to find citizens who receive farm subsidies. They can try to motivate farmers to vote based on environmental concerns pertinent to them. They can make these appeals because the data tell them who the farmers are and how to reach them. Campaigns can further request records from states that reveal which citizens have fishing and hunting licenses. They can approach these voters and encourage them to vote for protecting wildlife reservations. Again, they can do this because of data. They can also collect data to find homeowners and small business owners and speak to them as citizens who have a long-term stake in the environmental health of local communities. This tactic too they are able to pursue because of accessible data.

In short, an environment-focused campaign can begin assembling a coalition of like-minded citizens only if it can cobble together enough data about relevant constituencies. The campaign that emphasizes environmental policy is one example out of many that benefit from data, and the data from which they benefit come mostly from public records. Campaigns that serve niche political audiences of all kinds stand to benefit from this kind of data. And it is not just the elite organizations that benefit. Voters who care about specific issues may want to be mobilized on these issues. To be mobilized, the voters need to be identified. And to identify them, campaigns need data.

Individual-level records found in campaign databases can help politicians provide representation to the "long tail" in the electorate. The "long tail" is a concept in the study of consumer preferences. In the consumer marketplace, there are a few products that many people like and a large number of products that just a few people like. In many markets, *most* of the distribution of consumers is in the tail, meaning that the majority of people like lots of different niche products. While physical stores must dedicate their shelf space to the popular products, Internet-based firms, such as Amazon.com can offer products that have small and dispersed audiences (Anderson, 2006; Benkler, 2006; Brynjolfsson, Hu, and Smith, 2003). As in the consumer market, the political market may have a "long tail." The political parties tend to focus on big groups of voters that are their core constituents. More information is the key to extending a campaign's reach beyond these groups to the pockets of people who care about specific issues. If campaigns, for example, have data that allow them to perceive environmentalists, they can mobilize these voters based on the issues the voters care about. Without the data, their task is much harder. By helping organize these kinds of voters, data provides organizational strength to important voices that are otherwise absent from political discourse. This is the virtue of the use of personal data and targeting strategies in campaign politics.

## Argument Opposed to Microtargeting

What is the viewpoint opposed to microtargeting? Two primary arguments can be articulated for why individual-level voter contact based on the kinds of data available in campaign databases is bad for democracy. One argument is that these strategies distort the perceptions of politicians and their campaign workers; a second argument is that they distort voters' own attitudes.

When voter registration records contain information about voters' party and race, these data allow campaigns not only to target their supporters; they also allow them to figure out which individuals are unlikely to support them. Fine-grained segmentation strategies may be troubling because they reduce the portion of the electorate that a politician needs to care about. If politicians can focus their campaigns just on the 51 percent of electorate that is likely to support them, then they might begin to see their job as representing the 51 percent and not the entire electorate. Recall the 2012 presidential candidate Mitt Romney's infamous remark to a room full of donors: "There are 47 percent of the people who will vote for the president no matter what... who are dependent upon government, who believe that they are victims... and so my job is not to worry about those people."[6] This is the kind of perspective that is informed by an attention to data that identify likely supporters and likely opponents.

Even the use of basic party identifiers can permit a political party or campaign to think of its constituents not as the public at large but as a narrower coalition of perceived supporters. This violates a long-standing ideal in American politics that politicians should not see their role as representing factions. Just as data can help politicians expand the electorate to include more people with diverse interests, data can also be used to contract the audience that a campaign interacts with, which may do harm to the ideal of representation by encouraging factional appeals.

Whether or not the use of public records in microtargeting distorts the perceptions of politicians and their campaigns, the use of these data can also alter the experience of voters. It can do so by limiting the voter's exposure to alternative political viewpoints. This is the second argument against microtargeting strategies. In data-rich environments, such as in states that collect party and race data in voter files, voters are less likely to have unplanned encounters with representatives of their political opponents, and this might do a disservice to voters. When campaigns have access to these resources, they can use them to estimate the likely partisan leanings of voters before ever making contact with voters. Parties will often decide that their time is better spent on voters who are more likely to be supportive than on people who are confidently predicted as opponents. As I demonstrated in Chapter 5, in data-poor environments, both parties will more often engage with partisan opponents. A voter may be strongly partisan, but without data, the campaigns do not know that.

In 2012, President Obama's reelection campaign offered volunteers a smart phone application that flags their neighbors by party affiliation. As reporter Lois Beckett explained, "the app ... includes a Google map for canvassers that recognizes your current location and marks nearby Democratic households with small blue flags."[7] With this public-data-supported technology, volunteer canvassers can avoid uncomfortable conversations with their neighbors and only approach homes that are marked as Democratic. As I have shown, the campaign can only effectively direct canvassers to the intended doorways when the public record outs voters as supporters or opponents.

Voters and canvassers alike may appreciate a reduction in unplanned encounters with political opponents that results from access to party registration records (Mutz, 2002). However, a reduction in unplanned encounters with political opponents may be detrimental to a voter who is developing and refining his or her ideas about politics. Consider the concerns expressed by Cass Sunstein about online political behavior. If Web-based political discourse takes place in isolated environments where people only encounter like-minded peers, Sunstein (2007) worries, citizens will be less likely to face the arguments of their political opponents. Having chance encounters with people who express uncomfortable and oppositional views "help[s] promote understanding" (p. 27). Sunstein argues that common spaces are important in a democracy not just because speakers have a right to express their views in public but because the people hearing those views gain insights they would otherwise have missed.

Whereas in Sunstein's analysis people have fewer chance encounters because they *voluntarily* filter out uncomfortable viewpoints online, in my analysis voters have fewer chance encounters because of a data-generating process over which they personally exert no control. Your neighbor who volunteers for a campaign will not be sent to your door if the campaign predicts you are an opponent. In all likelihood, this is a decision you will never know was made. But the result will be neighbors having fewer conversations with their political adversaries – fewer conversations that might help voters understand what motivates people who have reached different conclusions from themselves.

To public opinion scholars, this isolating effect can be expressed in terms of information flows. Among the forces that shape voters' attitudes are partisan elites who transmit messages to voters through broadcast, targeted, and social mechanisms. When voters only receive elite messages from one side of a political debate, the considerations they will bring to bear in their own judgment of the debate will come from that one side. They will not be equipped with the considerations presented by the other side. When campaigns can shift from targeting whole neighborhoods to targeting specific voters within neighborhoods, which they can do if they have access to public records of partisanship, then fewer citizens will be the accidental recipients of arguments from the opposing side. With increased precision in targeting, voters are less likely to benefit from the "by-product learning" that happens when they have unplanned encounters with alternative viewpoints (Prior, 2007). In turn, this might make it harder for them to make reasoned decisions about their own political choices.[8]

## Resolving the Debate

The two sides to the debate about the effects of targeting on democratic representation are just as relevant with the knowledge that targeting happens largely through the vehicle of public records than if one presumed campaigns have more detailed and secretive knowledge of voters' dispositions. Public records stemming from the voter registration system, open records requests, and the Census Bureau can enable politicians to form clearer perceptions of their constituents than they otherwise would, which may lead to better representation. On the other hand, even the simplest types of public records, such as party and race on registration files, can also permit politicians to cease contact with large swaths of the electorate, which may lead to more factionalized representation and may result in voters having less contact with representatives of the party they tend not to support. Neither of these arguments depend on a presumption that campaigns have detailed, accurate profiles of all the relevant political traits of every voter, but depend only on the fact that campaigns are engaging in individual-level voter contact based on perceptions gleaned from their databases.

Framing the debate about campaign targeting as a debate about public records laws focuses the discussion in a productive way. Participants in this debate can consider one kind of record at a time and develop an argument for the effects of campaigns using that record on targeting decisions. For example, I have shown that party registration, when available, is especially important to campaign perceptions of supporters. Does party registration data help campaigns perceive the public and mobilize like-minded supporters? Does the data lead campaigns to narrow their attention to subgroups and avoid political opponents in the mass public? Does the data result in voters having less contact with representatives of the opposite party? From my assessment of this item in campaign databases, the answer to all three of these questions is yes. Whether this means that, on balance, democratic values are furthered or hindered by campaigns' use of party registration records is still an open question.

Answers to this question can be developed by a research agenda that continues to pursue the arguments of the debate as testable empirical claims. For instance, what tests can we pursue to study whether voters have less contact with political opponents because campaigns are using targeting data? What evidence would convince us that a change in voters' exposure to canvassers from the opposite party is detrimental to their political decision making? How do public records like Census neighborhood statistics and state licensing data affect how campaigns perceive the electorate? Do the perceptions that campaigns form about neighborhoods or about groups of listed licensees result in better representation of these cohorts' interests or do they serve to polarize these groups in ways that do not help them achieve their political goals?

Rather than a discussion about vague potential consequences of campaign targeting strategies, these sorts of specific questions that are tied to specific types of records found in campaign databases can help inform one's evaluation of the merits of targeting. In turn, the evaluation of the merits of targeting can result in specific policy recommendations for how governments should collect and disseminate records of politically relevant personal information. If the evidence suggests that the democratic process benefits from political organizations having clearer perceptions of voters' characteristics, then one may conclude that campaigns should have more data about voters' personal information. For example, maybe the democratic process would benefit from looser restrictions on data sharing between candidate campaigns and independent groups. On the other hand, if the evidence suggests that democratic process suffers when political organizations have clear perceptions of voters' characteristics, then one may conclude that policymakers should restrict campaigns' access to some of the public records that campaigns currently utilize. In this way, a discussion of the increasing prevalence of microtargeting can be placed on firmer ground by continuing to explore the uses and effects of specific kinds of targeting data and continuing to pay attention to the policy decisions that generate politically relevant public records.

In addition to the recommendations made above of a Franking Commission–equivalent to oversee targeting in constituent services and heightened public scrutiny of state-level data legislation, I now offer one final policy recommendation that can help the public evaluate the relative merits of campaign targeting and to decide whether the use of various forms of public records in targeting is a net gain or loss for the conduct of elections. The policy recommendation is to create the equivalent of free credit reports for campaign database entries. Ordinary voters ought to be able to at least access and perhaps comment on the profiles that political campaigns, parties, and associated companies build about them. In the end, opening up databases to voters might be in the interest of political campaigns and parties as well, not just of voters.

Imagine a Web-based interface like the one developed by NGP VAN and discussed in Chapter 4, but in this interface any voter can authenticate their identity and then review their profile. They can see how they are listed; they can see what campaigns know about them. In their own profiles, perhaps voters would be able to change some information (like their demographics or issues they care about), and they may be able to indicate by what means, if any, they would be comfortable with campaigns contacting them. However, campaigns would not necessarily need to abide by the contacting preferences indicated by voters.

There are several rationales for granting voters access to their political profiles through a mechanism like this. One is that voters may plainly have an interest in accessing the information that politicians know about them and use in campaign targeting. A second rationale is that voters may have an interest in being engaged by campaigns based on some characteristic about themselves but not others, or they may want to be contacted in one way but not another. Few citizens would likely take advantage of the opportunity to review or alter their own political profile, but some may do so. Campaigns and parties may also have an interest in gathering self-reported data from voters because such data will allow campaigns to allocate their resources more efficiently. They will know, for some subset of the electorate, what the voters care about, how the campaigns may reach them, and if the voters want to be reached at all.

Arguing that political parties and campaigns should open up their databases to voters, even in a limited way, may initially seem far-fetched. Why should campaigns and their associated companies share their pro-prietary data that they collected in their state-of-the-art databases? The argument has legs because of what I have shown in this book: campaign databases are not primarily built from proprietary information; instead, they are glorified compilations of mostly public records. Even much of their contents that are not officially public records, such as predictions of voters' religion or purchasing habits, or microtargeting predictions of political support, are almost entirely derivative of records coming from the Census Bureau, voter registration system, and other public sources.

Campaigns and parties are indebted to the public for paying for the data that they find useful for their electioneering efforts. The public, therefore, may demand some transparency about how its own data are used. This is similar to the logic of the Fair Credit Reporting Act as well as to the "Share Alike" principle of open-source license agreements, such as those facilitated by Creative Commons. If at a great expense, the public generates personal information about registered voters and inexpensively makes this information available for noncommercial use, then derivative products built from that data (i.e., microtargeting models and databases) should be made available under the same terms: for free or minimal costs and for noncommercial use to anyone who wants access.

Would this kind of policy remove any incentive to build a campaign database, given that one campaign or party could simply access the records compiled by the other? No. Campaigns or parties could grant authenticated voters access to information about their own particular profiles without needing to release the entire database in a way that an opposing campaign could utilize it. The policy could accommodate both a party's interest in generating a state-of-the-art targeting database and a voter's interest in tracking how companies and parties use his or her own personal information. There could be a set of terms for disclosing political database entries to interested citizens that would be mutually agreeable to parties and the citizens alike. Once the technology is in place for any registered voter to authenticate themselves and access their campaign records, political parties would probably welcome the prospect of voters peering into their records and making adjustments, corrections, improvements, and maybe even telling campaigns they really do not like being solicited with political communications. Remember, the point of campaign databases is that they help campaigns sort and segment voters into those who may be amenable to their appeals. Campaigns build these databases because they do not have the resources to gather better information directly from voters. An open or semi-open database that allows voters to amend their profiles might actually help campaigns perceive voters even more clearly.

## 9.3 SUMMARY AND CONCLUSION

My objective in this book has been to examine how campaigns perceive voters in their targeting databases and to understand the consequences of those perceptions. Rather than studying campaigns from the perspective of the voters and asking how voters perceive campaigns, I have chosen to study voters from the perspective of campaigns. The population of *perceived voters* – the electorate as perceived by campaigns – differs in significant ways from how voters might describe themselves and from how social scientists typically describe them. The Perceived Voter Model forms predictions about how campaigns will interact with the electorate based on an understanding of the data that campaigns use to perceive voters' characteristics.

To engage in direct voter contact, campaigns assemble data to profile each voter and make an assessment of the voter's attributes. How likely is this voter to be a supporter? How likely is this voter to show up to the polls? How likely is this voter to be persuadable? Campaigns answer these questions by forming predictions so they can determine the right messages to use and the right voters to engage. The *perceived voters*, as I have defined them, represent the various predictions that campaigns make about the characteristics of voters that inform their contacting strategies.

The first important insight of the Perceived Voter Model is that campaigns, even sophisticated ones, do not have encyclopedic knowledge of voters. They do not have secret party records that list each voter with information garnered from local precinct captains and activists. They do not have survey responses that measure the issue positions, psychological dispositions, and personal habits of every voter. And they do not have microtargeting databases that provide precise measurements of voter attributes. Unlike popular accounts of contemporary electioneering, I have shown that campaigns do not "know you better than you know yourself."

In Chapter 2, I articulated a number of reasons why campaigns do not have encyclopedic knowledge of voters' dispositions. The large electorates that many candidates face contain hundreds of thousands to millions of voters. With so many voters, campaigns do not have the resources to record and track the details of most individuals. Voters are in flux, often moving across jurisdictional boundaries, and entering and exiting the election system. Campaigns, which generally are built up to face one election and then are dismantled after Election Day, have difficulty passing along information year to year, candidate to candidate, such that with time a party could learn intimate details about voters' political dispositions. Instead of possessing encyclopedic knowledge, campaigns use a predictable set of information shortcuts to perceive the characteristics of voters. They rely on a simple set of data available in public records that they receive from administrative agencies at almost no cost and that accurately describe politically relevant traits of millions of voters.

Among the critical reasons why campaigns have access to accurate and relevant public records that personally identify voters with politically relevant information is that the laws that generate these public records are passed by legislatures that are cognizant of the data's value in electoral politics. As I discussed in Chapter 3, politicians can use the power of their offices to require that administrative agencies collect politically relevant personal information and disseminate that information to campaigns. Campaigns can also supplement public data resources with alternative sources of data, such as consumer information, proprietary party records, and information gleaned from the social networks in which campaign activists are embedded. However, because of the limitations of these supplementary data sources, campaigns primarily perceive the electorate through the lens of public records.

Through an analysis of campaign strategy documents, interviews, and an investigation into two of the most prominent data resources in campaign politics, I have shown that the perceptions of voters that campaigns derive from their voter files are informed primarily by a simple set of public records. Sophisticated campaigns, such as the Obama campaign, and campaigns that contract with the vendor Catalist, certainly have access to hundreds of nonpublic records about each voter that can contribute to their perceptions of voters' characteristics. But even for these campaigns, the public records do most of the work in forming their perceptions.

After establishing how campaigns perceive voters, and how closely their perceptions are tied to public records, I then set out to measure the consequences of their perceptions. This was my main purpose. Knowing that elite perceptions of voters come primarily from a narrow set of public records, the Perceived Voter Model predicts strategic choices that are made in the ground campaign. Equipped with the understanding of how elites perceive voters in this context, it is possible to explain critical aspects of campaign strategy.

Past studies in campaign strategy have formed hypotheses about how campaigns will behave by thinking critically about how rational actors ought to behave. As I argued in Chapter 2, this scholarship has generally set aside the difficulty that campaigns have when implementing strategies that, in theory, would be optimal. Certainly, campaigns should focus their persuasion efforts on voters who are susceptible to persuasion. Certainly, campaigns should focus their mobilization efforts on voters who are likely to support their side. But the data that campaigns have to perceive voters may not allow them to connect with these kinds of voters. By first describing what *perceived voters* look like, it is possible to form hypotheses not about what campaigns should ideally do, but about what they do in reality.

The key hypotheses I tested predict consequences of the variability in public records across electoral jurisdictions. If, as I have argued, public records that reveal voters' races and party affiliations are important inputs to campaign perceptions, and if they cannot be substituted by alternative sources of data, then the availability of these public records in a given jurisdiction should affect how campaigns interact with voters. When public records of partisanship or race are available, campaigns will engage voters differently than if these records are not available.

In Chapter 5, I focused on perceptions of partisanship. In about half the states, campaigns can access individual-level records of voters' party affiliations; in the other states they cannot. I described the alternative ways campaigns might perceive partisanship in the absence of party registration data, such as with geographic estimates of precinct-level support and individual-level predictive models that employ commercial data and proprietary party data. These alternative perceptions are not only less accurate perceptions than those garnered from party registration records; they result in a different kind of voter being perceived as supportive. In Chapter 5, I showed that campaigns with access to party registration focus more on engaging individual partisans, more on strategies of mobilization, and they are likely to have less accidental contact with out-partisans. In electoral environments in which campaigns lack access to public records, campaigns focus more on persuasion and gear their mobilization appeals to voters who live in highly partisan precincts. I showed that voter behavior varies across jurisdictions consistently with differential strategies taken by campaigns. In states without party registration, turnout is more geographically contingent and turnout is less correlated with individual-level party identification.

In Chapter 6, I focused on perceptions of race. In eight southern states, campaigns are able to access individual-level public records that indicate voters' self-reported racial identity. In the rest of the country, campaigns must use geography and predictive models to estimate voters' races. I showed that in environments in which campaigns gather accurate public records of race, they focus more attention on the race of voters when pursuing their direct contacting efforts. In environments without racial identifiers, campaigns focus less on race, but they direct more attention to neighborhoods in which racial minorities are concentrated.

To test the downstream consequences of this difference in campaign strategy, I used a comparison between two similar states, Virginia and North Carolina, both 2012 swing states. In North Carolina, where voters are identified by race in the public record, turnout in 2012 was higher among blacks than it was in Virginia. But in Virginia, where campaigns must rely on geographic measures to perceive voters' race, turnout in homogenous black areas was higher than in similar areas in North Carolina. I also showed that the 5 percent of voters who live in racial registration states but who do not themselves list their race in their voter registration profile are consistently less likely to vote than voters who do list their race. After conducting a number of tests to explain this phenomenon, I attribute their lower turnout rate to the fact that campaigns in the south often only contact voters whom they can clearly perceive as a member of one racial group or another. Although voters without listed races have a racial identity, campaigns do not perceive that identity and so they limit their contact with them.

In Chapter 7, I focused on perceptions of persuadability. Whether campaigns use simple public records such as party affiliation, precinct location, and turnout history or whether they use sophisticated targeting models, I demonstrated that the kinds of voters who campaigns typically target with persuasion messages are quite distinct from the kinds of voters who scholars of public opinion and political psychology describe as persuadable. Unlike the disposition to be supportive of a political party, which can often be accurately estimated with basic voter registration records, the disposition to be persuadable is a trait that is very difficult to measure with public records. Having studied how campaign strategists construct lists of voters used for persuasion messages and having matched these kinds of lists to responses on public opinion surveys, I found that campaigns are essentially incapable of pinpointing persuasive messages to persuadable audiences. Lacking public records or any substitutes that are strongly indicative of persuadability, campaigns direct attention to voters who are likely to vote in upcoming elections and whose public profile does not signal a party choice, but who are unlikely to actually be persuadable. A key upshot of this chapter, which is consistent with the findings of practitioners and researchers who study campaign effectiveness, is that targeting strategies are more efficiently utilized to mobilize supporters than to persuade undecided voters.

The core chapters of the book, Chapters 5–7, investigated both how and why public record laws inform elite perceptions, which translate into campaign strategies, and then result in predicted behavioral patterns of voter turnout. In Chapter 8, I provided some additional analysis to help explain why perceptions stemming from public records and perceptions stemming from alternative sources are not perfect substitutes for one another. Finally, in the current chapter, I have explored how the centrality of public records in campaign perceptions should affect our collective normative judgment about the phenomenon of microtargeting. One implication of the results is that there is sometimes a troubling tension between the official and political incentives of politicians in the passage of data laws and the use of personal data. Most troubling is the process by which legislative offices contract to use microtargeting databases in their constituent services duties. Various government agencies produce individual-level records that have value to campaigns; parties and vendors collect these data and build databases that are used primarily for campaign targeting; legislative offices then utilize these campaign resources to employ targeting strategies in constituent services. Whatever one thinks of the virtues of microtargeting in the context of electoral campaigns, similar strategies used in responding to constituents who ask legislators for help is a real concern. As a result, I suggested that Congress ought to develop clear guidelines and auditing techniques to ensure that legislative offices are not using information such as a voter's history of past primary participation and predictions of voters' religion and race to determine whether or how to offer a voter assistance.

I offered two additional recommendations. First, given that public records are both important to campaign strategy and are generated by politicians who are well aware of the value of the data to their campaigns, I suggested that interest groups and the media ought to do a better job scrutinizing legislative action in this policy domain. The connection between the collection of personal data and the political incentives of elected leaders is easily overlooked, and the seemingly mundane local laws that call for the collection of more personal data generally go unnoticed. The public would benefit from greater attention to these laws when they are debated in legislative chambers.

Second, I suggested a policy by which voters can obtain records of their profiles as they are listed in the databases maintained by the major political parties and vendors. Similar to the benefits of credit report disclosure laws, this policy would enable the public to understand how taxpayer-funded public records are being used by political organizations to interact personally with them. This disclosure is especially important if databases of individual-level public records continue to be used, as they are now, in facilitating constituent services in official offices. If a system of disclosure could allow voters to interact with campaign records, this system could also allow parties to gain more information about the electorate that would help the parties achieve their goal of forming clearer perceptions of the political dispositions of the public. But it would do so at the discretion of individual voters.

There are a number of clear next steps in this research agenda. The first is to investigate in greater detail how congressional offices are using the same databases I study here to perform their constituent services duties. In the process of writing this book about direct voter contact, I discovered that the same databases used to facilitate campaign targeting are used in similar ways by congressional offices to interact with voters who have contacted their representatives. I have discussed this phenomenon in general terms. But much more can be done to study how offices are using these data and what effects they are having on representation.

Second, this book focused attention on the more prominent perceptions that campaigns develop about voters: perceptions about partisanship, race, and persuadability. In a more limited way, I have discussed how campaigns exploit open record laws to learn which voters are hunters, fishers, teachers, doctors, nurses, farmers, and members of other groups that are publicly listed on account of their needing licenses from governmental agencies. Just as the availability of party registration and racial registration affects strategic choices of campaigns, the availability of these databases of licensees should also affect the way these key constituencies are engaged by campaigns. Thus, a second extension to this book would be to test parallel hypotheses for these publicly listed subpopulations.

A third extension to this research agenda is to connect this study of campaign strategy with future studies of campaign effectiveness. Several new hypotheses arise about the circumstances under which direct contacting strategies will affect the behavior of targeted voters. For example, we know that campaigns often must use geographic data and model-based estimates to perceive a voter's likely party affiliation or racial identity. One can imagine field experiments that transmit messages geared toward partisans or racial minorities, utilizing the various perceptions that campaigns use to estimate these populations across different data environments. One could then measure the effectiveness of different perceptions and ask voters whether they actually identify with the targeted group so that researchers could determine how misperceived voters react to campaign messages. Such a study of campaign effectiveness would help further explain the consequences of the Perceived Voter Model for behavioral outcomes among the mass public.

Finally, I hope that this book will inspire future political science research to study elite behavior with a focus on investigating elite perceptions. Political elites are no longer making strategic decisions based on gut feelings and intuitions; they are looking at quantitative data to inform their decisions. There is much we can learn if we can access their data. This book was inspired by the idea that to study elite decision making, scholars need not confine themselves to investigating downstream, observable consequences of decisions. By partnering with elite organizations, we can study the informational inputs that lead to elite decisions. Scholars should continue to partner with organizations that manage data used by elite actors so that we can gain a better understanding of how politicians learn about and engage with voters based on the information at their disposal.

# Appendices

To consider in more detail how elite perceptions might affect resource allocation to geographic- or individual-level targeting, consider a refinement on Kramer's (1966) pioneering model of canvassing (see also Imai and Strauss, 2009). I briefly reconstruct Kramer's model and advance it by introducing a data-quality parameter. Assume that a Democratic campaign wants to maximize its vote plurality in a two-party race. In each jurisdiction, the campaign must decide whether to blindly target the entire electorate or selectively target its likely supporters. In either case, the campaign's message only encourages voting; the message does not persuade. In each jurisdiction, let:

$N_R$ equal the number of eligible registered voters in the population,

$P_V$ equal the proportion of registrants who will vote without any encouragement,

$\theta$ equal the proportion of registrants who support the Democratic candidate,

and $1 - \theta$ equal the proportion of registrants who support the Republican candidate.

The propensity to vote is assumed to be independent of partisanship. Following Kramer's model, the expected Democratic plurality without any interference by campaigns is

$$(\theta - (1 - \theta))P_V N_R$$
$$= (2\theta - 1)P_V N_R. \qquad (A.1)$$

In a blind canvass, the entire jurisdiction is targeted. Turnout increases because some people who would not have voted are encouraged to do so by the campaign. Given this canvassing strategy, the expected Democratic plurality becomes:

$$(2\theta - 1)(P_V + \alpha(1 - P_V))N_R, \tag{A.2}$$

where $\alpha$ represents the effectiveness of the campaign. If a campaign pursues a blind canvass, turnout increases by the fraction $\alpha$ of people who would not have voted without a reminder.

Kramer argues that a political campaign can identify its partisan supporters at the individual level. Just as the campaign can estimate $\theta$ from a poll or past election result, the campaign can find all of the Democratic supporters and contact only these voters. Under this assumption, Kramer generates an expected plurality equation as:

$$(P_V + \alpha(1 - P_V))\theta N_R - P_V(1 - \theta)N_R$$
$$= \alpha(1 - P_V)\theta N_R + (2\theta - 1)P_V N_R. \tag{A.3}$$

In this formulation, the voters consist of Democratic and Republican partisans who would have voted in absence of the canvass, plus some fraction of Democratic partisans who would not have voted. The key difference between this model and the blind canvass model is that in the blind model some Republican partisans were mobilized by the Democratic campaign.

One implication of the Perceived Voter Model is that at the individual level, a campaign cannot mobilize Democrats, Republicans, or people possessing any other relevant trait. They can only mobilize people whom they predict possess those traits. Thus, consider an alternative specification. Suppose that some fraction, $p$, of voters who look like Democrats are actually Democrats but $1 - p$ are actually Republicans. For simplicity, assume that the quality of prediction is the same for Republicans (i.e., $p$ voters who look like Republicans are actually Republicans and $1 - p$ are actually Democrats). In reality, a campaign may be better at predicting some groups than others.

Note that Kramer includes an extension to his own model that incorporates defection, in that some voters do not vote how they were predicted by the campaign. But in Kramer's model, defection happens at the same rate in geographic and individual targeting. Here, I am showing that since the data at the root of targeting may be very different at the geographic and individual levels (e.g., precinct returns used at the geographic level; party registration at the individual level), the quality of data will likely be very different at these levels. Here, for the sake of clarity, I assume that the geographic-level predictions are accurate and the individual-level predictions are noisy.

If a Democratic campaign chooses to target selectively under the assumption that the individual-level estimate is noisy, it must account for the fact that it will leave out Democrats who appear as Republicans and will accidentally target Republicans who appear as Democrats. Thus, the expected Democratic plurality can more realistically be summarized as

$$[(P_V + \alpha(1 - P_V))(p\theta - (1 - p)(1 - \theta)) + P_V((1 - p)\theta - p(1 - \theta))]N_R,$$

which simplifies to

$$[P_V(2\theta - 1) + \alpha(1 - P_V)(\theta + p - 1)]N_R. \qquad (A.4)$$

This equation accounts for the extent to which false-positives (Republicans who appear as Democrats) and false-negatives (Democrats who appear as Republicans) are engaged by campaigns. Notice a couple of key properties of Equation A.4. First, when the campaign is able to perfectly predict Democrats and Republicans (i.e., when $p = 1$), Equation A.4 becomes identical to Equation A.3. Second, when the probability of a true-positive ($p$) is exactly the same as the probability that a voter is a Democratic supporter ($\theta$), Equation A.4 becomes equal to Equation A.2, the representation of a blind canvass.

It is now possible to examine how these models would lead to different campaign strategies. Consider how a campaign might allocate its resources to the sixteen imaginary states listed in Table A.1 on the basis of the models just developed. In this election, states 1–4 are heavily Democratic, states 5–8 lean Democratic, states 9–12 are toss-ups, and states 13–16 lean Republican. Furthermore, the states take one of four values for $p$: in some places the prediction of a voter's partisan leanings is just a little better than 50/50; in other places it is almost always correct. To focus just on the relationship between $\theta$ and $p$, all other parameters are kept constant. $P_V$ is set to 0.75, $N_R$ is set to 1000, and $\alpha$ is set to 0.4. I find the maximum gain in plurality for blind canvassing, Kramer's selective canvassing model, and my extension to Kramer's model of selective canvassing, calculated using the equations just derived by subtracting the plurality under no canvassing from the plurality expected from canvassing every relevant voter in each state.

There are three key implications from the results in Table A.1. (1) In every state under Kramer's selective canvassing model, the campaign

TABLE A.1 *The Maximum Expected Vote Gain in States That Vary in the Accuracy of Campaign Perceptions*

| | | | | Votes Added to Plurality by Canvassing | | |
|---|---|---|---|---|---|---|
| State | $\theta$ | $p$ | Plurality with No Canvass | Blind Canvass | Selective Canvass (Kramer) | Selective Canvass (with uncertainty) |
| 1 | 0.9 | 0.95 | 600 | 80 | 90 | 85 |
| 2 | 0.9 | 0.85 | 600 | 80 | 90 | 75 |
| 3 | 0.9 | 0.65 | 600 | 80 | 90 | 55 |
| 4 | 0.9 | 0.55 | 600 | 80 | 90 | 45 |
| 5 | 0.7 | 0.95 | 300 | 40 | 70 | 65 |
| 6 | 0.7 | 0.85 | 300 | 40 | 70 | 55 |
| 7 | 0.7 | 0.65 | 300 | 40 | 70 | 35 |
| 8 | 0.7 | 0.55 | 300 | 40 | 70 | 25 |
| 9 | 0.5 | 0.95 | 0 | 0 | 50 | 45 |
| 10 | 0.5 | 0.85 | 0 | 0 | 50 | 35 |
| 11 | 0.5 | 0.65 | 0 | 0 | 50 | 15 |
| 12 | 0.5 | 0.55 | 0 | 0 | 50 | 5 |
| 13 | 0.3 | 0.95 | −300 | −40 | 30 | 25 |
| 14 | 0.3 | 0.85 | −300 | −40 | 30 | 15 |
| 15 | 0.3 | 0.65 | −300 | −40 | 30 | −5 |
| 16 | 0.3 | 0.55 | −300 | −40 | 30 | −15 |

*Note:* All sixteen hypothetical states are assumed to have the same number of registered citizens ($N_R = 1000$) and the same baseline voting rate ($P_V = 0.75$). Campaigns are assumed to be equally effective in all states ($\alpha = 0.4$). Varying only the rate of Democratic support ($\theta$) and the rate of predicting which voters are Democratic ($p$) affects the optimal mobilization strategy for the Democratic campaign.

gains more votes than it would by canvassing blindly; in my extension, this is not the case. When $p < \theta$, blind canvassing is preferable. While it would take a poor predictive model for $p$ to be less than $\theta$ in reality, it is quite realistic for $p$ to be not all that much larger than $\theta$. In such cases, targeted canvassing will rarely be worthwhile. (2) Kramer's insight is that selective canvassing is most useful in places where the campaign has fewest supporters. My extension makes clear that selective canvassing will provide the most benefit in places where the campaign has the fewest supporters *and* the data is most predictive. (3) Under the Kramer model, with unlimited resources and perfect data, all states could be targeted in some fashion and reap positive results. However, once one takes the data quality into account, it is clear that in the two states with the fewest Democrats and the worst data, the Democratic campaign must abandon its supporters or risk losing votes.

## APPENDIX B: HISTORICAL ALABAMA VOTER REGISTRATION APPLICATION

### APPLICATION FOR REGISTRATION, QUESTIONNAIRE AND OATHS

**PART I**

(This is to be filled in by a member of the Board of Registrars or a duly authorized clerk of the board. If applicant is a married woman, she must state given name by which she is known, maiden surname, and married surname, which shall be recorded as her full name.)

Full Name: ................................................................................................................................................................
         Last                                         First                          Middle

Date of Birth: ............................................................................ Sex ......................................... Race ..................

Residence Address: ...................................................................................................................................................

Mailing Address: .......................................................................................................................................................

Voting Place: Precinct ............................................... Ward .................................... District ...............................

Length of Residence: In State ............................................... County ...................................................................

      Precinct, ward or district .............................................................................................................................

Are you a member of the Armed Forces? ................................................................................................................

Are you the wife of a member of the Armed Forces? ............................................................................................

Are you a college student? ........................ If so, where ...................................................................................

Have you ever been registered to vote in any other state or in any other county in Alabama?............. If so, when and in

    what state and county and, if in Alabama, at what place did you vote in such county?....................................

........................................................................................................................................................................

Highest grade, 1 to 12, completed ........................ Where ...............................................................................

Years college completed ........................................ Where ...............................................................................

**PART II**

(To be filled in by the applicant in the presence of the Board of Registrars without assistance.)

I, ............................................................................, do hereby apply to the Board of Registrars of ..........................

County, State of Alabama, to register as an elector under the Constitution and laws of the State of Alabama and do here-
with submit my answers to the interrogatories propounded to me by the board.

........................................................................................
(Signature of Applicant)

1. Are you a citizen of the United States? .................................................................................................................

2. Where were you born? .........................................................................................................................................

3. If you are a naturalized citizen, give number appearing on your naturalization papers and date of issuance ...............

........................................................................................................................................................................

4. Have you ever been married? .............. If so, give the name, residence and place of birth of your husband or wife ...........

........................................................................................................................................................................

    Are you divorced? ..................................................................................................................................................

FIGURE B.1 Reproduction of February 1964 Voter Registration Application from Alabama, Page 1.

*Source:* Image provided courtesy of Professor Brian K. Landsberg.

5. List the places you have lived the past five years, giving town or county and state ...... ...

... ... ...................... ....... .... .... ...

6. Have you ever been known by any name other than the one appearing on this application?... ... If so, state what name

..... .... ...

7. Are you employed?............If so, state by whom. (If you are self-employed, state this.)...............

... ... ... ....................... ......

8. Give the address of your present place of employment ........................

9. If, in the past five years, you have been employed by an employer other than your present employer, give name of all employers and cities and states in which you worked .... ... ..............................

... ... ... ....................

............. .............. .... .... ... ...

10. Has your name ever been stricken for any reason from any list of persons registered to vote?......... If so, where, when, and why?......

........................

11. Have you previously applied for and been denied registration as a voter?............. If so, when and where?.......

.......................

12. Have you ever served in the Armed Forces?.........................If so, give dates, branch of service, and serial number

............................

13. Have you ever been dishonorably discharged from military service?.................................

14. Have you ever been declared legally insane?.................If so, give details...............

.......................

15. Give names and addresses of two persons who know you and can verify the statements made above by you relative to your residence in this state, county and precinct, ward or district........................

........................

16. Have you ever seen a copy of this registration application form before receiving this copy today?...........If so, when and where? ....

17. Have you ever been convicted of any offense or paid any fine for violation of the law?........... (Yes or No) If so, give the following information concerning each fine or conviction; charge, in what court tried, fine imposed, sentence, and, if paroled, state when, and if pardoned, state when. (If fine is for traffic violation only, you need write below only the words "traffic violation only.")........................

........................

........................

(Remainder of this form is to be filled out only as directed by an individual member of the Board of Registrars.)

**PART III**

Part III of this questionnaire shall consist of one of the forms which are Insert Part III as herein below set out. The insert shall be fastened to the questionnaire. The questions set out on the insert shall be answered according to the instructions therein set out. Each applicant shall demonstrate ability to read and write as required by the Constitution of Alabama, as amended, and no person shall be considered to have completed this application, nor shall the name of any applicant be entered upon the list of registered voters of any county until after such Inserted Part III of the questionnaire has been satisfactorily completed and signed by the applicant.

FIGURE B.2 Reproduction of February 1964 Voter Registration Application from Alabama, Page 2.

*Source:* Image provided courtesy of Professor Brian K. Landsberg.

APPENDIX C: MATCHING TECHNIQUE ASSESSING THE EFFECT
OF RACIAL IDENTIFICATION ON TURNOUT

To balance key covariates for the analysis in Table 6.3, I use coarsened exact matching (Blackwell et al., 2009). The motivation for this methodological strategy is to find individuals who did and did not register with their race but who are otherwise as similar as possible. The method is comparable to estimating a fully interacted regression model, but is easier to interpret than such a model, which would require the estimation of hundreds of independent variable coefficients.

As reviewed in Chapter 6, voters listed without their races live in slightly higher socio-economic-status neighborhoods than voters listed with their races. However the relationship reverses and strengthens when we restrict the analysis of unlisted races to voters whose race can be confidently predicted by a model. The reason why some voters' races can be predicted with a high degree of confidence is that they live in more racially homogenous areas and their names are more unique to their race. Past research has found that racially distinct names are especially prevalent among the lower class (Fryer Jr. and Levitt, 2007). Thus, demographic differences between the groups emerge, and so it is necessary to match on these characteristics in statistical modeling. Ideally, it would be possible to balance not only on geographic measures of income and education but on individual-level measures as well. Since the data are from public records rather than survey responses, such information is not available.

Before matching, variables are coarsened into theoretically sensible groups. The income and education measures are divided into quintiles. The percentage black measure is divided into census block groups that are more than 75 percent black, 50–75 percent black, 25–50 percent black, and less than 25 percent black. In testing the effect of racial identification for whites, percentage white is used. That variable is coarsened into just three categories rather than four: greater than 75 percent white, 50–75 percent white, and less than 50 percent white. Age is coarsened into seven categories: 18–21-year-olds, 22–25-year-olds, 26–29-year-olds, 30–39-year-olds, 40–49-year-olds, 50–59-year-olds, and those over 60.[1] Registration year is divided into three categories: those who registered between 2005 and 2008, those who registered between 2001 and 2004, and those who registered before 2000. Because there are some key differences across states, I match on state of residence. The party registration variables are only relevant to the three states that allow for party registration. For black voters, a dummy variable separates registered

TABLE C.1 *Matching on Covariates for Registrants Listed as Black on the Voter File and Registrants Who Are Predicted with High Confidence as Being Black, But Whose Race Is Not Listed on the Public Record*

| | Before Matching | | After Matching | |
|---|---|---|---|---|
| | Predict. Black | Voter File Black | Predict. Black | Voter File Black |
| *Voter File Variables* | | | | |
| Pct. Female | 58 | 59 | 64 | 64 |
| | (6,981) | (144,168) | (3,102) | (9,428) |
| Ave. Age | 40 | 44 | 46 | 46 |
| | (6,068) | (140,510) | (2,927) | (8,896) |
| Ave. Reg. Year | 2000 | 1997 | 1996 | 1995 |
| | (7,502) | (144,210) | (3,104) | (9,433) |
| Pct. Democrat | 53 | 84 | 89 | 89 |
| | (1,181) | (70,522) | (636) | (2,765) |
| *Behavioral Variables (%)* | | | | |
| Mail Responsive | 49 | 49 | 55 | 56 |
| | (5,483) | (124,392) | (2,719) | (8,263) |
| Mag. Subscriber | 21 | 24 | 25 | 28 |
| | (5,483) | (124,392) | (2,719) | (8,263) |
| Mail Orderer | 20 | 19 | 20 | 20 |
| | (5,483) | (124,392) | (2,719) | (8,263) |
| Summary Measure | 54 | 54 | 61 | 61 |
| | (5,483) | (124,392) | (2,719) | (8,263) |
| *Census Variables* | | | | |
| Med. HH Income | $27K | $35K | $33K | $34K |
| | (7,525) | (144,352) | (3,105) | (9,436) |
| Pct. w/ B.A. | 14 | 18 | 17 | 17 |
| | (7,520) | (143,186) | (3,105) | (9,436) |
| Pct. Black | 74 | 50 | 73 | 72 |
| | (7,526) | (144,352) | (3,105) | (9,436) |

*Note:* Observations are in parentheses. Census variables are measured at the level of block-group. The behavioral summary measure is an indicator variable that equals 1 if a respondent has a positive value for at least one of the three behavioral items. The party registration variable is only applicable to the three states with party registration (FL, LA, NC). Note that in addition to the variables listed in this table, the treatment and control groups are also matched on state of residence.

Democrats from those not registered as Democrats. For whites, two dummy variables are used: one for Democrats and one for Republicans. This coding decision reflects the fact that so few black voters register as Republicans.

The three "form-filler-outer" variables in the Catalist database are combined into a summary measure, which is matched upon. The first

TABLE C.2 *Matching on Covariates for Registrants Listed as White on the Voter File and Registrants Who Are Predicted with High Confidence as Being White, But Whose Race Is Not Listed on the Public Record*

| | Before Matching | | After Matching | |
| --- | --- | --- | --- | --- |
| | Predict. White | Voter File White | Predict. White | Voter File White |
| *Voter File Variables* | | | | |
| Pct. Female | 51 | 53 | 54 | 54 |
| | (26,898) | (465,723) | (24,588) | (133,565) |
| Ave. Age | 45 | 50 | 54 | 54 |
| | (26,893) | (465,723) | (24,424) | (132,677) |
| Ave. Reg. Year | 2000 | 1995 | 1997 | 1994 |
| | (31,863) | (469,528) | (24,587) | (133,558) |
| Pct. Democrat | 27 | 42 | 31 | 31 |
| | (4,681) | (277,973) | (11,714) | (63,643) |
| Pct. Republican | 28 | 42 | 48 | 48 |
| | (4,681) | (277,973) | (11,714) | (63,643) |
| *Behavioral Variables (%)* | | | | |
| Mail Responsive | 68 | 70 | 79 | 80 |
| | (27,660) | (437,463) | (23,799) | (129,281) |
| Mag. Subscriber | 39 | 44 | 52 | 53 |
| | (27,660) | (437,463) | (23,799) | (129,281) |
| Mail Orderer | 32 | 32 | 37 | 37 |
| | (27,660) | (437,463) | (23,799) | (129,281) |
| Summary Measure | 73 | 75 | 86 | 86 |
| | (27,660) | (437,463) | (23,799) | (129,281) |
| *Census Variables* | | | | |
| Med. HH Income | $46K | $46K | $53K | $53K |
| | (31,893) | (469,876) | (24,588) | (133,567) |
| Pct. w/ B.A. | 25 | 25 | 29 | 29 |
| | (31,837) | (465,854) | (24,566) | (133,447) |
| Pct. White | 88 | 81 | 89 | 89 |
| | (31,893) | (469,876) | (24,588) | (133,567) |

*Note:* Observations are in parentheses. Census variables are measured at the level of block-group. The behavioral summary measure is an indicator variable that equals 1 if a respondent has a positive value for at least one of the three behavioral items. The party registration variable is only applicable to the three states with party registration (FL, LA, NC). Note that in addition to the variables listed in this table, the treatment and control groups are also matched on state of residence.

variable, *mail responsiveness*, equals one if the household of the voter has ever responded to a commercial mail advertisement. The second variable equals one if the household subscribes to magazines or periodicals. The third variable equals one if there is evidence that the household has made mail order purchases in the last four years. These measures are combined into a 0–1 variable, where 1 implies a positive value for one or more of the component variables. The balance on all uncoarsened variables before and after matching is reported in Tables C.1 and C.2, for black voters and white voters, respectively.

### APPENDIX D: MEASUREMENT NOTES FROM CHAPTER 7

In utilizing the 2008 Cooperative Congressional Election Study (Ansolabehere, 2009), unregistered respondents as well as respondents who were not identified in the Catalist database are excluded. Also excluded are noncitizens and all residents of Virginia. At the time of the survey validation, Virginia had a rule limiting vote history data only to active campaigns in the state. Because vote history plays a significant role in campaign targeting, respondents from Virginia must be excluded. Survey weights are used in all analyses of the CCES.

General election vote history data used in the construction of target groups include records of participation in the 2000, 2002, 2004, and 2006 general elections. In Figure 7.1, in which the entire Catalist 1% sample is used rather than just data matched into the survey, additional general elections are employed in the construction of the target measures, such as odd-year elections. Data on these additional elections, however, were not made available for the survey respondents.

*Construction of Cross-Pressure Measures.* Twelve issue measures are utilized in assessing whether an independent or partisan is cross-pressured: (1) CC309, preference to cut domestic spending, cut military spending, or raise taxes (Republican position: cut domestic spending); (2) CC310, abortion opinion (Republican position: support restrictions on abortion/outlaw abortion); (3) CC310, trade-off between environmental protection and jobs (Republican position: jobs more important); (4) CC312, social security privatization (Republican position: support privatization); (5) CC313, affirmative action (Republican position: oppose affirmative action); (6) CC316a, legislation to withdraw troops from Iraq (Republican position: oppose); (7) CC316b, legislation to increase minimum wage (Republican position: oppose); (8) CC316c, legislation to allow stem cell research (Republican position: oppose); (9) CC316d, legislation to allow spy agencies to eavesdrop on overseas terrorist suspects without a court order (Republican position: support); (10) CC316e, legislation to fund health insurance program for poor children (Republican position: oppose); (11) CC316f, constitutional amendment to ban gay marriage (Republican position: support); (12) CC316g, legislation for federal assistance to homeowners facing foreclosure (Republican position: oppose). Note that all of these issue positions are highly correlated with partisan identification. Other issue positions that were asked of respondents but were not highly correlated with partisanship (e.g., support for NAFTA; support for the bank bailout) were not included in the cross-pressure measures.

# Notes

## I INTRODUCTION

1. Catalist, the main political data vendor I study in this book, is also an official vendor to congressional offices for constituent services data. In Chapter 9, I describe how Catalist and other approved congressional data vendors facilitate targeting strategies in constituent services.
2. In a 2012 voting rights case, *Texas v. Holder*, the U.S. Department of Justice hired Catalist to predict the races of Texas voters who were believed not to have valid forms of identification and thus would be impacted by a voter identification requirement. See Representative Lamar Smith, Letter to Attorney General Eric H. Holder, Jr. July 5, 2012, http://judiciary.house.gov/news/pdfs/Smith%20to%20Holder%207%205%2012.pdf, retrieved October 1, 2013. Disclosure: I served as a consultant in this case.
3. See Sasha Issenberg, "How President Obama's Campaign used Big Data to Rally Individual Voters," *MIT Technology Review*, December 19, 2012.
4. See Steven Levy, "In Every Voter, A 'Microtarget,'" *Washington Post*, page D01, April 23, 2008; Jon Gertner, "The Very, Very Personal Is the Political," *New York Times Magazine*, February 15, 2004; Peter Wallsten and Tom Hamburger, "The GOP Knows You Don't Like Anchovies," *Los Angeles Times*, June 25, 2006; Allison Brennan, "How Campaigns Know You Better Than You Know Yourself," CNN, November 5, 2012; Kate Hinman, "'Microtargeting' Lets Pols Turn Data into Votes,'" ABC Nightline, October 22, 2012.
5. These two sides are summarized in Steven Levy, "In Every Voter, A 'Microtarget,'" *Washington Post*, April 23, 2008, page D01. They are also summarized in Hillygus and Shields (2008).

## 2  THE PERCEIVED VOTER MODEL

1. John Sides, "What Matters Between Now and the Election," www
.themonkeycage.org, July 11, 2012.
2. See, for example, the work done by the Analyst Institute, www
.analyistinstitute.org.
3. Note that there is a separate class of information theories that focus on
the strategic interaction among multiple players. For example, a politician's
decision about a policy position might be affected by uncertainty about an
opponent's decision. See Shepsle (1972); Ferejohn and Noll (1978); Glazer
(1990); Snyder Jr. and Ting (2002); Canes-Wrone and Shotts (2007); Tomz
and Van Houweling (2009). The Perceived Voter Model is best characterized
as a single-player game. Opposing campaigns generally know which types of
voters the other campaign would like to mobilize or persuade. What is at
issue is that both campaigns may have trouble perceiving which voters bear
the characteristics that are known to correlate with propensities to turn out,
be persuadable, or support one candidate over the other.
4. See also Abramson and Claggett (2001) and Hanmer (2009).
5. Quoted in Hillygus and Shields (2008).
6. See Hill and Dunbar (2003) on the size of social networks.
7. There is a useful analogy for a campaign's use of shortcuts in the field of
economics. Economists studying hiring decisions by firms have asked whether
workers are hired and compensated based on their actual skills or based on
shortcuts that are signals of skill, like educational attainment. In other words,
who gets hired: a worker with an impressive résumé but a poor skill-set or a
talented worker with an unimpressive résumé? This literature has found that
at the start of a career, wages are more closely tied with superficial shortcuts
that appear on résumés. However, as workers spend time in the workforce,
their wages become increasingly correlated with measures of actual ability.
Unlike national parties and campaigns that have trouble learning the true
dispositions of voters over time, employers are in a smaller-scale setting,
and they develop more intimate knowledge of their workers. See Farber and
Gibbons (1996); Altonji and Pierret (November 1997); Lange and Topel
(2006); Lange (2007).

## 3  THE POLICY ROOTS OF ELITE PERCEPTIONS

1. See DeCanio (2000) on public ignorance as a barrier to oversight of democratic institutions.
2. *The Alton Telegraph*, Page 1, October 16, 1868.
3. *The World*, Page 4, October 12, 1892.
4. The notion that the parties found value in the voter registration system, even
while the system was being promoted by anti-party reformers, bears similarity
to Ware's (2002) historical analysis of the direct primary. In that study, Ware
finds that political parties were not particularly strong opponents of the direct
primary, even though they had been portrayed that way.

5. *The World*, October 31, 1892.

6. On early political uses of voter databases, see also Duverger (1954).

7. An interesting aside: decades prior to experimental research on social pressure and voting (e.g., Gerber, Green, and Larimer, 2008; Mann, 2010), Harris noticed that the public printing and posting of registration lists may have increased turnout because neighbors wanted to demonstrate to others that they were participating. Reflecting on a practice in Milwaukee in which twenty-five lists of voters were posted in each precinct, Harris writes: "People are curious about their neighbors and scrutinize the list to satisfy their curiosity... quite probably that the posting of registration lists of voters has some effect in encouraging registration" (p. 279).

8. Introduction of Senate Bill 8, Ohio State Senate, December 9, 2009, Senator Bill Seitz (R-Cincinnati), transcribed from video from www.ohiochannel .org/MediaLibrary/Media.aspx?fileId=123587\&startTime=235\ &autoStart=True

9. Nancy Vogel, "Bill to Seek Voters' Racial Data Signed," *Los Angeles Times*, September 18, 2003.

10. Mark Ridley-Thomas, qtd. in Committee hearing on AB 587, Assembly Committee on Elections, Redistricting, and Constitutional Amendments, John Longville (chair), California State Assembly, April 22, 2003.

11. Rebecca Edwards, Floor Statement regarding H.B. 304, Utah House of Representatives, January 26, 2012, transcribed from video at www.le.state.ut.us/ asp/audio/FloorPlayer.asp?sess=2012GS\&house=H\&bill=HB0304\ &ID=73101

12. Blog of Becky Edwards, March 13, 2012, accessed November 5, 2012, www .utahbecky.com/blog/2012/03/my-bills-where-did-they-end-up/

13. Billy Hasterman, "Bill Would Protect Birth Dates on Voter Info," *Daily Herald*, February 14, 2012.

14. Committee Reports on HB 1139, State of New Hampshire House Record, Second Year of the 160th General Court, March 12, 2008, www.gencourt .state.nh.us/house/caljourns/journals/2008/houjou2008_24.html

15. Calvin Trillin, "Onward and Upward with the Arts: You Can't Wear Out a List," *The New Yorker*, September 24, 1966. I thank David Mayhew for referring this article to me.

16. "Business Uses of Census Data and Nielsen Company Capabilities," The Nielsen Company, 2010.

17. Interview with the author, June 1, 2011.

18. Issenberg (2012) provides a brief history of direct marketing applications to political campaigns.

19. This story was told to me by Bob Blaemire in an interview.

20. On the relationship between election officials and political parties, see also Persily (2001).

21. www.fec.gov/hava/law_ext.txt

22. See "The Help America Vote Act at 5," www.electionline.org, Pew Center on the States, November 29, 2007.

## 4   CAMPAIGN PERCEPTIONS QUANTIFIED

1. Daniel Tynan, "GOP Voter Vault Shipped Overseas," *PCWorld*, September 24, 2004.
2. Lev Grossman, "Campaign '04: Technology: What Your Party Knows About You," *Time Magazine*, October 18, 2004.
3. See Eliana Johnson, "The GOP's Data Surge," POLITICO, January 16, 2014.
4. The figure appears to show a rather high predicted turnout rate for a midterm election year. This is attributable to the relatively small group of voters who are almost sure to vote being concentrated in just a few cells while most voters are spread thin. To give some perspective, only 17% of registrants have a turnout score over 90 (out of a 100) and 58% of registrants have a score over 50.
5. Plotting voters in this way demonstrates the shortcomings of one-dimensional political science models of mobilization. Trying to back out a campaign strategy from a regression model in which self-reported contact is the dependent variable and no interaction is allowed between turnout propensity and partisanship will clearly lead to faulty inferences. The work on contingent mobilization by Arceneaux and Nickerson (2009) begins to confront this problem.
6. For more information on the Catalist heatmap analysis, see Nickerson and Rogers (2014).
7. Formerly registered voters are either individuals who Catalist had a record of but who moved from their registration address and did not yet reregister at their new address, or they are individuals who have been purged from the rolls since Catalist began tracking voters.

## 5   THE PERCEIVED PARTISAN

1. These states are AZ, CA, CO, IA, MA, MD, ME, NC, NH, NJ, NM, NV, NY, OR, PA, RI, and WV.
2. These states are AK, CT, DC, DE, FL, KS, KY, LA, NE, OK, SD, UT, and WY.
3. These states are AR, GA, OH, IL, IN, MS, SC, TN, TX, VA, and WA.
4. These states are AL, HI, ID, MI, MN, MO, MT, ND, VT, and WI.
5. Prior to the change in the Michigan law, the primary data was available to political parties, just not to private data vendors or members of the public. See *Practical Political Consulting v. Secretary of State*, Docket No. 291176, Michigan Court of Appeals, 2010, March 9.
6. See "Primary Runoffs," National Conference of State Legislatures, August 16, 2012, www.ncsl.org/legislatures\-elections/elections/primary-runoffs.aspx
7. See, e.g., Hanmer (2009).
8. Author's interview with Sean Gilliland, April 7, 2010.
9. I replicated Figure 5.12 with a preliminary version of the 2012 Cooperative Congressional Election Study, with validated turnout. In this dataset, the

pattern from 2008 was not apparent; party registration swing states were not different from non–party registration swing states. At the time of this writing, it is not clear whether the final version of the 2012 CCES will reveal the same pattern.

## 6 THE PUBLIC CODE OF RACIALIZED ELECTIONEERING

1. A copy of a 1922 Alabama registration application was transmitted to me by law professor Brian Landsberg, which he had collected from evidence presented in court cases that led up to the passage of the VRA.
2. This note on Louisiana comes courtesy of election historian Morgan Kousser.
3. It should be noted that I have asked dozens of legal experts, historians, and political scientists about the origins of these laws. While I can exclude the VRA and white primaries as the reasons, it is indeed a mystery to me why these states but not others collect race data.
4. See Fraga (2012) on race-based electoral coalitions.
5. This claim, it should be noted, comes from data from the 1990s, but to my knowledge, no newer, analogous data is available. About 60–75% of blacks claim in surveys that they attend church regularly (Verba, Schlozman, and Brady, 1995; Tate, 1996), and that number is surely inflated due to misreporting. More importantly, only 35% of black churchgoers report that they have heard any announcements or discussions in church about an upcoming presidential race (Calhoun-Brown, 1996). Calhoun-Brown finds that all effects of church mobilization on participation are concentrated among this 35% of churchgoers who attend a politicized church. As a back-of-the-envelope calculation, assuming (charitably) that 75% of blacks attend church regularly, but of these only 35% attend a politicized church, church-based mobilization strategies may be reaching at most 26% of blacks.
6. This problem is not only evident to campaign strategists but also to social scientists who have used name-matching techniques themselves to identify the race of voters for research purposes. Such studies tend to focus on the behavior of Latinos and Asians because of the difficulty of distinguishing black from white names (Barreto, Segura, and Woods, 2004; Tam Cho, 2003).
7. Because most falsely predicted black voters are white and most falsely predicted white voters are black, and because I expect to find an effect of racial registration on turnout for both racial groups, I need not worry that a small portion of the racial predictions is inaccurate.
8. In Table 6.3, I can focus on the simple difference of means between these two groups because the matching procedure is analogous to a fully interacted regression model with all the covariates just described and without unrealistic linearity assumptions. As a robustness check, I can estimate a logistic regression model on the matched dataset, while incorporating the uncoarsened independent variables as controls. There is a serious drawback to running this test, however. Neither voting nor campaign targeting are linear functions of independent variables such as age or registration date. Nevertheless,

running this model produces similar results as in Table 6.3, except for that in two of the six racial-group/election-year estimates, the effect is not statistically significant.

## 7  PERSUADABLE VOTERS IN THE EYES OF THE PERSUADERS

1. See, for example, work done by the Analyst Institute.
2. For a conceptualization of swing voters based on voters' positions relative to candidates' positions in a spatial model, consult Hill (2010).
3. See Ghitza (2009); Aida and Rogers (2014) on the predictive value of vote history.
4. The leaked Catalist memo, dated Summer 2009, was titled, "Aggregate Activities of Progressive Organizations in 2008: Compilation from Catalist Subscribers." It is discussed online by Marc Ambinder, "Exclusive: How Democrats Won the Data War in 2008," *The Atlantic*, October 5, 2009, www.theatlantic.com/politics/archive/2009/10/exclusive-how-democrats-won-the-data-war-in-2008/27647/, and by Nancy Scola, "The Fine Art of Data Husbandry: A Look at What Catalist Is Teaching Democrats," *Tech President*, October 6, 2009, http://techpresident.com/blog-entry/fine-art-data-husbandry-look-what-catalist-teaching-democrats. Both websites linked to the full text of the document, but the document has since been removed.
5. See New Organizing Institute, "An Organizer's Guide: What Is GOTV?" 2010, http://neworganizing.com/wp-content/uploads/2010/10/What-is-GOTV-1.pdf.
6. See also Alvarez, Hopkins, and Sinclair (2010) on the mobilization of low-turnout voters. It is worth emphasizing that the goal here is to subset the electorate into typical persuasion and GOTV target universes, not to identify groups that will be most responsive to persuasion and GOTV messages. This distinction is important in light of work by Arceneaux and Nickerson (2009) on contingent mobilization. Arceneaux and Nickerson generate turnout propensity scores for voters and show that in a series of field experiments the effect of turnout messages on voters was contingent on turnout propensity and on campaign intensity. In high-intensity campaigns, like the 2008 presidential election, they show that it is the lowest propensity types of voters who are most responsive to appeals. This finding, however, does not change the fact that campaigns relying on conventional strategic approaches may still gear GOTV campaigns to those who seem as if they have middling turnout propensities.
7. The precinct data I am able to incorporate here comes from the 2008 presidential election. Precincts that are 65% or more Democratic (Republican) are those that gave 65% or more of their vote share to Obama (McCain). Using 2008 data is inconsistent with the simulation of a campaign working ahead of the 2008 election. Nevertheless, the precincts that are overwhelmingly partisan in one election are likely to be overwhelmingly partisan in another election, and so for the illustrative purposes of this chapter, data on 2008

precincts is a suitable proxy for precinct-level data from earlier elections. As a robustness check, I used county-level data from 2000 and 2004 presidential returns (removing voters from the persuasion universe if their county voted overwhelmingly partisan), and this had no effect on the results of the analysis.

8. See John Sides and Lynn Vavreck, "Obama's Not-So-Big Data," *Pacific Standard*, January/February 2014, and Sasha Issenberg, "How President Obama's Campaign Used Big Data to Rally Individual Voters," *MIT Technology Review*, December 19, 2012.

9. For a recent methodological discussion of this type of information measure, consult Levendusky (2011).

## 8  VOTERS PERCEIVED IN SOCIAL NETWORKS AND CONSUMER FILES

1. The lack of interest in targeting more than a few segments of voters was related to me by Hal Malchow, who has been a leader in microtargeting strategies.

2. Note that in a similar exercise, Jackman and Vavreck (2011) measure a voter's "cosmopolitanism" using behavioral questions such as whether the voter has traveled overseas, eaten at an Indian restaurant, or gone hunting. Their measure of cosmopolitanism, like the consumer variables I assess here, is highly correlated with education, income, and other basic demographic and geographic variables. However, controlling for an array of demographic and attitudinal measures, Jackman and Vavreck's measure of cosmopolitanism is correlated with candidate support. Our analyses are difficult to compare on account of different data available in Catalist's consumer records as was available in their survey and their controlling for attitudinal measures such as ideology and issue preferences, which is not possible with Catalist records.

3. Note that IDs from professional survey firms are likely to be more accurate that IDs from volunteer canvassers. The Obama campaign was particularly focused on generating IDs from professional polling firms.

4. This quote was referenced in an interview with Patrick's 2006 campaign manager and subsequent chair of the Massachusetts Democratic Party, John Walsh.

5. See Dan Rather's reporting on CBS of the Nixon campaign's use of commercial targeting data, January 18, 1972, www.youtube.com/watch?feature=player_detailpage\&v=9HPnW4EBed4\#t=3s

## 9  CONCLUSION

1. Repurposing data for political ends is often innocuous, but history has shown that administrative collections of personal data are sometimes used in damaging ways. Voter registration lists, as well as lists of organizational members, petition signers, party supporters, and political donors, collected for some purported administrative end, can be used as a tool for intimidation and

harassment (see *NAACP v. Alabama* (1958), *Brown v. Socialist Workers* (1984), and Justice Thomas's opinions in *Doe et al. v. Reed* (2010), and *Citizens United v. FEC* (2010), as well as Kousser, 1999.). And, of course, one of the most egregious examples of data misuse is the Roosevelt administration's repurposing of Census data to intern Japanese Americans in 1942. See J.R. Minkel, "Confirmed: The U.S. Census Bureau Gave Up Names of Japanese-Americans in WWII," *Scientific American*, March 30, 2007.

2. Nikita Stewart and Mike DeBonis, "Mayor Gray's 2010 Campaign Had Database of Public Housing Residents," *Washington Post*, July 22, 2012.

3. Josh Speerstra, "New Feature: Issue Fields for Audiences," Blog Post, Fireside21, February 23, 2012. www.fireside21.com/new-feature-issue-fields-for-audiences/ (accessed August 9, 2012).

4. Telephone interview with Ken Ward, Fireside21, August 23, 2012.

5. *Advisory Opinion No. 1* of the House Standards Committee, qtd. in House Ethics Manual, p. 151.

6. Mother Jones, "Full Transcript of the Mitt Romney Secret Video," September 19, 2012, www.motherjones.com/politics/2012/09/full-transcript-mitt-romney-secret-video\#47percent

7. Lois Beckett, "Want to Know If Your Neighbor Is a Democrat? The Obama Campaign Has an App for That." *ProPublica*, August 6, 2012.

8. The concern about how targeting might affect voters' judgment that is expressed in this section has a parallel in an odd law once proposed by California Assemblyman Walter Karabian. Karabian's bill, as recounted by Ferejohn and Noll (1978), would have restricted opinion polls from being publicized during election campaigns. Karabian was concerned that voters were not evaluating candidates solely on their merits but were factoring in the candidates' current popularity when making their decisions. Karabian thought this was corrosive to the electoral process.

## APPENDICES

1. The reason to have more fine-grained age cohorts among young people is that the voting behavior of young people is much more volatile and nonlinear than among those over thirty years old (Ansolabehere, Hersh, and Shepsle, 2012).

# Bibliography

2012 *Obama Campaign Legacy Report*. 2013. Technical report Obama for America.

Abramson, Paul R. and William Claggett. 2001. "Recruitment and Political Participation." *Political Research Quarterly* 54(4):905–916.

Aida, Masahiko and Todd Rogers. 2014. "Vote Self-Prediction Hardly Predicts Who Will Vote, and Is (Misleadingly) Unbiased." *American Politics Research* 42(3):503–528.

Aldrich, John H. 1995. *Why Parties? The Origin and Transformation of Political Parties in America*. Chicago: University of Chicago Press.

Alter, Jonathan. 2013. *The Center Holds: Obama and His Enemies*. New York: Simon & Schuster.

Althaus, Scott L. 1998. "Information Effects in Collective Preferences." *American Political Science Review* 92(3):545–558.

Altonji, Joseph G. and Charles R. Pierret. November 1997. "Employer Learning and the Signaling Value of Education." Discussion Paper, National Longitudinal Survey.

Alvarez, R. Michael. 1999. *Information and Elections*. Ann Arbor: University of Michigan Press.

Alvarez, R. Michael. 2005. "Voter Registration: Past, Present and Future." Written Testimony Prepared for the Commission on Federal Election Reform. Pasadena: Caltech/MIT Voting Technology Project Report.

Alvarez, R. Michael, Asa Hopkins, and Betsy Sinclair. 2010. "Mobilizing Pasadena Democrats: Measuring The Effects of Partisan Campaign Contacts." *Journal of Politics* 72(1):31–44.

Anderson, Christopher. 2006. *The Long Tail: Why the Future of Business is Selling Less of More*. New York: Hyperion.

Ansolabehere, Stephen. 2009. "Cooperative Congressional Election Study, 2008: Common Content." [Computer File]. Cambridge, MA: MIT [producer].

Ansolabehere, Stephen. July 15, 2011. "Guide to the 2008 Cooperative Congressional Election Survey, Data Release No. 4." Cambridge, MA: Harvard University.

Ansolabehere, Stephen and Eitan Hersh. 2012. "Validation: What Survey Misreporting Reveal about Survey Misreporting and the Real Electorate." *Political
Analysis* 20(4):437–459.

Ansolabehere, Stephen and Eitan Hersh. 2014. "Voter Registration: The Process
and Quality of Lists." In *The Measure of American Elections*, ed. Barry C. Burden and Charles Stewart III. Cambridge: Cambridge University Press, pp. 61–
90.

Ansolabehere, Stephen, Eitan Hersh, and Kenneth Shepsle. 2012. "Movers, Stay-
ers, and Registration: Why Age Is Correlated with Registration in the U.S."
*Quarterly Journal of Political Science* 7(4):3333–3363.

Ansolabehere, Stephen and Shanto Iyengar. 1995. *Going Negative: How Political
Advertisements Shrink and Polarize the Electorate*. New York: Free Press.

Ansolabehere, Stephen D., Shanto Iyengar, and Adam Simon. 1999. "Replicating
Experiments Using Aggregate and Survey Data: The Case of Negative Advertising and Turnout." *American Political Science Review* 93(4):901–909.

Ansolabehere, Stephen and Jonathan Rodden. 2011. "Harvard Election Data
Archive." Online http://projects.iq.harvard.edu/eda

Arceneaux, Kevin and David W. Nickerson. 2009. "Who Is Mobilized to Vote?
A Re-Analysis of 11 Field Experiments." *American Journal of Political Science*
53(1):1–16.

Bailey, Michael A., Daniel J. Hopkins, and Todd Rogers. 2013. "Unresponsive
and Unpersuaded: The Unintented Consequences of Voter Persuasion Efforts."
Working Paper.

Balkin, Jack M. 2008. "The Constitution in the National Surveillance State."
*Minnesota Law Review* 93(1):1–25.

Balkin, Jack M. and Reva B. Siegel. 2005. "Principles, Practices, and Social Move-
ments." *University of Pennsylvania Law Review* 154:927–950.

Barreto, Matt A., Gary M. Segura, and Nathan D. Woods. 2004. "The Mobilizing
Effect of Majority-Minority Districts on Latino Turnout." *American Political
Science Review* 98(1):65–75.

Bartels, Larry M. 1996. "Uninformed Votes: Information Effects in Presidential
Elections." *American Journal of Political Science* 40(1):194–230.

Bartels, Larry M. 1998. "Where the Ducks Are: Voting Power in a Party System".
In *Politicians and Party Politics*, ed. John Geer. Baltimore: Johns Hopkins
University Press, pp. 43–79.

Baumgartner, Frank R., Beth L. Leech, and Christine Mahoney. August 28–31,
2003. "The Co-Evolution of Groups and Government." Annual Meeting of the
American Political Science Association, Philadelphia. Unpublished Conference
Paper.

Beck, Paul A. and Erik. Heidemann. September 2–5, 2010. "Changing Strategies in Grassroots Canvassing: 1856–2008". Annual Meeting of the American
Political Science Association, Washington, DC. Unpublished Conference Paper.

Bedolla, Lisa García and Melissa R. Michelson. 2012. *Mobilizing Inclusion:
Transforming the Electorate through Get-Out-the-Vote Campaigns*. New
Haven: Yale University Press.

Benkler, Yochai. 2006. *The Wealth of Networks: How Social Production Trans-
forms Markets and Freedom*. New Haven: Yale University Press.

Bimber, Bruce. 2003. *Information and American Democracy: Technology in the Evolution of Political Power*. Cambridge: Cambridge University Press.

Blackwell, Matthew, Stefano Iacus, Gary King, and Giuseppe Porro. 2009. "cem: Coarsened Exact Matching in Stata." *Stata Journal* 9(4):524–546.

Box-Steffensmeier, Janet M. 1996. "A Dynamic Analysis of the Role of War Chests in Campaign Strategy." *American Journal of Political Science* 40(2):352–371.

Bradburn, N.M., L.J. Rips, and S.K. Shevell. 1987. "Answering Autobiographical Questions: The Impact of Memory and Inference on Surveys." *Science* 236(4798):157.

Brady, Henry E., Richard Johnston, and John Sides. 2006. "The Study of Political Campaigns". In *Capturing Campaign Effects*, ed. Henry E. Brady and Richard Johnston. Ann Arbor: University of Michigan Press, pp. 1–26.

Brady, Henry E., Kay Lehman Schlozman, and Sidney Verba. 1999. "Prospecting for Participants: Rational Expectations and the Recruitment of Political Activists." *American Political Science Review* 93(1):153–168.

Brynjolfsson, Erik, Yu Hu, and Michael D. Smith. 2003. "Consumer Surplus in the Digital Economy: Estimating the Vallue of Increased Product Variety at Online Booksellers." *Management Science* 49(11):1580–1596.

Bullock, John G. 2011. "Elite Influence on Public Opinion in an Informed Electorate." *American Political Science Review* 105(3):496–515.

Burden, Barry C. and Steven Greene. 2000. "Party Attachments and State Election Laws." *Political Research Quarterly* 53(1):63–76.

Burden, Barry C. and D. Sunshine Hillygus. 2009. "Opinion Formation, Polarization, and Presidential Reelection." *Presidential Studies Quarterly* 39(3):619–635.

Butler, Daniel M. and David E. Broockman. 2011. "Do Politicians Racially Discriminate Against Constituents? A Field Experiment on State Legislators." *American Journal of Political Science* 55(3):463–477.

Butler, Daniel M. and David W. Nickerson. 2011. "Can Learning Constituency Opinion Affect How Legislators Vote? Results from a Field Experiment." *Quarterly Journal of Political Science* 6(1):55–83.

Calhoun-Brown, Allison. 1996. "African American Churches and Political Mobilization: The Psychological Impact of Organizational Resources." *Journal of Politics* 58(4):935–953.

Campbell, Andrea L. 2003. *How Policies Make Citizens: Senior Political Activism and the American Welfare State*. Princeton: Princeton University Press.

Campbell, Angus. 1960. "Surge and Decline: A Study of Electoral Change." *Public Opinion Quarterly* 24(3):397–418.

Campbell, Angus, Philip E. Converse, Warren E. Miller, and Donald E. Stokes. 1960. *The American Voter*. New York: Wiley.

Campbell, James E. 2008. "Do Swing Voters Swing Elections?" In *The Swing Voter in American Politics*, ed. William G. Mayer. Washington, DC: Brookings Institution Press, pp. 118–132.

Canes-Wrone, Brandice and Kenneth W. Shotts. 2007. "When Do Elections Encourage Ideological Rigidity?" *American Political Science Review* 101(2):273–288.

Chong, Dennis and James N. Druckman. 2007. "Framing Theory." *Annual Review of Political Science* 10:103–126.

Cohen, Marty, David Karol, Hans Noel, and John Zaller. 2008. *The Party Decides: Presidential Nominations Before and After Reform*. Chicago: University of Chicago Press.

Cohen, Staney E. 1965. "The Census: More Help For Marketers." *Management Review* 54(4):41.

Converse, Philip. 1964. "The Nature of Belief Systems in Mass Publics." In *Ideology and Discontent*, ed. David Apter. New York: Free Press, pp. 206–261.

Cox, Gary W. 1990. "Centripetal and Centrifugal Incentives in Electoral Systems." *American Journal of Political Science* 34(4):903–935.

Cruz, Jose E. and Jackie Hayes. Fall 2009. "Adding Race and Ethnicity: Electoral Data Collection Practice and Prospects for New York State." NYLARNet, SUNY Albany.

Darr, Joshua P. and Matthew S. Levendusky. 2009. "Relying on the Ground Game: The Placement and Effect of Campaign Field Offices." *American Politics Research* 42(3):529–548.

DeCanio, Samuel. 2000. "Beyond Marxist State Theory: State Autonomy in Democratic Societies." *Critical Review* 14(2-3):215–236.

DeNardo, James. 1980. "Turnout and the Vote: The Joke's on the Democrats." *The American Political Science Review* 74(2):406–420.

Dimock, Michael, April Clark, and Juliana Menasce Horowitz. 2008. "Campaign Dynamics and the Swing Vote in the 2004 Election." In *The Swing Voter in American Politics*, ed. William G. Mayer. Washington, DC: Brookings Institution Press, pp. 58–74.

Downs, Anthony. 1957. *An Economic Theory of Democracy*. New York: Harper.

Duverger, Maurice. 1954. *Political Parties: Their Organization and Activity in the Modern State*. Trans. Barbara and Robert North. New York: Wiley.

Eckler, A. Ross. 1970. "Profit from 1970 Census Data." *Harvard Business Review* 48(4):4–180.

Ellis, Richard B. 1979. "Business Use of Census Data: Suggestions from the Perspective of Bell System Use." *Review of Public Data Use* 7(2):2.

Enos, Ryan D. and Eitan D. Hersh. 2015a. "Campaign Perceptions of Electoral Closeness: Uncertainty, Fear, and Overconfidence." Forthcoming. *British Journal of Political Science.*

Enos, Ryan D. and Eitan D. Hersh. 2015b. "Party Activists as Campaign Messengers: The Ground Campaign as a Principal-Agent Problem." Forthcoming. *American Political Science Review.*

Farber, Henry S. and Robert Gibbons. 1996. "Learning and Wage Dynamics." *Quarterly Journal of Economics* 111(4):1007–1047.

Fenno, Richard F. 1978. *Home Style: House Members in Their Districts*. Boston: Little, Brown.

Ferejohn, John A. and Roger G. Noll. 1978. "Uncertainty and the Formal Theory of Political Campaigns." *American Political Science Review* 72(2):492–505.

Finkel, Steven E. and Howard A. Scarrow. 1985. "Party Identification and Party Enrollment: The Difference and the Consequences." *Journal of Politics* 47(2):620–642.

Fraga, Bernard L. 2012. "The Dynamics of Party Coalitions in Congressional Elections." Working Paper.

Fryer Jr., Roland G. and Steven D. Levitt. 2007. "The Causes and Consequences of Distinctively Black Names." *Quarterly Journal of Economics* 119(3):767–805.

Geer, John G. 1996. *From Tea Leaves to Opinion Polls: A Theory of Democratic Leadership*. New York: Columbia University Press.

Geer, John G. and Prateek Goorha. 2003. "Declining Uncertainty: Presidents, Public Opinion, and Polls." In *Uncertainty in American Politics*, ed. Barry C. Burden. Cambridge: Cambridge University Press, pp. 139–160.

Gerber, Alan S. and Donald P. Green. 2000. "The Effects of Canvassing, Telephone Calls, and Direct Mail on Voter Turnout: A Field Experiment." *American Political Science Review* 94(3):653–663.

Gerber, Alan S., James G. Gimpel, Donald P. Green, and Daron R. Shaw. 2011. "How Large and Long-lasting Are the Persuasive Effects of Televised Campaign Ads? Results from a Randomized Field Experiment." *American Political Science Review* 105(1):135–150.

Gerber, Alan S., Donald P. Green, and Christopher W. Larimer. 2008. "Social Pressure and Voter Turnout: Evidence from a Large-Scale Field Experiment." *American Political Science Review* 102(1):33–48.

Gerber, Alan S., Gregory A. Huber, David Doherty, and Conor M. Dowling. 2009. "Reassessing the Effects of Personality on Political Attitudes and Behaviors: Aggregate Relationships and Subgroup Differences." Working Paper.

Gershtenson, Joseph. 2003. "Mobilization Strategies of the Democrats and Republicans, 1956–2000." *Political Research Quarterly* 56(3):293–308.

Ghitza, Yair. 2009. "Partisan Electoral Outcomes and Validated Voter Turnout: A Surprisingly Balanced Electorate." Working Paper.

Glaser, James M. 1996. *Race, Campaign Politics, and the Realignment in the South*. New Haven: Yale University Press.

Glazer, Amihai. 1990. "The Strategy of Candidate Ambiguity." *American Political Science Review* 84(1):237–241.

Goldstein, Kenneth M. and Travis Ridout. 2002. "The Politics of Participation: Mobilization and Turnout Over Time." *Political Behavior* 24(1):3–29.

Gosnell, Harlold F. 1933. "The Political Party versus the Political Machine." *Annals of the American Academy of Political and Social Science* 169:21–28.

Green, Donald P. and Alan S. Gerber. 2008. *Get Out The Vote*. Second ed. Washington, DC: Brookings.

Grimmer, Justin. 2013. *Representational Style in Congress: What Legislators Say and Why It Matters*. Cambridge: Cambridge University Press.

Hacker, Jacob S. 2002. *The Divided Welfare State: The Battle over Public and Private Social Benefits in the United States*. Cambridge: Cambridge University Press.

Hacker, Jacob S. and Paul Pierson. 2011. "The Case for Policy-Focused Political Analysis." Working Paper.

Hanmer, Michael J. 2009. *Discount Voting: Voter Registration Reforms and Their Effects*. Cambridge: Cambridge University Press.

Harris, Fredrick C. 1994. "Something Within: Religion as a Mobilizer of African-American Political Activism." *Journal of Politics* 56(1):42–68.

Harris, Joseph P. 1929. *Registration of Voters in the United States*. Washington, DC: Brookings Institution.

Hasen, Richard L. 2005. "Beyond the Margin of Litigation: Reforming U.S. Election Administration to Avoid Electoral Meltdown." *Washington and Lee Law Review* 62(3):937–999.

Hasen, Richard L. 2012. *The Voting Wars*. New Haven: Yale University Press.

Hendler, Josh. 2012. "Organizing Technology: The Marriage of Technology and the Field Campaign." In *Margin of Victory: How Technologists Help Politicians Win Elections*, ed. Nathaniel G. Pearlman. Santa Barbara: Praeger.

Hersh, Eitan and Clayton Nall. 2015. "The Primacy of Race in the Geography of Income-Based Voting: New Evidence from Public Voting Records." Forthcoming. *American Journal of Political Science*.

Hersh, Eitan and Brian Schaffner. 2013. "Targeted Campaign Appeals and the Value of Ambiguity." *Journal of Politics* 75(2):520–534.

Hersh, Eitan D. 2011. "Information-Based Candidate Strategy: Data Constraints and Voter Engagement" Ph.D. dissertation, Harvard University Cambridge, MA.

Hersh, Eitan. 2012. "Primary Voters Versus Caucus Goers and the Peripheral Motivations of Political Participation." *Political Behavior* 34(4):689–718.

Hersh, Eitan D. 2013. "Long-Term Effect of September 11 on the Political Behavior of Victims' Families and Neighbors." *Proceedings of the National Academy of Sciences* 110(52):20959–20963.

Hill, R.A. and R.I.M. Dunbar. 2003. "Social Network Size in Humans." *Human Nature* 14(1):53–72.

Hill, Seth J. 2010. "The Persuasion Region: A Theory of Electoral Change." Working Paper.

Hill, Seth J., James Lo, Lynn Vavreck, and John Zaller. 2007. "The Opt-in Internet Panel: Survey Mode, Sampling Methodology and the Implications for Political Research." University of California, Los Angeles.

Hillygus, D. Sunshine. 2005. "Campaign Effects and the Dynamics of Turnout Intention in Election 2000." *Journal of Politics* 67(1):50–68.

Hillygus, D. Sunshine, Norman H. Nie, Kenneth Prewitt, and Heili Pals. 2006. *The Hard Count: The Political and Social Challenges of Census Mobilization*. New York: Russell Sage Foundation.

Hillygus, D. Sunshine and Todd G. Shields. 2008. *The Persuadable Voter: Wedge Issues in Presidential Campaigns*. Princeton: Princeton University Press.

Hindman, Matthew. 2008. *The Myth of Digital Democracy*. Princeton: Princeton University Press.

Holbrook, Thomas M. and Scott D. McClurg. 2005. "The Mobilization of Core Supporters: Campaigns, Turnout, and Electoral Composition in United States Presidential Elections." *American Journal of Political Science* 49(4):689–703.

Hopkins, Daniel J. 2011. "Translating into Votes: The Electoral Impacts of Spanish-Language Ballots." *American Journal of Political Science* 55(4):813–829.

Huber, Gregory A. and Kevin Arceneaux. 2007. "Identifying the Persuasive Effects of Presidential Advertising." *American Journal of Political Science* 51(4):961–981.

Huckfeldt, Robert and John Sprague. 1992. "Political Parties and Electoral Mobilization: Political Structure, Social Structure, and the Party Canvass." *American Political Science Review* 86(1):70–86.

Huckfeldt, Robert and John Sprague. 1995. *Citizens, Politics, and Social Communication: Information and Influence in an Election Campaign.* Cambridge: Cambridge University Press.

Imai, Kosuke and Aaron Strauss. 2009. "Planning the Optimal Get-Out-the-Vote Campaign Using Randomized Field Experiments." Working Paper.

Issenberg, Sasha. 2012. *Victory Lab: The Secret Science of Winning Campaigns.* New York: Crown.

Jackman, Simon and Lynn Vavreck. 2011. "Cosmopolitanism." In *Facing the Challenge of Democracy: Explorations in the Analysis of Public Opinion and Political Participation,* ed. Paul M. Sniderman and Benjamin Highton. Princeton: Princeton University Press, pp. 70–96.

Johnson, William A. 1980. *Kansas City Votes, 1853–1979: Precinct Election Returns for the Offices of President, Governor and Mayor.* Kansas City: Committee for Urban and Public Affairs, University of Missouri–Kansas City.

Jones, Bryan D. and Frank R. Baumgartner. 2005. *The Politics of Attention.* Chicago: University of Chicago Press.

Jones, Jeffrey M. 2008. "Swing Voters in the Gallup Poll, 1994 to 2004." In *The Swing Voter in American Politics,* ed. William G. Mayer. Washington, DC: Brookings Institution Press, pp. 32–57.

Karpf, David. 2012. *The MoveOn Effect: The Unexpected Transformation of Amreican Political Advocacy.* Oxford: Oxford University Press.

Key, V.O. 1966. *The Responsible Electorate.* Cambridge, MA: Belknap Press of Harvard University Press.

Keyssar, Alexander. 2009. *The Right to Vote.* New York: Basic Books.

Klarman, Michael J. 2001. "The White Primary Rulings: A Case Study in the Consequences of Supreme Court Decision Making." *Florida State University Law Review* 29:55–107.

Kousser, D. Morgan. 1999. *Colorblind Injustice: Minority Voting Rights and the Undoing of the Second Reconstruction.* Chapel Hill: University of North Carolina Press.

Kramer, Gerald H. 1966. "A Decision-Theoretic Analysis of a Problem in Political Campaigning." In *Mathematical Applications in Political Science, Vol. 2,* ed. Joseph L. Bernd. Dallas: Southern Methodist University Press, pp. 137–160.

Krehbiel, Keith. 1991. *Information and Legislative Organization.* Ann Arbor: University of Michigan Press.

Kreiss, Daniel. 2012. *Taking Our Country Back.* New York: Oxford University Press.

Lange, Fabian. 2007. "The Speed of Employer Learning." *Journal of Labor Economics* 25(1):1–35.

Lange, Fabian and Robert Topel. 2006. "The Social Value of Education and Human Capital." In *Handbook of the Economics of Education*. Vol. 1, eds. Eric Hanushek and Finis Welch. Amsterdam: Elsevier, pp. 459–509.

Lau, Richard R. and David P. Redlawsk. 2001. "Advantages and Disadvantages of Cognitive Heuristics in Political Decision Making." *American Journal of Political Science* 45(4):951–971.

Lau, Richard R. and David P. Redlawsk. 2006. *How Voters Decide: Information Processing During Election Campaigns*. Cambridge: Cambridge University Press.

Leighley, Jan E. 2001. *Strength in Numbers? The Political Mobilization of Racial and Ethnic Minorities*. Princeton: Princeton University Press.

Leighley, Jan E. 2005. "Race, Ethnicity, and Electoral Mobilization: Where's They Party?" In *The Politics of Democratic Inclusion*, ed. Christian Wolbrecht and Rodney E. Hero. Philadelphia: Temple University Press, pp. 143–162.

Lenz, Gabriel S. 2009. "Learning and Opinion Change, Not Priming: Reconsidering the Priming Hypothesis." *American Journal of Political Science* 53(4):821–837.

Lessig, Lawrence. 2006. *Code: Version 2.0*. New York: Basic Books.

Levendusky, Matthew S. 2011. "Rethinking the Role of Political Information." *Public Opinion Quarterly* 75(1):42–64.

Logan, John R. 2001. "Ethnic Diversity Grows, Neighborhood Integration Lags Behind." Report by the Lewis Mumford Center, University of Albany.

Lowi, Theodore J. 1979. *The End of Liberalism: The Second Republic of the United States*. New York: W.W. Norton and Co.

Lupia, Arthur. 1994. "Shortcuts versus Encyclopedias: Information and Voting Behavior in California Insurance Reform Elections." *American Political Science Review* 88(1):63–76.

Maestas, Cherie D. 2003. "Risk and Uncertainty as Sources of Incumbent Insecurity." In *Uncertainty in American Politics*, ed. Barry C. Burden. Cambridge: Cambridge University Press, pp. 186–212.

Malchow, Hal. 2008. *Political Targeting*. Washington, DC: Predicted Lists, LLC.

Mancini, Michael. 2010. "Business Uses of Census Data." *Retail Property Insights* 17(2):20–27.

Mann, Christopher. December 2008. "How Data Improves Campaign Strategy." In *Data for Democracy*. Washington, DC: Pew Center on the States, pp. 18–19.

Mann, Christopher B. 2010. "Is There Backlash to Social Pressure? A Large-Scale Field Experiment on Voter Mobilization." *Political Behavior* 32(3):387–407.

Masket, Seth. 2009. *No Middle Ground*. Ann Arbor: University of Michigan Press.

Mayer, William G. 2007. "The Swing Voter in American Presidential Elections." *American Politics Research* 35(3):358–388.

Mayhew, David R. 1974. *Congress: The Electoral Connection*. New Haven: Yale University Press.

McClurg, Scott D. 2004. "Indirect Mobilization: The Social Consequences of Party Contacts in an Election Campaign." *American Politics Research* 32(4):406–443.

McGhee, Eric and John Sides. 2011. "Do Campaigns Drive Partisan Turnout?" *Political Behavior* 33(2):313–333.

Mendelberg, Tali. 2001. *The Race Card: Campaign Strategy, Implicit Messages, and the Norm of Equality.* Princeton: Princeton University Press.

Mettler, Suzanne. 2002. "Bringing the State Back In to Civic Engagement: Policy Feedback Effects of the G.I. Bill for World War II Veterans." *American Political Science Review* 96(2):351–365.

Miler, Kristina, C. 2009. "The Limitations of Heuristics for Political Elites." *Political Psychology* 30(6):863–894.

Mondak, Jeffrey J., Matthew V. Hibbing, Damarys Canache, Mitchell A. Seligson, and Mary R. Anderson. 2010. "Personality and Civic Engagement: An Integrative Framework for the Study of Trait Effects on Political Behavior." *American Political Science Review* 104(1):85–110.

Mutz, Diana C. 2002. "The Consequences of Cross-Cutting Networks for Political Participation." *American Journal of Political Science* 46(2):838–855.

Mutz, Diana C., Paul M. Sniderman, and Richard A. Brody, eds. 1996. *Political Persuasion and Attitude Change.* Ann Arbor: University of Michigan Press.

Nall, Clayton. 2014. "The Political Consequences of Spatial Policies: How Interstate Highways Facilitated Geographic Polarization." *Forthcoming in Journal of Politics.*

Nickerson, David W. 2006. "Hunting the Elusive Young Voter." *Journal of Political Marketing* 5(3):47–69.

Nickerson, David W. and Todd Rogers. 2014. "Political Campaigns and Big Data." *Journal of Economic Perspectives* 28(2):51–73.

Nielsen, Rasmus Kleis. 2012. *Ground Wars: Personalized Communication in Political Campaigns.* Princeton: Princeton University Press.

Noel, Hans. 2013. *Political Ideologies and Political Parties in America.* Cambridge: Cambridge University Press.

Oliver, J. Eric, Shang E. Ha, and Zachary Callen. 2012. *Local Elections and the Politics of Small-Scale Democracy.* Princeton: Princeton University Press.

Owens, Michael Leo and David J. Wright. 1998. "The Diversity of Majority-Black Neighborhoods." Rockefeller Institute Bulletin.

Parry, Janine, Jay Barth, Martha Kropf, and E. Terrence Jones. 2008. "Mobilizing the Seldom Voter: Campaign Contact and Effects in High-Profile Elections." *Political Behavior* 30(1):97–113.

Patashnik, Erik M. 2008. *Reforms at Risk: What Happens after Major Policy Changes Are Enacted.* Princeton: Princeton University Press.

Persily, Nathaniel. 2001. "Toward a Functional Defense of Political Party Autonomy." *New York University Law Review* 76(3):750–824.

Popkin, Samuel L. 1993. "Information Shortcuts and the Reasoning Voter." In *Information, Participation and Choice*, ed. Bernard Grofman. Ann Arbor: University of Michigan Press, pp. 17–35.

Prewitt, Kenneth. 2000. "The US Decennial Census: Political Questions, Scientific Answers." *Population and Development Review* 26(1):1–16.

Prior, Markus. 2007. *Post-Broadcast Democracy.* Cambridge: Cambridge University Press.

Rahn, Wendy. 1993. "The Role of Partisan Stereotypes in Information Processing about Political Candidates." *American Journal of Political Science* 37(2):472–496.

Reed, Virgil D. 1937. "Some Suggestions Uses for Census of Business Data." *Journal of Marketing* 1(4):310–316.

Rosenstone, Steven J. and John Mark Hansen. 1993. *Mobilization, Participation, and Democracy in America*. New York: Macmillan.

Schaffner, Brian F. and Matthew J. Streb. 2007. "The Partisan Heuristic in Low-Information Elections." *Public Opinion Quarterly* 66(4):559–581.

Scott, James C. 1998. *Seeing Like a State*. New Haven: Yale University Press.

Shaw, Daron R. 2006. *The Race to 270*. Chicago: University of Chicago Press.

Shaw, Daron, Rodolfo O. de la Garza, and Jongho Lee. 2000. "Examining Latino Turnout in 1996: A Three-State Validated Survey Approach." *American Journal of Political Science* 44(2):338–346.

Shepsle, Kenneth A. 1972. "The Strategy of Ambiguity: Uncertainty and Electoral Competition." *American Political Science Review* 66(2):558–568.

Sides, John and Andres Karch. 2008. "Messages that Mobilize? Issue Publics and the Content of Campaign Advertising." *Journal of Politics* 70(2):466–476.

Sides, John and Lynn Vavreck. 2013. *The Gamble: Choice and Chance in the 2012 Presidential Election*. Princeton: Princeton University Press.

Sinclair, Betsy. 2012. *The Social Citizen*. Chicago: University of Chicago Press.

Snyder Jr., James M. and Michael M. Ting. 2002. "An Informational Rationale for Political Parties." *American Journal of Political Science* 46(1):90–110.

Stokes, Susan, Thad Dunning, Marcelo Nazareno, and Valeria Brusco. 2013. *Brokers, Voters, and Clientelism: The Puzzle of Distributive Politics*. Cambridge: Cambridge University Press.

Strauss, Aaron B. 2009. "Political Ground Truth: How Personal Issue Experience Counters Partisan Bias." PhD Thesis, Princeton University.

Sunstein, Cass. 2007. *Repubic.com 2.0*. Princeton: Princeton University Press.

Tam Cho, Wendy K. 2003. "Contagion Effects and Ethnic Contribution Networks." *American Journal of Political Science* 47(2):368–387.

Tate, Katherine. 1996. "National Black Election Study." [Computer file]. ICPSR version. Columbus: Ohio State University [producer], 1997. Ann Arbor: ICPSR [distributor], 2004.

Tokaji, Daniel P. 2008. "Voter Registration and Election Reform." *William and Marry Bill of Rights Journal* 17(2):453–506.

Tomz, Michael and Robert P. Van Houweling. 2009. "The Electoral Implications of Candidate Ambiguity." *American Political Science Review* 103(1):83–98.

Turk, Michael. 2012. "Innovative Tactics: The GOP Goes Online." In *Margin of Victory: How Technologists Help Politicians Win Elections*, ed. Nathaniel G. Pearlman. Santa Barbara: Praeger.

Valentino, Nicholas A., Vincent L. Hutchings, and Ismail K. White. 2002. "Cues That Matter: How Political Ads Prime Racial Attitudes During Campaigns." *American Political Science Review* 96(1):75–90.

Vavreck, Lynn. 2007. "The Exxagerated Effects of Advertising on Turnout: The Dangers of Self-Reports." *Quarterly Journal of Political Science* 2(4):325–343.

Vavreck, Lynn. 2009. *The Message Matters: The Economy and Presidential Campaigns*. Princeton: Princeton University Press.

Verba, Sidney, Kay L. Schlozman, and Henry E. Brady. 1995. *Voice and Equality: Civic Voluntarism in American Politics*. Cambridge, MA: Harvard University Press.

*Voter Contact Summary*. 2012. Technical report Romney for President.

Waarden, Frans Van. 1992. "Dimensions and Types of Policy Networks." *European Journal of Political Science* 21(1):29–52.

Ware, Alan. 2002. *The American Direct Primary*. Cambridge: Cambridge University Press.

Weiss, Michael J. 1988. *The Clustering of America*. New York: HarperCollins.

Wielhouwer, Peter W. 2003. "In Search of Lincoln's Perfect List: Targeting in Grassroots Campaigns." *American Politics Research* 31(6):632–669.

Wielhouwer, Peter W. and Brad Lockerbie. 1994. "Party Contacting and Political Participation, 1952–90." *American Journal of Political Science* 38(1):211–229.

Wilcox, Walter F. 1914. "The Development of the American Census Office since 1890." *Political Science Quarterly* 29(3):438–459.

Winner, Langdon. 1980. "Do Artifacts Have Politics?" *Daedalus* 109(1):121–136.

Winner, Langdon. 1986. *The Whale and the Reactor: A Search for Limits in an Age of High Technology*. Chicago: University of Chicago Press.

Zaller, John R. 1992. *The Nature and Origin of Mass Opinion*. Cambridge: Cambridge University Press.

# Index

ABC (television network), 11
accuracy: of Catalist's commercial
    predictions, 171–6; of professional
    survey firms compared to volunteer
    canvassers, 239n2
ACLU, 68
AFL-CIO, 68
African-Americans: and Catalist, 127–8;
    Democratic campaigns and mobilization
    of, 126; and geographic-level strategies
    based on neighborhoods, 94; names and
    identification of, 128, 204, 227, 237n6;
    and political role of churches, 127,
    237n5; and voter turnout, 132–9,
    227–30. See also race and racial identity
age: identification of for registered voters
    in public records, 5–6; Obama election
    and reelection campaigns and young
    voters, 5–7; and Perceived Voter Model,
    29; and use of matching technique to
    assess effect of racial identity on voter
    turnout, 227; and voter registration
    system, 52; and voting behavior of
    young voters, 240n1
Alabama: and racial identity in public
    records, 123, 124, 125; and voter
    registration, 47–8, 61–62, 100, 103,
    109, 118, 225–6, 237n1
Alter, Jonathan, 11, 188
*Alton Telegraph* (Illinois), 48
Amazon.com, 207
Ansolabehere, Stephen, 67, 69, 75, 76,
    136, 143

Arkansas, and white-only primaries,
    125

Bartels, Larry M., 32–3
Beckett, Lois, 208
Blaemire, Bob, 61, 62
block-group level neighborhood data, and
    Catalist, 70
Bush, George W., and 2004 reelection
    campaign, 59

California: and effectiveness of 2012
    Obama campaign in persuading voters,
    152; and proposed law restricting
    opinion polls, 240n8; and voter
    registration, 51
"campaign," meanings of term in research
    on elections, 25
campaign databases: and conflicts of
    interest, 197–205; impact of on
    targeting strategies, 2. See also Catalist;
    public records
campaign strategies: author's contribution
    to literature on, 9; and comparison of
    persuadable voters and perceived voters,
    166–7; critique of mass survey-based
    studies on, 31–3; impact of data policies
    on, 2, 198–200; individual-level versus
    mass-level, 19; and information fallacy
    in academic research, 12; and
    perceptions of partisanship, 103–22;
    and perceptions of race, 129–32; and
    reemergence of direct targeting, 60–4;